Caribbean Realities and Endogenous Sustainability

Caribbean Realities and Endogenous Sustainability

Edited by

Debbie Mohammed

and

Nikolaos Karagiannis

The University of the West Indies Press

Jamaica • Barbados • Trinidad and Tobago

The University of the West Indies Press
7A Gibraltar Hall Road, Mona
Kingston 7, Jamaica
www.uwipress.com

A catalogue record of this book is available from the National Library of Jamaica.

ISBN: 978-976-640-642-4 (print)
978-976-640-643-1 (Kindle)
978-976-640-644-8 (ePub)

Cover design by The Invisible Creative, www.invisibleisland.com

Printed in the United States of America

In memory of my husband Nizam Anthony Mohammed

Debbie A. Mohammed

To my son Stylianos (Stelios) Karagiannis

Nikolaos Karagiannis

Contents

Acknowledgements

Our task would be incomplete if we were not to acknowledge those who kindly aided us in completing this edited book. We thank the distinguished contributors for their willingness to participate and respond to our suggestions, and also the advisors and staff of the University of the West Indies Press, who have provided excellent support throughout the preparation of this manuscript. Last, but not the least, we would like to thank our families for their continuous support and encouragement, as well as our colleagues and students for the inducements. We owe them more than we can recount.

Debbie A. Mohammed and Nikolaos Karagiannis
St Augustine, Trinidad and Tobago, and
Winston-Salem, North Carolina, USA
March 2017

Abbreviations

ACP	African, Caribbean and Pacific
ALBA	Bolivarian Alternative for the Americas
BA	business analytics
BWIA	British West Indian Airways
BWU	Barbados Worker's Union
CACM	Central American Common Market
CBI	Caribbean Basin Initiative
CARIBCAN	Canadian Programs for Commonwealth Caribbean Trade
CARICOM	Caribbean Community
CARIFORUM	Caribbean Forum
CCJ	Caribbean Court of Justice
CFL	CL Financial Limited
CLICO	Colonial Life Insurance Company (Trinidad) Limited
CSME	CARICOM Single Market and Economy
CTUSAB	Congress of Trade Unions and Staff Associations of Barbados
EAP	East Asia and Pacific
EPA	Economic Partnership Agreement
ERP	effective rates of (trade) protection
EU-28	twenty-eight countries of the European Union
EU-CAAA	EU-Central America Association Agreement
FTA	free trade agreement
GAL	guaranteed access level
GDP	gross domestic product
GSP	Generalized System of Preferences
IMF	International Monetary Fund
ISIS	Islamic State in Iraq and Syria

IT	information technology
NAFTA	North American Free Trade Agreement
NGO	non-governmental organization
OAS	Organization of American States
OWTU	Oilfields Workers' Trade Union
RCA	revealed comparative advantage
RCAV	revealed comparative advantage variation
RRCA	rival revealed comparative advantage
TCBL	Trade Confirmers (Barbados) Limited
TFP	total factor productivity
TNC	transnational corporation
UN	United Nations
UNEP	UN Environment Programme
WTO	World Trade Organization

Introduction

Debbie A. Mohammed and Nikolaos Karagiannis

The Caribbean region is more than a geographical expression. It is the designation of a cluster of nations with a distinctive political character and a diverse combination of races, religions, languages and cultures. Perhaps no other region of the world is so varied. As the Caribbean scholar Michel-Rolph Trouillot (1992, 21) states: "Caribbean societies are inescapably heterogenous. . . . The region – and indeed particular territories within it – has long been multi-racial, multi-lingual, stratified, and some would say, multi-cultural." This diversity, embedded in the pattern of settlement and in the social structure of the Caribbean countries, influences political power and mobilization as well as patterns of ethic formation and self-consciousness, which engender various claims with respect to resources and voice.

The Caribbean is also a distinctive socioeconomic order determined by experiences of a historical formation rooted in colonialism and the plantation system, and all the consequences manifested in social stratification, cultural contradictions and endemic economic limitations. As a result, the persistence of "plantation variables" is a fact, and the economies of the region eventually evolved typically into monocrop production, which is mostly foreign-owned and export-oriented. Later, since the 1960s, emphasis on crops such as sugar, coffee and bananas was replaced by an excessive emphasis on tourism, which has been heralded as the road to modernity and prosperity.

In the late twentieth century, substantial numbers of Caribbean people resided in North America, Great Britain, the Netherlands and France in what has been referred to as the "Caribbean diaspora". This phenomenon, which includes a substantial preservation of Caribbean cultural characteristics in predominantly Caribbean residential areas in the metropolitan countries, has created a new meaning of "Caribbean region" as including all areas of the world where Caribbean people have migrated and established themselves as distinct subcommunities (Premdas 1996, 8).

Recently, even though Caribbean countries are signatories to a wide variety of conventions and international agreements, economies and societies in the region and all over the world have been grappling with the challenges of globalization and the tyranny of financialization: the astonishing pace of technological innovation, widening poverty gaps, food shortages, climate change, rising energy costs, environmental problems and global financial crises, along with vexing social ills such as unemployment and underemployment, rising criminality, health and educational challenges, and the like. Taking these facts into consideration, it becomes crucial that the present preoccupation of Caribbean societies be social transformation from societies enduring colonial woes to self-reliant, economically viable, technologically responsive, politically stable and culturally secure entities pursuing "the quest for endogenous holistic sustainability". A "holistic" approach utilizes four pillars of sustainability: social, cultural, environmental and economic.

Evidently, globalization has already impacted the economies and societies of the Caribbean: exacerbation of economic instability, rising current account and fiscal deficits alongside high debt obligations, a slowdown in productivity growth, limited adjustment in traditional sectors, high unemployment and underemployment, reduction and deterioration of public services and the quality of infrastructure, degradation of the environment and natural resources, increasing social problems (including crime and violence), the growing distance between rich and poor, marginalization and social exclusion and unfair competition arrangements which put Caribbean nations in a situation of ever-increasing inferiority. Besides, the nature of the current financial integration of Caribbean countries has created new forms of external vulnerability. As the effects of globalization will more likely intensify, and given its complexity and its potentially disruptive power, together with its opportunities, there is clearly an urgent need to understand it, to take advantage of whatever benefits it offers and to minimize potentially negative outcomes.

The Caribbean also has several strengths as regards globalization: the region is democratic; adheres to a system of laws; has embraced economic liberalism, particularly since the beginning of the 1990s; has a relatively high level of education compared with other less developed countries and is mostly English-speaking and geographically close to the United States, the largest single market in the world (United Nations 2004). But a positive, realistic, and forward-looking stance will not be possible without a good understanding of this new world order which is shaping and will continue to shape the contemporary Caribbean and the rest of the world. Consequently, the question that arises is this: What are realistic development options for Caribbean territories given the policy space available to their national institutions at present?

This era of neoliberal globalization and financialization, however, challenges old-fashioned areas of intellectual concern to discovery, explanation and theory. To effectively deal with the multidimensional problems of the region requires capable theoretical analyses and thorough and technically proficient policy responses and interventions for building social resilience for local sustainable socioeconomic development while enhancing institutional strength in the region. This multidisciplinary edited book, *Caribbean Realities and Endogenous Sustainability*, emphasizes the need for a sound understanding of the nature of modern realities and seeks to offer concrete policy suggestions to national and regional institutions as well as the local business community while engaging scholars, policymakers, professionals, students, and all persons interested in the burning issues associated with this theme.

The Structure of the Book

Caribbean Realities and Endogenous Sustainability discusses alternative theoretical perspectives, sustainable growth-inducing economic policies and special challenges in this era of neoliberal globalization. These perspectives, policies and challenges have to be boldly and seriously considered if appropriate administrative and economic interventions towards changing the Caribbean status quo and eliminating social and political ills are to be pursued. With important contributions by distinguished academics and scientists, the book evaluates past efforts and policies, criticizes failed perspectives, and offers alternative strategies, policies and realistic options to address the region's current socioeconomic impasse and misery from a distinctly Caribbean viewpoint. While different areas of concern are addressed, the chapters are informed, to a greater or lesser extent, by such important factors as historical legacy, the role of institutions (including market and government), geopolitics and international relations, security, local culture and social psychology, which clearly stand in contrast to the starry-eyed analysis of the current orthodoxy. Overall, the contributions to this edited book not only expand the body of knowledge but, more important, provide a rich menu of alternative strategies and policies related to Caribbean international relations and social and governance ills in the twenty-first century.

This volume is structured around three main themes – which are also the titles of the three parts of the book. Part 1, "Theoretical Issues and Alternative Perspectives", contains chapters 1 to 4. In the opening chapter, Emilio Pantojas-García seeks to explain why, despite changes, the Caribbean continues to play a subordinate role in the new global economy. The author concludes that, even though the structure and role of the region in the world economy have changed, subordination and vulnerability persist. In chapter 2, Ron R. Sookram explores the corporate governance landscape of the Caribbean by considering the major corporate failures and their impacts as well as the region's responses to these failures. The author proposes a responsible leadership approach to corporate governance linked to sustainability which, consequently, broadens the framework within which good governance is assessed. Chapter 3, by Ronald Marshall and Russell Foote, adds to the discussion on the fashioning of a Caribbean identity. By examining social, cultural, educational and political policies, the authors argue that there is a multicultural social dynamic influencing behaviours that are prompted by various policy positions, which could shed more light on the identity question. In chapter 4, Jacqueline A. Braveboy-Wagner reviews the foreign policies of the small Caribbean nations, seeking to find out how well they are adapting to global changes while focusing on general patterns applicable to most if not all the states of the region.

Part 2, "Economic Policies for Sustainable Growth", comprises chapters 5 to 8. Chapter 5, by Dave Seerattan, reviews the economic performance of Caribbean countries over time in the context of the emerging global environment, evaluates key areas of weakness and suggests the main planks on which political reforms can be prosecuted to address the region's vulnerabilities and improve its overall performance. In chapter 6, Anthony Peter Gonzales's findings offer support to theories on the positive links between trade openness and overall competitiveness as well as the empirical work on trade competitiveness

Part 1

Theoretical Issues and Alternative Perspectives

CHAPTER 1

The Caribbean in the Age of Globalization: From Plantations to Resorts

Emilio Pantojas-García

The Caribbean was the fulcrum for the rise of European empires. It was the linchpin of capital accumulation and mercantilist expansion from the sixteenth century to the eighteenth. Unlike any other region of the world, the Caribbean was the site where modern global empires were born. The emergence of Spain, England, France, the Netherlands and Portugal as world powers would not have been possible without their Caribbean plantations or the strategic bastions they established there to collect and control the gold and silver of New Spain and New Granada; sell slaves; produce sugar, molasses and rum; and export European manufactures. This statement is not intended to diminish the role of Africa as a major contributor to the making of both European empires and Caribbean countries. It simply puts in perspective the fact that without the Caribbean the "age of imperialism" would not have come to pass as it did. The infamous trade triangle that produced European empires built on the export of European manufactures to Africa and the West Indies, the "import" of African slaves to the "new world", and the export of Caribbean sugar, molasses and rum to Europe and the Atlantic World, could not have materialized without the existence of a Caribbean archipelago that allowed competing European powers to establish a network of plantations and legal and illegal trading posts. The Caribbean was not just one of the angles of the triangle; it was its axis.

In the initial stages of colonization and settlement, the Caribbean served Spain as the platform for the "discovery" and colonization of the American continent. For Spain's rival powers (England, France, the Netherlands and Portugal), the Caribbean became a strategic outpost used to trade and smuggle with settlers in Spanish colonies and also to launch raids against the Spanish fleet to plunder its gold and silver upon its return to Seville. Thus, initially the Caribbean archipelago was mostly used and seen as the site for strategic manoeuvring for the European metropolises (Curtin 2006, 77–78).

Some authors have characterized the Caribbean as a "repeating island" based on plantation economies as their common denominator (for example, see James 1989; Benítez-Rojo 1996). Clearly, since the European colonization, the history of the Caribbean as a region has been driven and defined by its role as a link in a "global" chain of economic, social, political and cultural exchanges. But it would be inaccurate to argue that the formation of Caribbean economies and societies followed a linear process of evolution. This process included diverse experiences ranging from export production in haciendas (coffee, tobacco, cocoa) in the Spanish Caribbean to import-substitution industrialization through regional integration and export-led industrialization in the twentieth century.

Throughout history, however, Caribbean countries and territories have been "price takers" and "policy takers" in the international economic and political systems. The prices of traditional Caribbean commodities associated with "plantation economies" (sugar, spices, bananas, tobacco, coffee, cocoa), as well as other internationally traded manufactures (rum, textiles) and non-traditional commodities (bauxite, oil), were set in the commodities exchanges in London, New York and other European capitals or by parent corporations located outside the region, which controlled global commodity chains. The same is true for the international services which have become the dynamic sector of the Caribbean economies in the twenty-first century; tourism, entertainment, offshore financial centres and so on. In spite of many attempts to develop alternative development models, external reliance and subordination in global production and value chains continue to be features of Caribbean economies.

Likewise, the Caribbean countries and territories have traditionally been "policy takers". Small and fragmented politically and linguistically, the governments of the region have found themselves weak in the international arena. Many are non-independent territories, and regional integration has proved elusive. Recent negotiations on free trade agreements with North America and on economic partnership agreements with the European Union have demonstrated that these weaknesses reinforce the vulnerable position of the countries in the region as "policy takers" (see, for example, Clegg 2002; Cooper 2011).

The objective of this chapter is to provide a conceptual framework that will help us to understand why, in spite of changes, the Caribbean continues to play a subordinate role in the new global economy. The aim is to understand the dynamics of the transformation of Caribbean economies in the context of asymmetric international politico-economic relations. As the formation of the Caribbean has been at the core of the formation of modern capitalism and European empires, the dynamics of these societies have continuously been dictated by global economic expansion. Yet, although the structure and role of the Caribbean in the global economy have changed, subordination and vulnerability persist. The question is why?

From Plantations to Resorts

The "theory of plantation economy" gained ascendance in the Caribbean in the 1970s. The notion of plantation economies and societies persists beyond the original theory to characterize "how Caribbean economies work, by reference to their historical origins. The theory explains why Caribbean economies undergo alternating cycles of 'boom' and 'bust', why periods of boom are not self-sustaining, and why adjustment during the bust does not free the economy from dependence on the 'plantation sector' – broadly defined as that which is foreign-owned and export-oriented" (Girvan 2009, xvii–xviii). This metahistorical definition of "plantation" is used as an heuristic principle to refer to the outward-orientated character, heavy external reliance and international subordinate role of Caribbean economies throughout history.

Like the concept of plantation, the notion of "resort" is used here as a conceptual construct, an ideal type that refers to a larger complex of international or global services. In the tourism industry, a resort typically refers to a self-contained facility that meets all the lodging, food and entertainment needs of its clients. In many respects, it is an enclave where the patrons can satisfy all their needs and wants for leisure and recreation without leaving the premises but which relies on external linkages for inputs, customers and finances. This means that "resort economies", as "plantation economies", are externally oriented and have low levels of domestic forward and backward linkages and local value added.

The Plantation Complex

In the seventeenth century, a number of events coalesced to transform the Caribbean economies from small- to large-scale agriculture. The decline of the price of tobacco by the mid-seventeenth century was a factor in the decision of British and French colonists to engage in sugar production. This decline coincided with the Portuguese recapture of Pernambuco in Brazil and the displacement of Dutch sugar planters and merchants. Dutch immigrants from Pernambuco settled in the Lesser Antilles with support from the Dutch West India Company, establishing sugar plantations as well as introducing advanced distilling techniques which led to the creation of rum. Superior in quality to the spirits distilled earlier from sugar-cane molasses – tafia and kill devil – rum became a trademark of the Caribbean. From the side of consumption, Mintz argues that by the second half of the seventeenth century the popularity of sugar had grown in England, along with that of tea, coffee and chocolate (Mintz 1985, 52, 108–12; see also Smith 2005, 13–18).

As sugar demand grew, the Caribbean experienced what Higman calls the "sugar revolution". The effects of the sugar revolution were a massive boost to the Atlantic slave trade, which provided an engine for a variety of triangular trades, altered European nutrition and consumption, increased European interest in tropical colonies and contributed vitally to the industrial revolution (Higman 2000, 213). According to Higman:

> The plantation came to be understood as a unit of landholding and people-holding, each plantation a microcosm of colonization and each colony in turn shaped by this newly defined plantation. The principal features of plantation economy were found in the large scale of landholdings, dependence on enslaved and other forms of forced labour, hierarchical management, monoculture, export-orientation, high population densities, high ratios of African to European people, and high-value per capita output. The plantation provided a model that was rapidly embraced by the colonists and made difficult, if not impossible the consideration of alternatives. (Higman 2005, 5)

But, as the islands of the Caribbean are not equal, and as time and technology evolved, plantations also evolved. Aware of this, Philip D. Curtin refers to a "plantation complex" rather than a "plantation economy". According to Curtin, "The sugar revolution of the seventeenth century was only one among many." As the plantation complex moved onward from Madeira to Brazil, to the Eastern Caribbean, to Jamaica and St Domingue (Haiti), it changed and adapted. After the Haitian Revolution, sugar production moved to Cuba, the Dominican Republic and Puerto Rico. Incorporating new technologies and transportation innovations, such as railways, made large sugar plantations economically viable on these larger islands (Curtin 2006, 10–13, 73–77).

A number of authors have questioned the view of a "repeating island" and a homogeneous "plantation economy" as historically accurate. In the book *Un Caribe sin plantación* (a Caribbean without plantations), Abello and Bassi (2006) question the usefulness of associating the Caribbean with plantation economies. The Caribbean region of Colombia was characterized by cattle haciendas rather than sugar plantations.[1] Haciendas dominated the Spanish Caribbean economies until the nineteenth century. Initially used as strategic outposts for the settlement of Spanish America and the trans-shipment of gold and silver from the continent, the Spanish Crown developed sugar production for export in Cuba, Santo Domingo and Puerto Rico mainly after the Bourbon reforms in the eighteenth century. However, these islands cannot be simply characterized as "plantation economies". Large-scale plantations in the Spanish Caribbean emerged after the Haitian revolts and independence to fill demand in the international markets, but the Hispanic Caribbean continued to export other commodities, such as coffee and tobacco, produced in haciendas under different conditions and social relations of production (see García Muñiz 2005).

For the purpose of our analysis, the notion of "plantation economy" is used throughout this chapter as an ideal type and a heuristic principle to illustrate and explain the dynamics of economies linked in a subordinate manner from their inception to international production and commercial chains.

From Export Platforms to Resorts

In spite of transformations, until World War II the axis of Caribbean economies continued to be agricultural commodity exports. During the post-war period there was a range of experiments and processes of diversification ranging from mineral exports to regional industrial integration to export-oriented industrialization.

The oil shocks of the 1970s plunged the commodities-export-based economies of the Greater Caribbean into severe economic crises. The hike in oil prices begot deteriorating terms of trade, leading to increased external borrowing to finance oil and other imports and eventually to a major debt crisis in most Caribbean and Central American economies. As a response, metropolitan and Caribbean policymakers and entrepreneurs adopted a set of economic policies intended to stimulate a shift, from export of commodities to export of assembly manufactures through the establishment of *maquiladoras*, and from state-centered to market-oriented development strategies. These market-centered policies would be anchored on preferential treatment by developed countries for Caribbean manufactured exports.

The preferential regimes driving economic development in the 1980s started with the launching of the US Caribbean Basin Initiative (CBI) in 1982, followed by the signing of the European Economic Community's Lomé III Convention in 1984. A third component of this system of trade preferences was the Canadian Programs for Commonwealth Caribbean Trade Investment and Industrial Cooperation (CARIBCAN), established in 1986. With the exception of the CBI, none of the other initiatives included Central America, except for Belize.[2]

These preferential agreements were framed in the context of structural adjustment packages and market fundamentalism. Such was the case of the Nassau Understanding, signed by Caribbean Community (CARICOM) leaders at their annual summit in July 1984, calling for fiscal restraint and trade liberalization. Nonetheless, the CBI, CARIBCAN and Lomé III constituted neoprotectionist programmes that provided preferential market access for selected Caribbean assembled manufactures and non-traditional export goods (for example, fruits and vegetables) to the United States, Canada and Europe. These preferential regimes, especially the CBI, fostered a process of economic restructuring centered on labor- and import-intensive, export-processing industries or *maquiladoras*. Such *maquila*-type operations, with limited production linkages to the domestic economy, multiplied in newly established free trade zones which Caribbean Basin governments created, often with private-sector assistance. Among the products most benefited by the CBI and these new offshore sourcing arrangements were light manufactures and agro-industrial products (Pantojas-García 1988).

The category that grew fastest, apparel, was not included in the CBI. The rapid growth in apparel assembly was fuelled by another US special-preference programme established in 1986 known as the GAL (guaranteed access level programme, or "807a" for the applicable section in the US Customs Code). The GAL ensured unrestricted access to the US market for apparel assembled in the Caribbean Basin (the Caribbean and Central America) from fabrics made and cut in the United States. Under this programme, exports of assembled apparel from the Caribbean Basin to the United States more than doubled in only four years, from $1,125.4 million in 1987 to $2,589.6 million in 1991, an annual growth rate of 23.2 per cent. By 1995, 807 exports (including those covered by section 807a) to the United States rose to $5,544.6 million, an annual growth rate since 1991 of 21 per cent (USITC 1996, table 6).[3]

In spite of growth in particular industries, the early impact of these preferential regimes on export production in the Caribbean Basin was disappointing. Between 1984 and 1988, exports from CBI-beneficiary countries to the United States declined from $8.9 to $6.2 billion. Exports moved up to $8.4 billion in 1991, partly due to the addition of Guyana to the list of CBI countries in 1988. In the short run, the CBI-induced exports did not compensate for the decline in traditional agricultural exports. By 1994 Caribbean Basin exports to the United States reached $12.2 billion; over a third of these, $4.6 billion, were assembled apparel. The value-added content of these assembled products averaged 25 per cent or less, and the foreign exchange earnings were estimated to be less than those of traditional agricultural exports.

By 1994, a group of researchers studying the global production chain for the textiles and apparel industries described a production "triangle" for Asian and American corporations in which the Caribbean had become one of the key axes (Bonacich and Waller 1994, 21–41; Bonacich et al. 1994, 3–4). The Multi Fibre Agreement, which regulated international trade in textiles and apparel under the General Agreement on Tariffs and Trade, allowed the restriction of imports of these products to the United States and other developed countries through a complex system of quotas. The system of quotas assigned to firms and countries led to the creation of international commodity chains that allowed companies to assemble goods for export from multiple production sites, thus increasing their share of the import quotas. In the 1980s, American and Asian producers established assembly plants in the Caribbean to take advantage of the CBI/GAL programme, thus increasing exports to the United States from different countries. In the Insular Caribbean, this programme especially benefited the Dominican Republic, Jamaica and St Lucia. But the major beneficiaries were El Salvador, Honduras and Guatemala in Central America.

The CBI/GAL regime was short-lived. The enactment of the North American Free Trade Agreement (NAFTA) re-established the comparative disadvantages of the Caribbean vis-à-vis Mexico as an export platform for apparel *maquiladoras*. In the short run, Mexico's low wages and proximity to the United States, combined with NAFTA's duty-free treatment, seem to have provided a nearly insurmountable competitive advantage for Mexico over Caribbean production locations. In the textile and apparel industries in particular, freer market access under NAFTA caused the value of Mexican textile and apparel exports to the United States to grow exponentially, while the combined value of the four larger Caribbean exporters sagged. In the first two years after the beginning of NAFTA (1994–96), the value of Mexican textile and apparel exports to the United States grew by 123 per cent, while the combined exports of the Dominican Republic, Jamaica, St Lucia and Haiti grew by only 14 per cent (USITC 1996).

Dale Mathews points out that two other critical events dealt a fatal blow to the Caribbean Basin textile and apparel industries. First was the creation in 1995 of the World Trade Organization (WTO), which included the Agreement on Textiles and Clothing, which initiated a ten-year phase-out of all textile quotas ending in 2005. Second was the 2001 accession of China to the WTO, which opened the US market to imports from the largest and cheapest producer of textiles in the global commodity chain supplying that market (Mathews 2011). Table 1.1 captures the process of the rise and decline of the Caribbean and Central American textile manufacturing industries in the 1990s and the first decade of the twenty-first century for two kinds of products: knitted or crocheted (industrial classification HTS61) and not knitted or crocheted (HTS62). US textile and apparel imports from all Caribbean and Central American countries except Haiti grew at a healthy rate before NAFTA (1989–94). After NAFTA (1994–2001), Mexico outperformed all countries except those with a low base (such as Nicaragua and Guatemala), which increased US imports at a higher rate. In general, Mexico outperformed China and the major producers of the Caribbean Basin. After China's accession to the WTO, that country outperformed everyone, and the Caribbean Basin economies experienced substantial declines. Between 2001 and 2010, US imports from the Caribbean Basin and Mexico declined steadily. After 2005, with the termination of quota restrictions under the Agreement on Textiles and Clothing, even China's imports grew slower as new exporters entered the scene, such as India and Vietnam (Mathews 2011).

Table 1.1. US Imports for Consumption of Apparel and Clothing, 1989–2010 (US$ Million) (2000 = 100)

	HTS 61 Knitted or Crocheted					HTS 62 Not Knitted or Crocheted				
Country	**1989**	**1994**	**2001**	**2005**	**2010**	**1989**	**1994**	**2001**	**2005**	**2010**
China	1,181	1,608	2,409	6,762	13,214	1,759	3,595	4,332	10,577	13,873
Change (%)		36.2	49.8	180.7	95.4		104.4	20.5	144.2	31.2
Mexico	81	505	3,436	2,354	1,221	480	1,244	4,781	3,776	2,112
Change (%)		521.2	580.4	−31.5	−48.1		158.8	284.4	−21.0	−44.1
Caribbean[1]	364	735	1,180	1,281	688	764	1,290	1,567	997	357
Change (%)		102.1	61.9	7.6	−46.3		68.8	26.6	−36.4	−64.2
Central America[2]	125	840	4,410	5,148	4,767	502	1,556	2,695	2,174	1,204
Change (%)		571.3	427.4	16.2	−7.4		209.8	74.1	−19.8	−44.6

Sources: Data in this table have been compiled and calculated using tariff and trade data from the US Department of Commerce and the US International Trade Commission http://dataweb.usitc.gov/scripts/query.asp, and the US Bureau of Labor Statistics, Import/Export Price Indexes, http://data.bls.gov/cgi-bin/surveymost?ei (accessed 19 October 2011).

Notes: HTS = harmonized tariff schedule. HTS61 and HTS62 are the industrial classifications for those products.

[1]Dominican Republic, Jamaica, Haiti, St Lucia.

[2]Costa Rica, El Salvador, Guatemala, Honduras, Nicaragua.

By the end of the 1990s, employment in export manufacturing in the Caribbean declined, free trade zones stopped expanding, migration of the working populations increased, and tourism and remittances were becoming two important sources of foreign exchange and income for the region.

In the 1970s, Caribbean policymakers began focusing on the tourism and leisure industries as potential axes of growth. In 1976, for example, the first "all-inclusive" resort in the Caribbean was developed in Negril, Jamaica, as a joint venture of government and local entrepreneurs. This was also the decade when the cruise-ship industry entered the Caribbean market, with Norwegian companies Royal Caribbean and the Norwegian Caribbean Line (later Norwegian Caribbean Cruises) and the American company Carnival Cruises leading the way.[4] With the expansion of both resorts and cruises, tourism and leisure became a key sector in the economic development strategy for the region, with tourism receipts growing at an annual rate of 9 per cent in the 1980s (World Bank 1994, xii). The promise of sun, sand and sea accessible to the North American and European middle classes fuelled the growth of Caribbean resorts.

The experts of the World Bank's Caribbean Division argued that the region had great growth potential in international services (cf. World Bank 1996). Beyond tourism, in spite of significant social inequalities, most Caribbean countries have an educated labour force with experience in other services such as finance, data processing and entertainment. Knowledge of the English language, shared Western cultural understandings, geographical proximity, and a shared time zone with the United States are some of the advantages of the region as a site for international services. Caribbean countries have a middle class often educated in the United States or Europe that is familiar with the Western business culture and moves between urban centres in the region and these continents.

Besides the human resource advantage, existing service companies operating in the Caribbean were positioned to take advantage of new investment opportunities. Since the 1960s, in some cases earlier, many Caribbean countries had developed international banking centres or offshore financial centres that served as tax havens for international companies and entrepreneurs involved in legal and illegal tax avoidance schemes. Secret networks of international business existed side by side with networks of US, Canadian, British, Dutch and French banks, and international financial service companies. The transnational corporate side of this network was already in place. It was estimated that a total of US$9 trillion resided in or passed through the Caribbean each year in the form of bank funds and capital from insurance businesses and private trust companies. Bermuda alone was home to 75 per cent of the Fortune 100 companies (Marshall 2007, 931).

Likewise, informatics and entertainment services drove the expansion of the telecommunications networks in countries like the Dominican Republic and

Jamaica. In the 1990s, the Dominican Republic hosted one of twelve Internet relay stations in the world and quickly became a major international processing centre for telemarketing. Telecommunications transnational corporations (TNCs) used the advantage of geographical proximity, shared time zones, and other incentives to establish regional call and customer service centres. For example, Claro, the Mexican telecommunications TNC that bought the assets and operations of Verizon in the Dominican Republic and Puerto Rico, services operations in Puerto Rico and other Spanish-speaking countries in the region from Santo Domingo. In entertainment, before the onset of Facebook and other Internet-based networks, the Dominican Republic was the base for operations of a gamut of telecommunications services, from psychic readings and "party lines" to illegal gambling in US sports, focusing on the US Latino market. In Jamaica, under the pressure of its structural adjustment agreement with the International Monetary Fund and the World Bank, the government succeeded in promoting the establishment of a digital port facility, the Jamaica Digiport International. Owned by a private consortium (Telecommunications of Jamaica, Cable and Wireless and AT&T), the Jamaica Digiport International provided low-cost data transmission and telemarketing services to international clients (Mullings 1998, 4).

In 1994, the WTO achieved the first global accord on trade in services, the General Agreement on Trade in Services, designed as the framework for progressive multilateral liberalization of trade in services. The agreement entered into effect with the creation of the WTO in January 1995, with negotiations on basic telecommunications and financial services successfully concluded in 1997. By 2011, services accounted for over 60 per cent of global production and employment, yet they represented no more than 20 per cent of total trade (WTO 2011).

A key factor in the growth of international services was the "technological revolution" of the end of the twentieth century. Changes in technology permitted the segmentation of services or the exact reproduction of services and knowledge-based products on a global basis. Changes in telecommunications, management techniques, transportation, informatics, and other services to industry have made possible the vertical segmentation of corporate production lines as well as services. Nowadays a company can design a product in one country, have it produced by contractors in various countries continents apart, and sell the product with its brand name by telemarketing or Internet almost anywhere in the world, with other contractors (international carriers) delivering the product. The services involved (design, sales, financing, delivery) can be done by different actors in different locations without any of them ever meeting face to face or making direct physical contact with one another, with the exception perhaps of the courier service that delivers the final good.

Existing infrastructure in international services, trade liberalization in services and deteriorating advantages of Caribbean economies as manufacturing export platforms pushed the region toward a second wave of economic restructuring.

The Caribbean in the New Global Political Economy

During the first decade of the twenty-first century, the repositioning of the Caribbean in the new global economy has centered on international services, especially tourism, entertainment and financial services. Tourism has become the most dynamic sector in most Caribbean economies. According to the World Travel and Tourism Council, in 2010 this sector contributed 9.4 per cent of the world's gross domestic product (GDP), 4.8 per cent of global exports and 9.2 per cent of investment (Blanke and Chiesa 2011, xi).

Tourism grew steadily even after the terrorist attacks of 9/11 in New York. Between 2002 and 2006, the average annual growth in tourism was 4.2 per cent for the world, 1.9 per cent for the Americas, 3.9 per cent for the Caribbean and 11.6 per cent for Central America. In that same period, tourist spending grew by 56.1 per cent overall and 17.1 per cent for the Americas, while it grew by 26.6 per cent for the Caribbean and 84.9 per cent for Central America (OMT 2008, anexos 9, 10, 13). Put another way, after 9/11, travel spending in the Caribbean grew at a lower rate than in the world but at a greater pace than in the Americas.

The global recession of 2008 affected Caribbean tourism significantly. According to the Caribbean Tourism Organization, between 2008 and 2009 the number of visitors declined by an average of 3.6 per cent, although this was below the decline in visitors to the United States, 4.4 per cent, and Europe, 8.9 per cent. Cuba and the Dominican Republic were the exceptions to this trend. The number of cruise passengers also declined by 3 per cent in 2008 (CTO 2010).

Nonetheless, tourism continued to contribute significantly to the Caribbean economies' GDP and investment through the recession. Table 1.2 shows the contribution of tourism to GDP and investment in the Caribbean, Central America and the world. It is clear that between 2006 and 2010, the contribution of tourism remained stable, even in the context of the recession. The table suggests that, although these contributions did not grow or contract during the recession, the contributions of other sectors did contract, as the shares of the contributions to production and investment remained stable, albeit showing negative growth. The contribution of tourism did not grow during the

Table 1.2. Direct Contribution of Tourism to GDP and Investment, 2006–2010 (Per Cent)

	2006	2007	2008	2009	2010
Caribbean					
GDP	10.7	10.6	9.8	9.9	10.1
Growth	6.6	4.1	–5.1	–4.3	1.9[a]
Investment	18.0	19.3	20.5	20.2	19.6
Growth	26.9	23.1	12.3	–11.0	–1.1
Central America					
GDP	6.0	6.3	6.0	5.7	5.4
Growth	12.7	9.6	1.3	–4.9	–2.5
Investment	7.7	8.6	9.0	9.4	9.2
Growth	27.5	24.5	17.0	–3.7	7.4
Greater Caribbean[b]					
Share GDP	8.8	8.7	8.2	8.1	8.2[a]
Growth	7.0	4.6	–3.4	–4.8	0.8[a]
Investment	14.3	15.3	16.1	15.9	15.4
Growth	23.7	20.2	10.6	–9.2	–0.3
World					
GDP	2.9	2.9	2.8	2.8	2.8
Growth	2.4	2.8	–1.5	–3.4	3.2
Investment	4.7	4.9	5	4.8	4.5

Source: www.wttc.org/research/economic-data-search-tool/ (accessed 16–18 January 2012).

[a]Excludes Haiti.

[b]Caribbean and Central America.

recession, but its shares of GDP and investment in the Caribbean and Central America held steady. In the midst of the global recession, hotel and tourist services corporations continued to view the Caribbean as a region with growth potential; a substantial portion of investment in this sector was related to construction of resorts and second-home communities in the region (Blázquez and Murray 2011, 377–83).

In 2013, according to data from the Cruise Lines International Association, the Caribbean continued to be the principal destination in the cruise industry, accounting for 36 per cent of the bed/days occupancy in the industry.[5] Although this represents a decline from 2011, when bed/days occupancy in the Caribbean was 40 per cent of the global industry total, the reduction is the result of growth in other regions, not a contraction in Caribbean cruises. Overall, bed/days occupancy in the Caribbean grew steadily by 37 per cent from 2003 to 2013 (BREA 2012, 18, and 2013, 16). Tourism's direct contribution to the Caribbean GDP in 2014 was estimated at 4.5 per cent, 4 per cent of employment, 18 per cent of total exports and 12.5 per cent of total investment (WTTC 2015, 3–5).

The share of local earnings of tourism for every dollar spent by visitors is estimated to range between ten and thirty cents per dollar. This is due to the high import content of goods consumed by tourist and external links in the tourism value chain. The majority of the Caribbean countries are net food importers (Castañeda 2009, 13; Graziano da Silva 2009, 1–2). This means that a share of the money spent in "local gastronomy" is "leaked" through the import of foodstuffs. And international transportation and lodging are dominated by international airlines and hotels. There are competing regional chains, but the lion's share of international tourism is controlled by TNCs (Blázquez and Murray 2011, 377–83; Jiménez Martínez 2011).[6]

Figure 1.1, reproduced from Pedro Monreal (2005), presents the value chain for international tourism. It shows that Caribbean countries are receivers of tourists and that most of the value generated is appropriated by the originating countries, where the tours are organized and sold. The "value added" in the Caribbean is limited mostly to lodging, local transport, gastronomy, entertainment and retail trade. And even within these locally produced components there are high rates of external inputs. This asymmetry in the value chain is reflected in the triangle-shaped bar at the bottom of the figure, which reflects a diminishing share of value accruing to "receiving" countries.

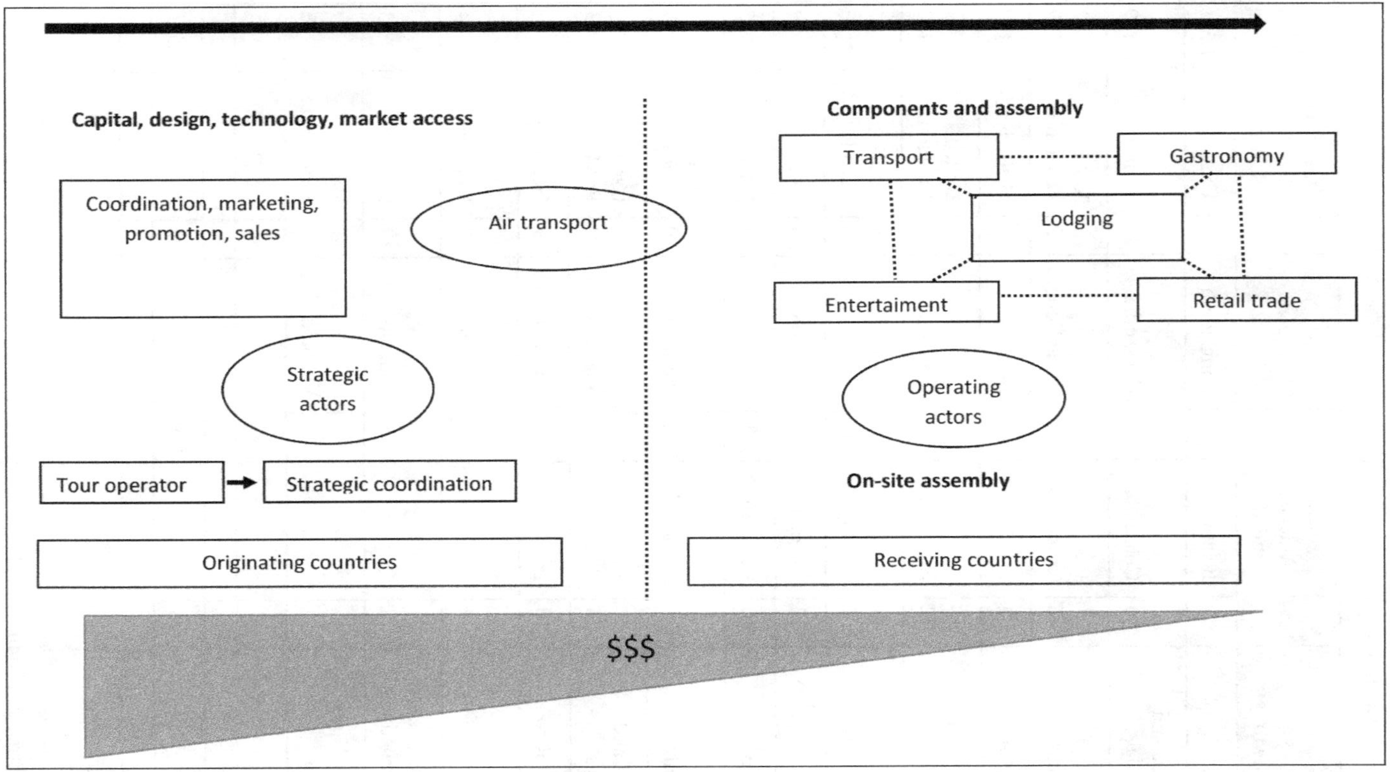

Figure 1.1. Value chain for international tourism
Source: Monreal (2005).

Table 1.3. Casinos in the Caribbean, Tropical Asia and the World, 2011

Caribbean		Central America and G3		Tropical Asia		Others with 25 or More Casinos	
Aruba	10	Belize	2	Bangladesh	0	USA	1,511
Antigua and Barbuda	6	Colombia	19	Cambodia	14	France	189
Bahamas	6	Costa Rica	40	Hong Kong	2	Russian Federation	169
Barbados	2	El Salvador	2	India	6	Netherlands	167
Dominican Republic	32	Honduras	3	Indonesia	0	United Kingdom	140
Guadeloupe	2	Nicaragua	10	Macau, China	33	Canada	110
Haiti	2	Panama	36	Malaysia	4	Argentina	79
Jamaica	10	Venezuela	5	Myanmar	4	Estonia	75
Martinique	2	Mexico	2	Philippines	19	South Africa	45
Netherlands Antilles	26			Singapore	2	Czech Republic	43
Puerto Rico	18			Sri Lanka	9	Germany	35
St Kitts and Nevis	2			Thailand	0	Ukraine	34
St Vincent and the Grenadines	2			Vanuatu	2	Spain	33
Trinidad and Tobago	3			Vietnam	2	Kazakhstan	28
US Virgin Islands	1					Egypt	25
Total	124		119		95		2,683
Greater Caribbean			243				

Source: Ernst and Young (2011).

Casinos and Offshore Financial Centres

Casinos have become a major part of the Caribbean tourist industry, generating millions of dollars in revenue and foreign exchange. Table 1.3 shows that the Caribbean and the Greater Caribbean have one of the largest concentrations of casinos in the world, aside from Europe and the United States.

The proliferation of casinos in the Caribbean is linked to the growth of tourism but also to increasing tax evasion and money-laundering practices. Although casinos are not financial institutions, they have the legal capacity to transfer money to and receive transfers from banking institutions around the world, issue cashier's checks, rent safe deposit boxes and exchange currencies. Even though they are regulated, it is not unheard of for casinos to launder money using these mechanisms (FATF 2009). In theory, anyone can walk into a casino, purchase chips paying cash, play, and then cash the chips and ask for a receipt from the casino, thereby transforming the original cash purchase into a legal payment from the casino. As long as such a transaction is under US$5,000, the casino is not obligated to report it to authorities. A study from the Financial Action Task Force of the Organization for Economic Co-operation and Development reports that certain gambling junkets do not transact payments through regular financial channels but rather deal directly with the casinos, affording them the opportunity to launder money (FATF 2009, 47–49).

The Greater Caribbean is also one of the regions of the world with a greater concentration of casinos and offshore financial centres than is found elsewhere. At the beginning of the twenty-first century there were fifty-eight offshore financial centres in the world, of which nineteen were in the Caribbean, sixteen in Asia and fourteen in Europe. At the end of the first decade in the new century there were sixty-two, of which nineteen were in the Greater Caribbean, another nineteen in Asia, fourteen in Europe, five in Africa, four in the Middle East and one in Latin America (Uruguay) (Godefroy and Lascoumes 2005, 273; OECD 2009; IMF 2011). Of the nineteen offshore financial centres located in the Caribbean, ten license casinos. In Asia, only six of the nineteen jurisdictions with offshore financial centres license casinos. Moreover, 132 casinos operate in Caribbean offshore financial centres, while only 62 operate in Tropical Asia (Tax Justice Network 2007; FATF 2009; IMF 2011).

Clearly, the economies of the Caribbean have transitioned from "plantations" to "resorts". The region has become a playground for its wealthy neighbours and a financial centre for TNCs based in the United States and Europe.

Modern buildings and paradisiacal resorts sprawl throughout the region, yet the asymmetries remain. Large portions of the Caribbean populations rely on transfer payments from members of their families living in developed countries for their subsistence. In 2012, personal transfers to Jamaica amounted to 14.6 per cent of its GDP; in Haiti they were 20.4, in Guyana 16.5 per cent and in the Dominican Republic 7.1 per cent. In Central America, Honduras received personal transfers equivalent to 16.5 per cent of its GDP, El Salvador 16.2 per cent, Guatemala 10.2 per cent and Nicaragua 9.2 per cent.[7] Unemployment and poverty have also fostered the expansion of the sex trade (cf. Brennan 2004; Gregory 2007; Pantojas-García, 2012).

Continuity and Change: Price Takers and Policy Takers

Caribbean economies have been historically "price takers", as well as "policy takers" in the global economy. As Lloyd Best and Kari Levitt argue, Caribbean economies were created as "the overseas operations of an integrated enterprise whose ultimate control was located in the metropole" (Best and Levitt 2009, 10–11).

The prices of internationally traded goods and services are set in global value chains controlled by international producers. Whether the Dutch West India Company, Kaiser Aluminum or Carnival Cruises, the prices of internationally traded goods and services – sugar, bauxite or cruises – are set by a combination of international demand driven by consumers in advanced economies and the cost and profit structure of the international companies that produce them.[8] In the words of Best and Levitt:

> Thus, the hinterland is a *price taker* not only in the obvious sense that hinterland producers have little or no control over the selling price of commodity exports or the purchase price of imports, but in the more fundamental sense that the *internal structure of prices is determined by (external) prices corresponding to the requirements of resource allocation and accumulation in the metropolitan centres.* The internal structure of prices is a derivative of the external or world price structure. (Best and Levitt 2009, 55)

In terms of international economic policy, the new governance structures of the WTO have created a framework that constrains the ability of small governments to influence international economic policies. Studying the banana conflict between the United States and the European Union, Clegg demonstrates how the new dispute-settlement regime of the WTO marginalized Caribbean banana-producing countries in the process of settling the dispute. The conflict centered on trade practices between the United States and the European Union and the marketing TNCs and placed producers in the role of "third parties" with little ability to influence the process (Clegg 2002, 173).

In a more recent dispute on Internet gambling, in the WTO Antigua complained that the United States was using unfair trade practices in banning Internet betting. Although the US government was found guilty of unfair trade practices and sanctioned, the ban was not lifted. The government of Antigua was granted permission to ignore copyrights on US products (films, music) and to sell US copyrighted merchandise up to an amount equivalent to the lost income from Internet gambling. The amount of the penalty was such that the United States did not lift the ban (Cooper 2011, chap. 6).

This is the new framework of Caribbean international economic and political relations. Colonialism and plantations are long gone, and the economy and the polity of both the Caribbean and its metropolises have changed. The subordinated nature of these relationships have changed and been redefined. Caribbean countries, many of them microstates and small economies, participate in the world as sovereign nations, and even those territories that are not independent enjoy a measure of autonomy. Caribbean countries and territories are not mere appendages or subsidiaries of overseas powers. They are, however, small and weak actors in international politics and in the international economy.

Unlike in the initial bipolar metropolis-satellite relation of seventeenth- and eighteenth-century plantation economies, in the modern international economy it is not countries that set the conditions of international exchange but TNCs, cartels such as OPEC, international commodities exchange and other international organizations such as the International Monetary Fund and the WTO. Transnational commodity chains and value chains set not only prices but the distribution of benefits among participants in the modern global economy.

Both Caribbean plantations and resort economies are export-oriented; import fundamental inputs and consumer goods; have low domestic backward and forward linkages; rely on external investment; have low wages; pay substantial profits, royalties and dividends to international capital; and are highly vulnerable to international economic cycles. The more things change, the more they are the same.

Acknowledgements

The author wishes to thank Lou Anne Barclay of the University of the West Indies, Mona, Jamaica, who provided important comments to an earlier version of the chapter.

Notes

1. Haciendas are distinctively different from plantations in many respects. Two key differences are that the owners live in and run the *hacienda* and a substantial share of its production is for the satisfaction of the consumption needs of both laborers and *hacendados* (landlords). A plantation is owned by an absentee corporation, and most of its production is for export.
2. Throughout this chapter "the Caribbean" refers to the Insular Caribbean plus Belize, Guyana and Surinam, and "the Greater Caribbean" refers to the Caribbean and Central America, including Panama. Mexico, Colombia and Venezuela are not included in any of these groupings.
3. All calculations on this section are from USITC 1992 and 1996 reports and from other unpublished data supplied by the US Department of Commerce.
4. John Issa, a Jamaican entrepreneur of Lebanese descent, credits himself with introducing the "all-inclusive" hotel concept to the Caribbean in 1976 with the Negril Beach Village resort. Issa explained on the Super Clubs home page that he devised the all-inclusive marketing strategy to counter the economic uncertainties of the mid-1970s. See www.superclubs.com/sc_about.sap (accessed 27 December 2001); see also, SuperClubs® and Hedonism II® chronology, www.jamaicajim.com/chronol.htm (accessed 7 April 2011). Norwegian Cruise Lines was created in 1966, Royal Caribbean in 1970 and Carnival Cruises in 1972 (see their histories on the websites for these companies).
5. In 2002 the Caribbean became the principal destination of cruises in the world, accounting for almost half of the bed/days occupancy (CTO 2002, 13; BREA 2012).
6. According to *Hotels Magazine*'s ranking of world hotel chains, three regional chains operated in the Greater Caribbean: Decameron, registered in Panama, ranked 187, operated 33 hotels with 6,075 bedrooms; Sandals, registered in Miami, ranked 234, operated 19 hotels with 4,749 bedrooms; Hoteles Real, registered in San Salvador, ranked 288, operated 18 hotels with 3,611 bedrooms. Super Clubs of Jamaica was not in the ranking but operates 11 hotels in the region, including one in Brazil (www.hotelsmag.com, September 2011). There are also regional airlines competing for shares of international transport and tourism packages. COPA, founded in Panama in 1947, bought Colombian Aero República in 2005, extending its regional coverage. In 2011, Salvadorean airline TACA merged with Colombian Avianca, consolidating a place in Central America, Colombia and Peru. (See www.taca.com/esp/fo1/abt/abtabotac.asp?id=26 and http://investor.shareholder.com/copa/overview.cfm [accessed 7 January 2012]).
7. Personal transfers consist of all current transfers in cash or in kind made or received by resident households to or from non-resident households. Personal

transfers thus include all current transfers between resident and non-resident individuals. Calculated from the World Bank, *World Development indicators*, http://data.worldbank.org/indicator/BX.TRF.PWKR.CD.DT (accessed 10 April 2015).

8. In the book *Up the Down Escalator*, former Jamaican prime minister Michael Manley describes in detail the negotiations between the government of Jamaica and the various bauxite companies operating on the island. The price of bauxite became a major issue, as government projections of revenue were based on calculations that did not take into account other factors, such as deteriorating terms of trade. Moreover, when the government of Jamaica imposed a levy on production in 1974, the companies reacted by reducing production in Jamaica while increasing production by a comparable amount in Guinea and Australia. Clearly, the control of the full value chain by TNCs allowed for that strategic manoeuvre against the levy. Because the levy made Jamaican prices higher, the companies increased production in other countries with a "lower" cost structure. If initially Australian and Guinean bauxite were less cost effective, with the levy in Jamaica they "became" more competitive. Control of global commodity chains allowed TNCs to outmanoeuvre not only Jamaica but eventually the International Bauxite Association, which included the major bauxite-producing countries (Manley 1987, chapters 2 and 3, esp. 46–48, 50–54 and 73–75).

References

Abello Vives, A., and E. Bassi Arévalo. 2006. Un Caribe por fuera de la ruta de la plantación. In *Un Caribe sin plantación*, comp. Alberto Abello Vives. San Andrés: Universidad Nacional de Colombia.

Best, L., and K. Polanyi Levitt. 2009. Essays *on the Theory of Plantation Economy: A Historical and Institutional Approach to Caribbean Economic Development*. Kingston: University of the West Indies Press.

Blanke, J., and T. Chiesa, eds. 2011. *The Travel and Tourism Competitiveness Report, 2011: Beyond the Downturn*. Geneva: World Economic Forum. www.weforum.org/reports/travel-tourism-competitiveness-report-2011.

Blázquez, M., and I. Murray. 2011. Una geohistoria de la turistización de las Islas Baleares. In *Turismo Placebo: Nueva colonización turística; del Mediterráneo a Mesoamérica y El Caribe. Lógicas espaciales del capital turístico*, 343–98. Managua: EDISA.

Benítez-Rojo, A. 1996 *The Repeating Island: The Caribbean and the Postmodern Perception*. Durham, NC: Duke University Press.

Bonacich, E., and D.V. Waller. 1994. Mapping a Global Industry: Apparel Production in the Pacific Rim Triangle. In *Global Production: The Apparel Industry in the Pacific Rim*, edited by E. Bonacich et al., 21–41. Philadelphia: Temple University Press.

Bonacich, Edna, Lucie Cheng, Norma Chinchilla, Nora Hamilton and Paul Ong, eds. 1994. *Global Production: The Apparel Industry in the Pacific Rim*. Philadelphia: Temple University Press.

BREA (Business Research and Economic Advisors). 2012. *Economic Contribution of Cruise Tourism to the Destination Economies*, vol. 1. www.f-cca.com/downloads/2012-Cruise-Analysis-vol-1.pdf.

———. 2013. The Global Economic Contribution of Cruise Tourism, 2013. www.cruising.org/docs/defaultsource/research/global_cruise_impact_analysis_2013.pdf?sfvrsn=2.

Brennan, D. 2004. *What's Love Got to Do with It? Transnational Desires and Sex Tourism in the Dominican Republic*. Durham, NC: Duke University Press.

Castañeda, Rodrigo. S. 2009. Contexto Regional. In *Política de reemplazo de importaciones agrícolas*. Rome: Food and Agriculture Organization of the United Nations. Annex 1. www.rlc.fao.org/es/temas/precios/pdf/politicas.pdf.

Clegg, P. 2002. The *Caribbean Banana Trade: From Colonialism to Globalization*. London: Palgrave.

Cooper, A. F. 2011. *Internet Gambling Offshore: Caribbean Struggles over Casino Capitalism*. London: Palgrave.

CTO (Caribbean Tourism Organization). 2002. Caribbean Tourism: One Year after 9/11. Prepared by Gail Clark, November. www.onecaribbean.org.

———. 2010. Caribbean Tourism: State of the Industry. www.onecaribbean.org.

Curtin, P.D. 2006. *The Rise and Fall of the Plantation Complex*, 2nd ed. New York: Cambridge University Press.

Ernst and Young. 2011 *The 2011 Global Gaming Bulletin Market Overview*. http://www.ey.com/Publication/vwLUAssets/2011-global_gaming-bulletin/$FILE/2011%20Global%20Gaming%20Bulletin.pdf.

FATF (Financial Action Task Force). 2009. *Vulnerability of Casinos and Gaming Sectors*. www.fatf-gafi.org/dataoecd/47/49/42458373.pdf.

García Muñiz, H. 2005. La plantación que no se repite: Las historias azucareras de la República Dominicana y Puerto Rico, 1870–1930. *Revista de Indias* 65 (233): 173–92.

Godefroy, T., and P. Lascoumes. 2005. *El capitalismo clandestino: La obscena realidad de los paraísos fiscales*. Barcelona, Ediciones Paidós.

Graziano Da Silva, J. 2009. *Política de reemplazo de importaciones agrícolas*. Rome: Food and Agriculture Organization of the United Nations. www.rlc.fao.org/es/temas/precios/pdf/politicas.pdf.

Girvan, Norman. 2009. Foreword. *Essays on the Theory of Plantation Economy: A Historical and Institutional Approach to Caribbean Economic Development*, edited by L. Best and K. Polanyi Levitt. Kingston: University of the West Indies Press.

Gregory, S. 2007. *The Devil behind the Mirror: Globalization and Politics in the Dominican Republic*. Berkeley: University of California Press.

Higman, B.W. 2000. The Sugar Revolution. *Economic History Review* 53 (2): 213–36.

———. 2005. *Plantation Jamaica: 1750–1850*. Kingston: University of the West Indies Press.

IMF (International Monetary Fund). 2011. *Offshore Financial Centers (OFCs): IMF Staff Assessments*. www.imf.org/external/np/ofca/ofca.asp.

James, C.L.R. 1989. *The Black Jacobins: Toussaint L'Ouverture and the San Domingo Revolution*. New York: Vintage.

Jiménez Martínez, A. 2011. Cadenas hoteleras: Estrategias y territorio en el Caribe Mexicano. Paper presented at the conference El Turismo en el Caribe ante los

Vaivenes de la Economía Global, Festival Cultural del Caribe, Universidad del Caribe, Cancún, México, 14 November.
Manley, M. 1987. *Up the Down Escalator: Development and the International Economy – A Jamaican Case Study*. Washington, DC: Howard University Press.
Marshall, D.D. 2007. The New International Financial Architecture and Caribbean OFCs: Confronting Financial Stability Discourse. *Third World Quarterly* 28 (5): 917–38.
Mathews, D.T. 2011. The Caribbean Clothing Industry and the Asian Competition. *Academy of Business Disciplines Journal* 3 (1): 45–59.
Mintz, Sydney W. 1985. *Sweetness and Power: The Place of Sugar in Modern History*. New York: Penguin.
Monreal, P. 2005. Repensando el turismo, la cultura y el desarrollo en el Caribe insular. Paper presented at the First Conference of the Cátedra del Caribe, Universidad de La Habana.
Mullings, B. 1998. Jamaica's Information Processing Services: Neoliberal Niche or Structural Limitation? In *Globalization and Neoliberalism: The Caribbean Context*, edited by Thomas Klak, 135–54. Lanham, MD: Rowman and Littlefield.
OECD (Organization for Economic Cooperation and Development). 2009. *A Progress Report on the Jurisdictions Surveyed by the OECD Global Forum in Implementing the Internationally Agreed Tax Standard*. www.oecd.org/dataoecd/38/14/42497950.pdf.
OMT (Organización Mundial del Turismo). 2008. *Panorama mundial y actualidad del turismo. Edición 2007: Tendencias de los Mercados Turísticos*. Madrid: OMT. www.unwto.org.
Pantojas-García, E. 1988. The CBI and Economic Restructuring in the Caribbean and Central America. *Caribbean Studies* 20 (3–4): 46–58.
———. 2012. Turismo y desarrollo en el Caribe: El auge de las industrias del Pecado. *Investigaciones Turísticas* 4: 49–76.
Smith, Frederick H. 2005. *Caribbean Rum: A Social and Economic History*. Gainesville: University Press of Florida.
Tax Justice Network. 2007. *Identifying Tax Havens and Offshore Finance Centres*. www.taxjustice.net/cms/upload/pdf/Identifying_Tax_Havens_Jul_07.pdf.
USITC (United States International Trade Commission). 1996. *Annual Statistical Report on U.S. Imports of Textiles and Apparel: 1995*. Publication 2987. Washington, DC: USITC. www.usitc.gov/publications/332/3322987.pdf.
World Bank, Caribbean Division. 1994. *Coping with Changes in the External Environment*. Report no. 12821, LAC. Washington, DC: World Bank.
———. 1996. *Prospects for Service Exports from the English-Speaking Caribbean*. Report no. 15301 CRG. Washington, DC: World Bank.
WTO (World Trade Organization). 2011. *The General Agreement on Trade in Services (GATS): Objectives, Coverage and Disciplines*. www.wto.org/english/tratop_e/serv_e/gatsqa_e.htm.
WTTC (World Travel and Tourism Council). 2015. *Travel and Tourism Economic Impact 2015 Caribbean*. https://www.wttc.org/-/media/files/reports/economic%20impact%20research/regional%202015/caribbean2015.pdf.

CHAPTER 2

Corporate Governance in the Caribbean: Failures, Impact and the Way Forward

Ron R. Sookram

Corporate governance became a key issue in the Caribbean after the 2009 financial meltdown of one of the largest conglomerates in the region: the Colonial Life Insurance Company (Trinidad) Limited (CLICO), and its parent company, CL Financial Limited (CFL). This collapse posed systemic risk not only to Trinidad and Tobago's financial sector but also to the wider Caribbean, with spillover effects in CARICOM member states, except for Jamaica and Haiti (Soverall and Persaud 2013, 17). The risk exposure of the Trinidad and Tobago economy was estimated to be as high as 10 per cent of gross domestic product, or TT$13.6 billion, while exposure in the Eastern Caribbean was as high as 17 per cent of gross domestic product, leading to costly government interventions (ibid.). CLICO/CFL's failure was attributed primarily to poor internal and external corporate governance and has raised questions concerning boards, regulators, executives and auditors.

The focus of this chapter, therefore, is on exploring the corporate governance landscape of the Caribbean by considering the major corporate failures and their impacts as well as the region's responses to these failures. As will be seen in our discussion, the responses were conservative, unsurprisingly concentrated on the financial and related industries. The chapter also suggests that researchers and practitioners need to develop a more holistic approach towards understanding corporate governance by going beyond traditional governance mechanisms and controls and incorporating responsible leadership levels of analysis into the equation.

Overview of Corporate Governance

Corporate governance, at its most basic level, establishes the rules to deal with issues related to the separation of ownership and control and so defines the framework in which relationships among a company's management, its board of directors, its shareholders, and other stakeholders interact. There is, however, no universally accepted definition of corporate governance, which is partly attributable to context specificity, emphasis on different aspects by different professional groups, and theoretical perspectives. Nonetheless, governance is relevant to the performance of both private- and public-sector organizations, and many of the principles and concepts of governance are applicable to both sectors.

With the series of corporate scandals and failures in North America and Europe in the early years of the twenty-first century and the more recent global financial crisis of 2008, corporate governance became a topic high on the agendas of all major economies (Crane and Matten 2010, 224). Understandably, achieving good governance became a central theme in most of the governance-related initiatives in these economies. There are a number of principles as well as structural and behavioral factors that are presented in the literature as ideals for good governance. The question of what constitutes good governance, however, is not as important or as relevant as the question of whether or not governance is present and whether it is the most appropriate form for the particular entity. This is why it is easier to identify the lack of governance through failure than the presence of sound governance mechanisms and structures through success. Good governance, nevertheless, is commonly presented as entailing the following characteristics: (1) shareholders elect directors who represent them; (2) directors vote on key matters and adopt the majority decision; (3) decisions are made in a transparent manner so that shareholders and others can hold directors accountable; (4) the entity adopts accounting standards to generate the information necessary for directors, investors and other stakeholders to make decisions; and (5) the organization's policies and practices adhere to applicable local laws (OECD 2015a).

Companies can derive various benefits by practicing good corporate governance. A well-governed entity will be more efficient and more likely to produce effective outcomes. Good governance improves access to capital and financial markets and attracts greater investment, and it strengthens management by shaping a sound company strategy that will generate better profit margins. Empirical research suggests that over 84 per cent of global institutional investors are willing to pay a premium for the shares of a well-governed company over one with a comparable financial record that is poorly governed (Papidze 2014). Also, good governance minimizes the incidence of corruption, improves the management of risks and helps prevent systemic banking crises even in countries where most firms are not actively traded on stock exchanges, as is the case in the Caribbean region (OECD 2015b).

The Corporate Governance Landscape of the Caribbean

The CARICOM community is comprised of fifteen emerging economies where organized markets are nascent and credible governance structures have historically been limited (ECCB 2003, 10). In each Caribbean state, there are several pieces of legislation designed to enforce order and discipline, regulate businesses, protect the public and enhance transparency, disclosure and accountability to ensure an efficiently functioning economy. But due to the individuality of circumstances in each member state, there are disparities within the regulatory system, ranging from penalties for offences to the effectiveness and interpretation of regulations. These disparities could make doing business difficult, as well as unintentionally allow inadequate controls for regulating a company's behavior and so pose greater risks to the region's financial stability (CARICOM Secretariat 2010, 344–59).

In CARICOM, developments in the area of corporate governance have been limited to the financial sector. These have largely been a result of the financial crisis in Latin America, Asia and Russia, which led to an increase in global sensitivity to risks in the international financial markets (ECCB 2003). In addition, concerns with respect to money laundering and terrorist financing have triggered pressure for governance-related developments in the region. These have driven central banks to improve the levels of supervision and regulation of financial institutions and the adoption of international standards. Nevertheless, within the non-financial sectors adoption of good governance measures has been inadequate. This is because corporate governance is generally considered in the context of promoting investor protection, but less than 1 per cent of the Caribbean population could be deemed an active investors (ECCB 2003). Thus corporate governance has not played an important role in regional corporations on account of the lack of institutional-and-retail-investor participation (ECCB 2003). Moreover, before the CLICO/CFL fiasco of 2009, the Caribbean did not experience the types of crises and losses of investors' and depositors' funds that have occurred in other regions. This absence of crises in itself retarded the pace at which corporate governance has developed in the region.

On the whole, CARICOM members face inherent governance problems and peculiarities based on their small size and economies as outlined in table 2.1. These peculiarities suggest that a formal governance framework in each of the islands is required and that there is a need for an overarching Caribbean response on corporate governance issues. The Caribbean Corporate Governance Code recommended in 2003, for example, was an appropriate regional response to be implemented through the Caribbean Single Market and Economy, but for various reasons this initiative never materialized (CARICOM Secretariat 2005, 362). However, there is a higher probability that individual national codes will be established instead, given the launch of governance codes in Jamaica (2006) and Trinidad and Tobago (2013).

A number of CARICOM member states have experienced major corporate failures. The collapse of Trade Confirmers (Barbados) Limited (TCBL) in 1987 triggered the establishment of a commission of inquiry in 1988. (See Commission of Inquiry into the Causes of the Collapse of Trade Confirmers [1988].) The commission was appointed to investigate and report on (1) the causes of the collapse of TCBL and (2) whether the business of Trade Confirmers was carried on negligently or with intent to defraud depositors or other creditors and shareholders, or in any way that was unfairly prejudicial to their interests or unfairly disregarded them. The commission was then to make such recommendations as were considered appropriate.

The commission found that TCBL was undercapitalized and in breach of various financial regulations. The Central Bank inspection in May 1984, one year after TCBL had become a financial institution, revealed that the funding of TCBL was provided by fixed deposits totaling US$4.3 million, share capital amounting to US$973,000 and bank borrowings amounting to US$2.8 million. The excess of deposits to share capital was a concern for the regulators, as was the narrow base of the deposits. Nine customers held deposits of US$100,000 or more, and two had balances of approximately US$800,000. This coupled with the fact that the majority of deposits (83 per cent) were for periods of two years

Table 2.1. Governance Peculiarities and Challenges in the Caribbean, Mid-2000s

Governance Peculiarities	Governance Problems or Challenges
Overreliance on the same pool to select directors (small director pool)	• Widespread cross-directorships • Difficulty in applying the concept of the independent director • Widespread conflicts of interest
Small number of public companies	• Low-volume stock markets • Under-resourced SECs (inability to attract and retain highly skilled persons) • Unsophisticated governance practices • Concentrated number of shareholders
Dominance of private companies	• Highly unregulated private sector • Development of boards and directors remains limited • Board governance is generally not professionalized
Dominance of large family-owned firms	• Little strategic change over time • Limited number of outside directors • Higher instances of CEO duality/executive chairpersons
Heavy state involvement in economic activities	• Governance that is conformance driven • State-owned enterprises with politicized board members
Preference for commercial bank financing	• Inability of stock markets to grow/expand
Lack of overarching regional regulator(s)	• Lack of commonality or coordination in times of regional crises • Poor monitoring and enforcement of governance-related requirements
Weak legislative frameworks	• Limitation on power/authority of regulators • Limited enforcement of laws • Loopholes conducive to a very risky venture
Culture of poor enforcement of laws	• Limited consequences for noncompliance

Source: Derived from an analysis of data from the Caribbean Trade and Investment Report, 2005–2010: Corporate Integration and Cross-Border Development, 2005, and Report on the Caribbean Corporate Governance Forum, 2003.

or less made the deposit base very volatile. Withdrawal of either or both of these deposits could have placed the institution in a serious liquidity situation.

During this first inspection, it was discovered that loans and advances were at US$8.7 million. This represented a loan-to-deposit ratio of 204 per cent and indicated that TCBL was severely overlent. There was also a lack of up-to-date financial information on borrowers, and many of them had poor credit ratings at other financial institutions. TCBL was also guilty of breaches of the Rate of Interest Act, the Hire Purchase Act, the Exchange Control Act and the stipulations in relation to unsecured loans to directors. In November 1984, a second inspection was conducted and revealed that very little had changed in the operations of TCBL. The number of deposits had decreased from ninety-seven to ninety-one, and borrowings from commercial banks had increased by 37 per cent. In addition, approximately 40 per cent of the loan portfolio was classified as "adverse", "sub-standard" or "doubtful".

The incompetence and negligence of the auditors were also factors in this case. The commission's inquiry found that both the audit senior and the audit partner had no experience in auditing financial institutions. Audit working papers that were reviewed by the commission showed a considerable lack of planning and failure to consider issues such as materiality, income recognition criteria and loan loss provisions.

The negligence, incompetence and irresponsible attitude of the board of directors and management also significantly contributed to TCBL's collapse. Although the company was in a dangerous and risky position, the board declared and paid a 7 per cent dividend in 1985 and 1986. The company's under-capitalization and the difficulty it was encountering with high-risk customers should have prompted a more prudent and responsible decision. The Commission of Inquiry eventually concluded as follows:

- The business of TCBL was carried on by the directors in a manner that unfairly prejudiced and unfairly disregarded the interests of the depositors, shareholders and creditors.
- The directors were negligent in that they failed to exercise due care and diligence in the management of the company.
- The chairman and the managing director withdrew funds of the company without the authority of the board of directors.
- The managing director caused fictitious entries to be made in the account books of the company, and several of these transactions appeared to be fraudulent.
- The auditors failed to adhere to generally accepted auditing standards in the acceptance and execution of the audit.

- The Central Bank of Barbados failed to exercise its powers under section 36 of the Central Bank Act, which allowed it to place restrictions on Trade Confirmers.

Although the Commission of Inquiry provided its findings to the director of public prosecutors, no one has been charged and/or prosecuted to date.

The second major governance-related failure in the Caribbean was Jamaica's financial-sector meltdown in 1995. This crisis resulted in the following being deemed insolvent: six of the nine existing commercial banks, which accounted for 60 per cent of the deposits; five life insurance companies, which accounted for 90 per cent of the premium income; one-third of all merchant banks and several building societies (Kirkpatrick and Tennant 2002, 30). Consequently, the Bank of Jamaica was forced to inject J$18 billion of special support to the local commercial banks and affiliated insurance companies to meet the demands of depositors for withdrawal. This crisis was due to weak governance and inadequate insurance and banking regulations (Kirkpatrick and Tennant 2002). These deficiencies can be further outlined as follows: (1) the absence of or failure to comply with proper internal control procedures, (2) poor risk management and inadequate portfolio diversification, (3) poor quality of management and strategic planning, (4) the failure to exercise due diligence and care, (5) a high incidence of connected party lending and (6) breach of fiduciary duty and fraud (CARICOM Secretariat 2005, 341).

Understanding the CLICO/CFL Meltdown

CLICO was the largest insurance company in the Caribbean, the flagship of its parent company, CFL. In turn, CFL was the largest privately owned conglomerate in the Commonwealth Caribbean, with operations spanning its core business, insurance, but also including financial services, real estate development, manufacturing, agriculture and forestry, retail and distribution, energy, media and communications (Soverall 2012, 167). CFL operated in thirty-two countries through its associated and joint-venture companies and through more than sixty-five subsidiaries spanning the Caribbean, Florida, Europe, the Middle East and Asia. Until 2009 it controlled assets in excess of TT$100 billion. CFL also had a 55 per cent majority ownership of Republic Bank, the country's largest commercial bank, as well as Methanol Holdings of

Trinidad Limited, then the world's largest methanol plant. It also controlled British American Insurance Company, which is one of the main insurance companies in the Eastern Caribbean. In addition, the four largest financial institutions in CFL managed assets of over TT$38 billion, which constituted approximately 25 per cent of Trinidad and Tobago's gross domestic product (Soverall and Persaud 2013, 18).

Yet CFL's business model was flawed. Although CLICO was a subsidiary of the parent company, CL Financial, it functioned as the primary source of deposits that were used to finance CFL's expansion through investments and acquisitions held in the names of other entities in the group (Soverall and Persaud 2013, 18). The nature of the ownership structure of these enterprises significantly varied. Some were wholly owned and managed by CFL, others were simply investments which CFL did not participate in managing and some were a mixture of both. In some cases, CFL borrowed from other subsidiary financial institutions to invest, and in most cases it used CLICO, Clico Investment Bank Limited, British American or Caribbean Money Market Brokers as the conduit for purchasing investments or borrowed from it to do so. In short, CLICO became the guarantor for many of CFL's assets, most of which were heavily pledged and, therefore, limited in terms of the potential proceeds to be derived from asset sales.

By operating with such a model, the Central Bank of Trinidad and Tobago alleged that CLICO operated an external ponzi scheme in which the insurance company took in new money from policyholders and mutual fund investors, as well as an internal ponzi scheme in which money was diverted or misappropriated away from CLICO to fund Clico Investment Bank, CFL, and other group entities with little or no prospect of return (Henry 2009). In other words, CLICO took large numbers of deposits on a short-term basis, paying high interest rates, and used them for long-term investments which resulted in significant cash-flow problems that precipitated its ultimate collapse.

There are always underlying vulnerabilities in the origin of a crisis. In the case of CLICO/CFL there were a mismatch between assets and liabilities, excessive leveraging of balance sheet assets, a preponderance of intragroup transactions, absence of an effective risk management framework and plain capital inadequacy (Soverall and Persaud 2013, 21). These were compounded by a weak legislative and regulatory infrastructure in which CFL – the holding company – was not subjected to adequate formal regulatory oversight and practiced poor internal governance when it did pay attention to such details (Soverall and Persaud 2013, 21). The previously stated factors are also related to a lack of good governance practices among the boards of directors, executives, external auditors, and regulators of CLICO/CFL. The consequences of years of persistent bad management and governance within CLICO/CFL, together with inaction by regulators, were eventually manifested in 2009. The global financial crisis of 2008 was simply the catalyst for the inevitable meltdown of CLICO/CFL (Jhinkoo 2013, 3).

The collapse of CLICO/CFL forced the intervention of the Government of the Republic Trinidad and Tobago because "the financial condition of CLICO, CLICO Investment Bank (CIB), and British American Insurance Company (Trinidad) Limited, subsidiaries of the parent company, CL Financial, threatened the interest of depositors, policy holders and creditors of these institutions and posed danger of disruption or damage to the financial system of Trinidad and Tobago" (GORTT 2009, 1–3). This intervention was formalized through a memorandum of understanding between the Trinidad and Tobago government and CFL dated 30 January 2009. The overarching aim of the memorandum of understanding was to protect the interests of the depositors, policyholders, and creditors of these institutions as well as to correct the financial problems of CLICO, Clico Investment Bank and British American.

In a move towards correcting the financial conditions of these companies, CFL agreed to sell all its shareholdings in Republic Bank Limited, Methanol Holdings (Trinidad) Limited, and Caribbean Money Market Brokers. CFL also agreed to sell all or any of its other assets as may be required to achieve the said correction (GORTT 2009). In addition, the proceeds of the sale of assets would be applied to satisfy the statutory fund requirements for CLICO and British American under the Insurance Act of 1980 and the balancing of the third-party assets and liabilities portfolio of Clico Investment Bank. However, in the event that there was a shortfall after the application of the proceeds realized from the sale of the assets, CFL warranted to provide collateral which could include a secured charge on the fixed and floating assets of CFL, CLICO and British American; this amount was to be sufficient to secure any financial assistance to be provided by the government with respect to that shortfall for the purpose of maintaining public confidence and stability in the financial system (GORTT 2009). Moreover, according to the memorandum of understanding, CFL agreed that "CLICO and BA [British American] will restructure its business and operations to conform to traditional life insurance business lines in a manner approved" by the Central Bank of Trinidad and Tobago, including "a reconstitution of the Board of Directors, Board Committees and senior management", selections of whose members were to be approved by the government (GORTT 2009). The corrective measures also included the need for CLICO/CFL to fundamentally change and adopt a more robust and less risky business model, and also to change its corporate governance structure (Williams 2009, 9).

The Commission of Inquiry into the failure of CLICO further revealed that the Central Bank had a number of concerns about the quality of CLICO's corporate governance, specifically the infrequency with which the CLICO board met and the limited number of independent directors on its board (Colman 2013, 14). The board's role seemed to be simply to rubber-stamp decisions made by the executive chairman. Furthermore, CLICO operated without an audit committee or risk committee as well as without an investment committee (Colman 2013). Therefore, there was no monitoring of decisions, risks and investments. Moreover, conflicts of interest were prevalent.

The previous discussion underscored the importance of internal and external governance practices in the financial sector. Internally, it is evident that the role of management and the core principles of management and risk management were inadequately exercised. Prudent leadership from the boards of directors would have ensured better monitoring of management's behavior as well as adequate risk management, which would, in turn, have protected the interests of depositors, shareholders, and other stakeholders. The directors, however, failed in their fiduciary duties and neglected to fulfil their roles with the duty of care and skills required. Therefore, while corporate governance frameworks existed from a statutory standpoint, in practice, compliance with these was mostly unobserved. Further, both management and boards in these cases may not have possessed the required competency to govern their respective institutions within the complexities of the ever-evolving innovative financial activities.

Externally, there were a number of key regulatory gaps. Regulators failed to properly supervise the institutions and take appropriate actions. This might have resulted from a combination of factors, such as incompetence, lack of resources and political interference. Without robust supervision and timely actions, the vulnerabilities increased over time, leading to these crises. Arguably, the smooth functioning of financial institutions will always depend on the quality of oversight by regulatory bodies. In addition, the legislative frameworks in the jurisdictions in which these cases occurred not only failed, in certain aspects, to provide regulators with the level of supervisory authority needed but also lagged in comparison to the rapidly evolving operations and complexities of financial institutions. The regulatory gaps, together with the deficiencies among the various boards, management teams and auditors, clearly demonstrate the importance of good corporate governance practices for firm performance and sustainability.

Recommendations and Measures to Be Taken Following the CLICO/CFL Meltdown

The region's pursuit of good corporate governance has been slow, with limited pressure from government, the media, civil society or even the professional and academic communities. Prior to the CLICO/CFL meltdown, the region had not experienced corporate failures that had regionwide consequences. Thus it was reasonable to expect that in the years following the CLICO/CFL meltdown there would have been pressure from various constituents for game-changing corporate governance reforms across the region. However, this was limited. On the national level, Trinidad and Tobago appointed a Commission of Inquiry into the failure of CLICO which also assessed the collapse of the Hindu Credit Union. The inquiry revealed details surrounding the circumstances leading to the failures of these two financial entities, but there would be no penalties or charges against the persons involved. Recommendations from the inquiry were to be used as guidelines for improving the regulatory and governance practices in Trinidad and Tobago.

In the legal sphere, the Insurance Act of Trinidad and Tobago was amended in 2009 in order to strengthen the role of the Central Bank, while the new Securities Act was proclaimed in December 2012. The Securities Act of 2012 is designed to provide protection to investors from unfair, improper or fraudulent practices; to foster fair and efficient securities and confidence in the securities industry of Trinidad and Tobago; to reduce systemic risk and to repeal and replace the Securities Industry Act of 1995 (Khan 2012). A new insurance bill was also introduced in 2013 to provide a new regulatory framework for the insurance industry, including the privately administered pension fund plans.

The bill introduced best practices in the areas of corporate governance, risk management, consolidated supervision, and consumer protection to the insurance industry. It also strengthened the powers of the inspector of financial institutions of the Central Bank of Trinidad and Tobago, which is legally empowered to oversee the operations of the insurance industry and to intervene in the sector when it becomes necessary (GORTT 2013).

Additionally, a Trinidad and Tobago Corporate Governance Code was launched in November 2013. The development of the code was based on a partnership initiative led by the Caribbean Corporate Governance Institute, the Trinidad and Tobago Chamber of Industry and Commerce and the Trinidad and Tobago Stock Exchange. The code seeks to enhance business governance and performance, strengthen transparency and efficiency in the market and improve the overall investment culture in Trinidad and Tobago. It is not rules-based but rather aspirational in philosophy, in keeping with international reporting trends, and strives for a high adoption rate among state and private corporations with public accountability, such as listed corporations, regulated corporations, and corporations with fiduciary accountability (Caribbean Corporate Governance Institute 2013).

On the regional level, the CLICO/CFL meltdown prompted calls by Caribbean leaders for greater regional cooperation on the regulation and supervision of such firms. CARICOM leaders recognized not only the need to affect appropriate reform in financial-sector policy but also the need to enhance national regulatory and supervisory systems, including the rationalization and consolidation of these systems across the region to ensure safety, soundness and stability in the financial services sector (CARICOM Secretariat, 2010, 21–22). Furthermore, in recognizing that there is significant financial integration across the region based on both organic growth and mergers and acquisitions, cross-border supervision – according to these leaders – needs to be critically enhanced by the regional regulatory organizations: the Committee of Central Bank Governors, the Caribbean Association of Insurance Regulators, the Caribbean Group of Securities Regulators, and the Regional Competition Commission (CARICOM Secretariat 2010, 21–22).

Throughout the region there has been ongoing governance training for directors, and governance-related guidelines have been revised accordingly. Nonetheless, these measures and recommendations have been channeled almost exclusively to the finance-related sector, although the region's corporate landscape is dominated by privately owned entities that are unregulated. Table 2.2 provides a timeline and overview of CLICO's operations across the Caribbean and the respective initiatives taken to address the meltdown.

Table 2.2. CL Financial Operations in the Caribbean: Costs and Actions Taken, 2009–2012

The Bahamas	February 2009: The Registrar of Insurance Companies in the Bahamas appointed a liquidator for Colonial Life Insurance Company (Bahamas) Limited (CLICO). March 2012: A settlement of US$1 million was made with the US Internal Revenue Service. This settlement results in a significant reduction of the IRS claim, thereby freeing up excess cash that is needed desperately. May 2012: Some 138.3 acres of the Wellington Preserve project were sold for US$13.384 million. After expenses related to the property's administration and homeowners' association were covered, it resulted in the recovery of US$10 million. This was the first recovery of funds for CLICO (Bahamas) Limited. Some 283 acres remain to be sold.
Barbados	February 2009: The Central Bank of Barbados deposited US$5 million into CLICO's mortgage subsidiary and provided access to a special credit window in the event that additional liquidity would be needed. May 2009: CLICO Holdings Ltd. signed a memorandum of understanding with the Barbados government for the establishment of an oversight committee to manage the sale of the regulated entities. June 2010: CLICO Mortgage Finance Company was acquired by the Barbados Public Workers Cooperative Credit Union Ltd. The CLICO International Life and CLICO General Insurance companies were placed under judicial management. October 2012: The judicial manager of CLICO International Life Insurance Limited (CIL) received sanction from the High Court of Barbados to pursue a restructuring plan for the company. The proposed plan would result in a write-down in value of all policyholders' liabilities (traditional policies and EFPAs) to match the estimated value of the company's net available assets. The restructured policyholder liabilities and all the assets of CIL will be transferred to a new company which will be separately governed and managed.

(*Table 2.2 continues*)

Table 2.2. (*continued*)

Eastern Caribbean Currency Union (ECCU)	April 2009: A memorandum of understanding was signed between the governments of the ECCU and the Central Bank of Barbados and Trinidad and Tobago to establish a liquidity support fund of US$80 million: Barbados – US$5 million; ECCU governments – US$10 million; Trinidad and Tobago – US$50 million via the Caribbean Community (CARICOM) Petroleum Fund; Regional and International Organisation – US$15 million. This was to be used to provide financial support to the Eastern Caribbean territories that were at risk following the meltdown of CLICO and BIACO. November 2012: The ECCU announced that they had sourced US$100 million, of which US$24 million came from the CARICOM Petroleum Facility, US$36 million from the Government of Trinidad and Tobago, and US$40 million from the Caribbean Development Bank. This was to be used to pay off policyholders.
Guyana	February 2009: CLICO (Guyana) was placed under judicial management. September 2010: The government offered guarantees to policyholders (excluding life insurance products) up to GY$30 million: • Policyholders with investments in the company of less than GY$30 million (US$145,000) as of February 2009 were to be repaid in full. The Guyana government was to make available GY$3.6 billion to finance the payout, of which about GY$2.7 billion would be used to pay off in full all holders of investment annuity policies and other insurance liabilities not in dispute, subject to a maximum limit of GY$30 million per policyholder. • A total of 4,366 holders of executive flexible-premium annuities and other undisputed claims against the company would be paid in full. The thirty-nine large policyholders of the company would then be given support, and a remaining GY$900 million would be utilized to pay these policyholders up to a maximum of GY$30 million each, with priority given to institutional policyholders. • With most of the liabilities remaining in government agencies such as the National Insurance Scheme, the Guyana Forestry Commission, the Dependents' Pension Fund and Guyoil, the government would also have to ensure that their interests were protected.

(*Table 2.2 continues*)

Table 2.2. (*continued*)

Trinidad and Tobago	January 2009: The CL Financial Group signed a memorandum of understanding with the Government of Trinidad and Tobago to provide financial support for the group's financial services. April 2009: The Government of Trinidad and Tobago announced it would be spending approximately TT$5billion during the following two years in the bailout of CLICO and BIACO. November 2010: The government established a Commission of Enquiry into the failure of CL Financial Limited, Colonial Life Insurance Company (Trinidad) Limited, CLICO Investment Bank Limited, British American Insurance Company (Trinidad) Limited and Caribbean Money Market Brokers Limited June 2011: The first sitting of the commission took place. November 2012: It was reported that between January 2009 and now an estimated TT$20 billion was spent by the Government of Trinidad and Tobago in the bailout. The majority of the TT$20 billion was spent on paying back policyholders of CLICO and the British American Insurance Company's Executive Flexible Premium Annuity. November 2012: As the extended shareholders agreement came to an end on December 12, 2012, the minister of finance identified three actions to be implemented by the government in 2013 to bring a conclusion to the bailout: • The establishment of a TT$1 billion CLICO Investment Fund (CLF) which would begin trading in January 2013. • The establishment of a new insurance company. The insurance policies of CLICO and British American would be transferred to the new, yet unnamed, company which would be set up that month to begin the transition. • A filing of a claim with CLF for money spent by the government. Unless CLF could meet the claim, the government had room to negotiate an extension to the memorandum agreement.

Source: Caribbean Centre for Money and Finance (2013).

Towards a Responsible Leadership Approach to Governance

The extent to which the region's compliance-focused regulations and laws would provide an impetus for change in corporate behavior is also questioned. This is based on the observation that where stiffer governance regulations or laws and penalties have been enacted, a decline in corporate scandals has not necessarily occurred. For instance, following the series of major corporate and accounting scandals affecting Enron, Tyco International, Adelphia, Peregrine Systems and Worldcom in the United States, the Sarbanes-Oxley Act (SOX) of 2002 was passed. This act established new or enhanced standards for all boards of US public companies, as well as management and public accounting firms. As a result of SOX, top management must individually certify the accuracy of financial information. In addition, penalties for fraudulent financial activity became much more severe. SOX elevated the requirements for the independence of outside auditors who review the accuracy of corporate financial statements and increased the oversight role of boards of directors.

Yet it was primarily irresponsible governance and leadership which caused the global economic crisis of 2008. This underscores the inherent limitations of regulatory and compliance-driven measures and forces us to consider other strategies to achieve effective governance and ultimately leadership (Pless and Maak 2011). SOX has neither prevented frauds nor instituted fairness (Malone 2008), but it has created the perception that stricter governance laws were needed to safeguard investors. However, it is arguable whether a fundamental change in the attitudes and behaviors of boards and executives has occurred. This suggests that board training and other strategies aimed at improving governance must give greater attention to the ethics and responsibility aspects of good governance.

It is based on this perspective that a compliance-regulatory focus needs to be significantly complemented with the building of a practice of responsible leadership. Responsible leadership represents a concept that bridges the fields of social responsibility and leadership and can be appropriately applied in the study and practice of corporate governance. Although the definition of responsible leadership is evolving, it can be considered to include intentional actions taken by leaders to benefit the stakeholders of a company and actions taken to avoid harmful consequences for corporate stakeholders and the larger society (Stahl and de Luque 2014). Responsible leadership crosses levels of analysis by considering individuals, groups and organizations as a whole. Compared to related forms of leadership, such as ethical or values-based leadership, responsible leadership has a unique applicability to the upper levels of organizations (Waldman and Galvin 2008). This includes executives and certainly boards of directors, who are charged with directing and controlling the decisions and behavior of an organization. Therefore, at the core of responsible leadership is a focus on how individual perceptions, decisions and actions, particularly those at senior levels, impact the social and financial performance of their organizations (Stahl and de Luque 2014).

Responsibility is one of the core pillars of corporate governance and requires that directors carry out their duties with honesty, probity and integrity while recognizing the rights of stakeholders established by law or through mutual agreements. This encourages cooperation between corporations and stakeholders in creating wealth, jobs and the sustainability of financially sound enterprises. This core pillar has been given limited attention in the attempts to improve corporate governance in the region. Responsible leadership not only addresses corporate scandals, but it also extends in scope to consider the changes in and new demands of business contexts. Responsible leadership therefore takes a stakeholder approach to governance whereby the importance of ethics and social responsibility to organizational effectiveness through engagement of diverse stakeholder groups accentuates the duties of businesses and boards of directors beyond profitability and shareholder returns (Singhapakdi et al. 1996). This is in contrast to the still dominant view that a business's sole responsibility is to maximize returns to shareholders.

Stakeholders demand that businesses and their leaders take active roles in fostering responsible behavior, internal and external to the organization, such as creating responsible organizational cultures, pursuing sustainability, and acting like good corporate citizens (Maak 2007). The scope of responsible leadership is directly linked to the increasing attention by various stakeholders to the roles and responsibilities of business leaders in the pursuit of a global common good. In this context, the scope of good corporate governance changes. Neither boards of directors, management nor regulators should focus only on shareholder interests, because society now demands that the interests of all key stakeholders be considered in a balanced manner. Profit remains critical, but the way in which it is derived becomes the key challenge with the new demands of and changes in business contexts. A responsible-leadership approach is integral to responding to these contexts.

Conclusion

This chapter has provided insights into the state of corporate governance in the Caribbean by examining three major governance failures, and it proposes a responsible leadership approach to corporate governance because it is much more relevant than earlier approaches to the changing business contexts of the region. Further research is certainly required, but the chapter has created a framework for continuing the discourse on Caribbean corporate governance.

References

Caribbean Community (CARICOM) Secretariat. 2005. *Caribbean Trade and Investment Report 2005*. Georgetown, Guyana: CARICOM Secretariat.

———. 2010. *Caribbean Trade and Investment Report 2010: Strategies for Recovery, Renewal and Reform*. Georgetown, Guyana: CARICOM Secretariat.

Caribbean Corporate Governance Institute. 2013. *Trinidad and Tobago Corporate Governance Code 2013*. Port of Spain: Caribbean Corporate Governance Institute. www.caribbeangovernance.org/Resources/Pictures/ttcode2013web.pdf.

Colman, A. 2013. *Commission of Enquiry into the Failure of CL Financial Limited, 2010–2013*. Port of Spain: Colonial Life Insurance Company (Trinidad) Limited, CLICO Investment Bank Limited, British American Insurance Company (Trinidad) Limited, Caribbean Money Market Brokers Limited and Hindu Credit Union.

Commission of Inquiry into the Causes of the Collapse of Trade Confirmers Ltd. 1988. Report of Commission of Inquiry into the Causes of the Collapse of Trade Confirmers (Barbados) Ltd., a Company Registered under the Companies Act Cap. 308.

Crane, A., and D. Matten. 2010. *Business Ethics: Managing Corporate Citizenship and Sustainability in the Age of Globalization*. Oxford: Oxford University Press.

ECCB (Eastern Caribbean Central Bank). 2003. Report on the Caribbean Corporate Governance Forum. Working document, September 2013. http://www.ecseonline.com/PDF/Caribbean%20Corporate%20Governance%20Forum%20Report.pdf.

GORTT (Government of the Republic of Trinidad and Tobago). 2009. Memorandum of Understanding between Minister of Finance and CL Financial Limited. Signed at the Central Bank of Trinidad and Tobago, Port of Spain, Trinidad, 30 January 2009.

———. 2013. Howai Delivers Insurance Bill 2013. www.news.gov.tt/content/howai-delivers-insurance-bill-2013#.WNEwV6IpDIV.

Henry, L. 2009. The CLICO Bailout: Issues, Impact, and Implications for T&T and the Wider Caribbean. Paper presented at the Department of Economics Forum, Learning Resource Centre, University of the West Indies, St Augustine, Trinidad and Tobago, 12 February.

Jhinkoo, J. 2013. The CL Financial Debacle: Four Years Later. *Caribbean Centre for Money and Finance Newsletter* 6 (1): 1–3.

Khan, Aleem. 2012. T&T Faces New Blacklist if Securities Act Not Passed. *Guardian*, 1 November. www.guardian.co.tt/business-guardian/2012-10-31/tt-faces-new-blacklist-if-securities-act-not-passed.

Kirkpatrick, C., and D. Tennant. 2002. Responding to Financial Crisis: The Case of Jamaica. *World Development* 30 (11): 1933–50.

Maak, T. 2007. Responsible Leadership, Stakeholder Engagement and the Emergence of Social Capital. *Journal of Business Ethics* 74 (4): 329–43.

Malone, M. 2008. Washington Is Killing Silicon Valley. *Wall Street Journal*, 22 December 2008. www.wsj.com/articles/SB122990472028925207.

OECD (Organization for Economic Co-operation and Development). 2015a. G20/OECD Principles of Corporate Governance: Report to G20 Finance Ministers and

Central Bank Governors. Report presented at the meeting of G20 Finance Ministers and Central Bank Governors, Ankara, Turkey, 4–5 September.

———. 2015b. *Risk Management and Corporate Governance.* Paris: OECD. www.oecd.org/daf/ca/risk-management-corporate-governance.pdf.

Papidze, M. 2014. Corporate Governance to Help Georgian Companies Attract Foreign Investors. *The Financial*, 22 December 2014. https://issuu.com/financial/docs/csr_2014_epaper.

Pless, N., and T. Maak. 2011. Responsible Leadership: Pathways to the Future. *Journal of Business Ethics* 98 (1): 3–13.

Singhapakdi, A., S. Vitell, K. Rallapalli and K. Kraft. 1996. The Perceived Role of Ethics and Social Responsibility: A Scale Development. *Journal of Business Ethics* 15 (11): 1113–40.

Soverall, W. 2012. CLICO's Collapse: Poor Corporate Governance. *American International Journal of Contemporary Research* 2 (2): 166–78.

Soverall, W., and W. Persaud. 2013. A Study of Corporate Failure and the Political Economy of Financial Regulation in Trinidad and Tobago and the Caribbean. *International Journal of Humanities and Social Science* 3 (16): 17–28.

Stahl, G., and M. Sully de Luque. 2014. Antecedents of Responsible Leadership Behavior: A Research Synthesis, Conceptual Framework, and Agenda for Future Research. *Academy of Management Perspectives* 28 (3): 235–54.

Waldman, D., and B. Galvin. 2008. Alternative Perspectives of Responsible Leadership. *Organizational Dynamics* 37 (4): 327–41.

Williams, E. S. 2009. Challenge of Regulation in T&T Financial Sector. *Barbados Business Authority*, 16 February, 9.

CHAPTER 3

Identity Formation in the English-Speaking Caribbean: Towards a Sociodynamic Perspective

Ronald Marshall and Russell Foote

The construction of a Caribbean identity has been elusive from the end of slavery to the present. Many attempts have been made by various writers who have interpreted the problem in various ways. Some have criticized the inhabitants of this geographic space as being responsible for the problem, and at times they chide them for slavishly imitating the identity of others while at the same time accusing them of displaying a lack of creativity in dealing with their own issues (Walcott 1974).

This chapter aims to add to the discussion on the fashioning of a Caribbean identity. It argues that a Caribbean identity is still in its formation stage, being held captive by policies and programmes without the best considerations for groups residing in its multicultural setting. In addition, it attempts to identify the location of the problem by examining the social, cultural, educational and political policies that hinder or fail to facilitate its development. In the main, we argue that there is a multicultural social dynamic influencing behaviours that are thrown up by various policy positions, and this dynamic needs to be examined in order to shed more light on the identity question.

The Legacy

The Caribbean is a region that encompasses a small space with a short history of transitions and transformations generated by "meetings and confrontations . . . of successive waves of migrants" (Ramchand 2004). The discovery of a chain of islands, collectively referred to as the "Caribbean", was the stimulus for a series of events that were largely interpreted in negative terms because of the foreign presence and management of the means of production in several sectors of Caribbean economies and the emergence and maintenance of a social class structure in which power, authority and influence resided in the "bowels" of the white upper class and everyone else gives their labour power (Williams 1979).

The cumulative effects of these factors precipitated dependency (Best and Levitt 2009), a plantation-type mentality (Beckford 1999), cultural pluralism (Smith 1965) and creolization (Brathwaite 2005). The impacts of these on various Caribbean peoples and contexts have also been captured in the following:

1. the music of the region (Manuel 2006);
2. the literature of the region (Aiyejina and Morgan 2006);
3. the West Indians' home-abroad relationship, which affects the formation of their individual and communal identities (Baugh 2006), along with colour;
4. how we govern ourselves amid contesting ethnic claims;
5. accounts of the growth of the Caribbean nations (Lewis 2004);
6. the development-related writings of Alex Dupuy (2001);
7. cultural discourses of orality, humour, rumour, social commentary, picong and the calypsos of the region (Rohlehr 2004);
8. a wide variety of commodified musical fusions and festivals, such as reggae and Carnival, which are reflective of a sense of agency emerging out of the regional socioeconomic struggles (Rohlehr 2004);
9. a mushrooming of indigenous religious denominations such as Rastafarianism, Orisha and the Pentecostal movement, among others; and
10. the emerging emphasis of Caribbean feminists on difference, reflective of self and the other (Reddock and Barrow 2001).

The historical influences and subsequent questioning of our development approaches, form of politics, economic means and ends, cultural contestations and educational emphases have all been reflected in the Caribbean region's preoccupation with forging its own identity. This has been particularly challenging as a result of the effects of colonization and counter-identities "and the distortions of living in a world culturally dependent on and dominated by some centre" (Hall 2001). For the Caribbean, attempts have been and continue to be made in terms of managing the nature, intensity and scale of these changes. Most of these efforts have been made at the institutional and organizational levels, thereby reinforcing a form and expression of this development. The extent of its successes has been debatable, given the absence of common understandings and definitions of development which are informed by a specific set of developmental needs of the Caribbean. Such efforts have also been stymied by individuals at various levels of the society, who at times prioritize self before country, conveniently shifting their "identities" and allegiances while at the same time voicing concerns about the lack of cohesion in the region. For example, West Indian people are offended that their nationality does not rank among those of Americans, British, or Canadians (Thomas 2012). They agonize that the Caribbean islands' image is "treated with disdain" and is noted only for "sun, surf and sand", something they attribute to cultural racism (Grosfoguel 1999; Heron 2001). Many blame the governments in the region for this impression.

Increasing exposure to education and extra-regional migration has fuelled a discursive reconstruction and consciousness of the impression, and this has been both revealing and gratifying in the midst of our diversity. Consequently, there is an ebb and flow emanating from these experiences. West Indians are proud, but this pride is sometimes constrained in the way we perceive ourselves by identifying with others' cultures. Brathwaite (2005), for example, aptly articulates struggles of the inner self in his poem "Red Rising" with the phrase "locomotives in me would like to straighten strange eye / self out". Clarke (2004) also argued that our people live in a douendom where it is believed that we are going forward, but we are really moving backwards. It was art, poetry and drama which were used to capture the mundaneness and excitements of the world, family and community life, which were considered "a new start, a culture" (King and Walcott 2000). In the Caribbean, this indigenous cultural expression continues to be reflected in our cuisine, creative and performing arts, fashion and dialect. We have been able to maintain these within the context of changes in the society wrought by the demands of modernization. These forms of expression also suggest the existence of a core set of values on which a West Indian identity might be built.

The extent to which we appreciate this lasting indigeneity is reflected in how we speak of ourselves and in what Ramchand (2004) sees as the centrality of dialect in West Indian literature. Caribbean dialects offer very useful understandings and assessments of our past and present experiences. We also interface with each other's culture in song, dance and dress, as well as participate in public celebrations such as Divali and Emancipation Day in Trinidad. The Caribbean's sense of identity is noticeable in the support of West Indian cricket (Dhondy 2001). It is also to be noted that the region's multiculturalism has been maintained due to increasing interethnic relationships and marriages among whites and West Indians, Africans and East Indians, as well as descendants of Spain and Africa. In addition, the mushrooming of many new religious groups has caused major traditional religions to lose much of their membership to some of the new ones. There is therefore a definite relationship between indigeneity and identity, in addition to what Nettleford (2003) calls "a legacy of a heritage of separate and shattered identities".

This indigeneity-identity relationship has been established in the works of Manuel's (1989) *Caribbean Currents*; Elder's (1968) *Congo Drum to Steelband*; and Nettleford's (1993) *Inward Stretch, Outward Reach: A Voice from the Caribbean.* Identity concerns have also been highlighted in the calypso music of the region. The unfolding narratives of resistance (Meeks 2000) reflect scenarios in which decision-makers were identifying with each other, while the masses were seriously troubled. Since the latter and the former subscribe to opposing discourses, both national and regional identity formations remain a challenging prospect. The absence of such nationalism is also featured in Naipaul's (1969) *Mimic Men,* a narrative of how people in the Caribbean diaspora began to aspire to be foreigners after yearning to finding a space to call their own, a theme emergent in Naipaul's *In a Free State* (1973) and *The Enigma of Arrival* (1987).

Dabydeen (2005), a Guyanese narrator of The *Intended,* shows how labelling of immigrants in the diaspora fuelled a sense of identity despite the presence of Naipaulian themes of mimicking other peoples' identity. For example, La Guerre (1974) recounts the leadership challenges immigrant Indians faced in the early stages of the development of a plural diaspora. Samaroo (2006) emphasizes the vicissitudes of race relations which generated varying degrees of both inclusion and exclusion of East Indians in the Caribbean. Look Lai (2006) describes similar concerns for the Chinese but suggests that because of their tightly knit lifestyle it was less problematic for those groups to adjust to their new realities. Studies of the ethnic minorities in the Caribbean have shown, for example, that

1. there is "the complexity of ethnic identity formation" (Morgan 2009, 195);
2. location contributed to the exclusion of the Amerindian communities of Guyana (Fox 1996); and
3. the Chinese in Jamaica initially resisted creolization because of their strong sense of ethnicity and business orientations but became more accommodating in later years even as they tended to define the extent of this accommodation (Bryan 1996).

Again, there are other reasons for this displacement of a Caribbean identity. There is a widening gap between the aforementioned aspects of the Caribbean's sociocultural landscape and its political–economic–educational base. While macro-level decision-making eventually impacted individuals and communities, some experienced difficulty in relating to and identifying with individuals at the micro level, even though the existence of common art forms and festivities speak to a oneness. But this is not the only challenge. As well, changing gender identities are tied very much to economic and cultural issues. Women could now relate to Bob Marley's vision of emancipating oneself from mental slavery. They envisioned and operationalized an agenda of new possibilities (Bailey, Leo-Rhynie and Barrow 2001) that is subsumed and propelled outwards under the banner of the feminist paradigm. At the same time, however, the increased risk of male marginalization has presented itself (Barrow 1995). This development has raised awareness surrounding male–female relationships, childhood care and adolescent growth and development, threatening to alter traditional family forms and functioning. In the process, identity formation has become a distraction.

The macroeconomic aspect is reflected in unemployment and the need for small entrepreneurship and job creation. Failure to address these problems has led to a market for the drug trade and consequential mental health issues, child abuse and neglect, and homelessness (Premdas 2007). Suffice it to say that the region's economic development within recent times has experienced several transitions, commencing with a state-led approach and proceeding to nationalization and to trade and income liberalization. This has created a backlash, since most of the groups who benefited from these initiatives appeared to have had an advantage over other groups such as Africans and East Indians. The high visibility of whites and Chinese in the financial sector triggered the 1970 Black Power riots in Trinidad as a response to these inequalities. This allowed for a greater influx of Africans and East Indians into the financial services sector.

The Caribbean's experience with structural adjustment have also had adverse effects in that it shrank the middle class and provided little social mobility except for the privileged few. This led to problems in Guyana, Jamaica and Grenada (Taylor 2011). During this period "class conflict" appeared muted, yet obvious, reflected in attitudes, relationships and institutional disruptions. The network of cleavages which emerged significantly influenced voting patterns as political parties continued subtly to appeal to tribal instincts as a means of gaining an edge over their rivals at the polls.

Given these nagging and paradoxical issues, developmental efforts towards political and economic integration have remained elusive, commencing with the establishment of the Caribbean Federation and proceeding to that of the Caribbean Free Trade Association, followed by CARICOM. During colonialism and up until independence, "the Caribbean has been characterized by a relatively low level of internal social dynamism" (Sankatsing 2001), a dynamism which owes its existence, in the first instance, to its economic approach. Caribbean countries tend to vacillate between fully embracing capitalism and retaining their traditional ways of life. This ambivalence has contributed in no small way to the way some groups perceive the natural resources of the various territories. For example, a frequently raised question is this: Should these resources belong to the indigenous groups, or should they be exploited by "newcomers" representing industrialists and foreign investors? Thus, the leaders of the region are caught between exploring their countries' natural resources for national development and leaving it up for the nationals to decide how they should be directed.

Conceptualizing Sociodynamism

This brings the focus of this debate to an appreciation of a constellation of social factors and what they mean for Caribbean identity. Sociodynamism is reflected in a cluster of simultaneous convergences and divergences – activities of social institutions and processes; constructions, misconstructions and deconstructions of societal issues and alignments, dealignments and realignments of individuals, groups, communities and institutions. These behaviours reflect the type of economic, cultural and ethnic issues that could meld into a West Indian identity. They speak to a repertoire of issues and disunities – some connecting, others not – brought about by ethnic, economic and political expectations.

In the circumstances, the dynamic impact of the interplay of micro and macro factors tends to redound to self and others as individuals struggle to give meaning to their own social space. The unfolding of such interactions has generated a variety of changes, anticipations and expectations. Therefore, what appears to be stable on the surface may often mask deep-rooted identity issues. Specifically, the model of sociodynamism refers to the ways in which new social forms tend to weave a pattern of economic, cultural and political behaviours which come to be regarded as acceptable normal social practices. But as community and national unity lie in waiting, it is sobering to continue to believe that we are "making progress" while our social existence and sense of self are mired in the incohesive constructions and contradictions of "indecisive", "focus-lacking", "region-specific" programmes and policies.

Sociodynamic society is seen in nation-building patterns in some territories with a heavy ethnic presence, such as Guyana, Suriname and Trinidad and Tobago. Jamaica's emphasis on nationalist ideologies in song (reggae), dance and attire remains instrumental in carving a Jamaican identity against a larger non-existent Caribbean one. It is reflected in the extent to which Caribbean people straddle the continuum from being "subjects" to being "objects", sometimes valuing the modern and sometimes the indigenous, sometimes the foreign and sometimes the local, but more the foreign rather than the local. This scenario establishes constraints and possibilities for the crystallization of nationalisms (Bhabha 2004; Puri 2004). The extent of such crystallization has been variously represented across time, as mentioned earlier, in music and drama, poetry, fiction and oral discourses on the various islands. The most serious challenge, however, is how the region can manage its ethnic and cultural cleavages within a multicultural economic base. We now attempt to delineate some of the possibilities.

Political Dynamism

The political dynamic is constitutive of several interweaving factors, each of which receives greater attention and importance at different points in time, and some of which operate in combination to shape political events (political campaigns, decision-making and voting patterns). It also has to do with who gets what, why and how. Some of these factors include the timing of entry into the political arena, personality, alliances with individuals and organizations, communication style (Trent and Freidenberg 2008), the resource base of the economy, growing population needs, institutional operations and development strategies. Central to this dynamism is the role of the heads of government and their leadership styles:

1. Forbes Burnham of Guyana declared himself president for life and did whatever was necessary to make this a reality;
2. Michael Manley of Jamaica appeared to vacillate between ideologies and failed in his efforts to appease the black masses and the capitalist class simultaneously (Lamming 1996);
3. Eric Gairy of Grenada was eventually overthrown by others who persistently denounced his oppressive regime;
4. Eric Williams of Trinidad and Tobago appeared enigmatic but emphasized rights and freedom for all, the role of education in providing people with the knowledge and skills needed for all types of occupation that are required in the development process, despite his unpredictable personality (Ryan 2009); and
5. Under Errol Barrow's leadership, Barbados strived to be a noteworthy economic entity.

These leaders understood and were able to expand their support networks (Gray 2004). Subsequent leaders made appeals based on ethnicity, social class, religion and gender. These support bases come alive on specific occasions, particularly during elections. While these political maneuverings increased the likelihood of leaders being returned to power, there has always been some level of political disaffection (Meeks 2000) borne out of the interactions of different interests, the degree of acceptance of countervailing arguments and emotional attachments (Offe 2006; Hodder 2011) to a known or imagined cause.

One therefore has to be wary about these strategies because they are likely to undermine political goodwill, no matter how well-intentioned. Examples include increased marginalization and aligning with gangs, as is the case in Jamaica; allegations of rigging the election machinery in Guyana; and the loss of the traditional community spirit due to feelings of alienation in Trinidad. Generally speaking, increased claims of fear or favour and other issues tend to render the public/private political domain highly problematic.

In this atmosphere there are claims and counterclaims of competing interests, competition and cleavages deriving from region, class (Garner 2008) and political alignments. The extent to which governments are able to reduce social problems is often influenced by voting behaviours. But these issues cannot be fully understood until we acknowledge the presence and contribution of various ethnicities in society. The influx of diverse groups brought "new social problems, conflicts . . . divergent economic, social and political interests" (Moore 1995). To be sure, Caribbean identity is caught up in this revolving scenario. It is not that these scenarios are problematic in themselves. Rather, it is that policies and programmes that are distinctly "Caribbean" are not utilized in harnessing a cohesive instrument to fashion a Caribbean identity among the prevailing divergent factors. Instead of being generic, these programmes appear to have a selective variant by appealing to specific ethnic and cultural support groups, representing the various subcultures, who conveniently tend to champion their own cultural cause while portraying little appreciation to the needs of other groups in society.

Educational Dynamism

In most instances, Caribbean education systems are managed through a historically established State/Board arrangement, particularly in Trinidad and Tobago. Schools controlled by various religious denominations (Catholic, Anglican, Baptist, Hindu, Muslim, and so on) are populated by students of the respective faiths. The majority of the staff is usually of one denomination. More often than not, cultural factors tend to influence the behaviours of staff and students of similar religious denominations. In these settings, ethnicity, religious persuasion, culture and class tend to overlap and influence the nature of work attitudes, identity and school activities. Such experiences continue to influence children's behaviours well into adulthood and, if and when carried to their logical conclusions, they tend to resonate in the workplace, church and family life. While significant progress has been made with respect to teacher training, curriculum expansion, school-building and scholarship-awarding, the ongoing emphasis on academic achievement has intensified competition between ethnic and religious groups as reflected in the allocation of financial resources, examination results, placement of students and entry into the job market.

Cultural Dynamism

The challenge of locating a West Indian identity remains manifest in the construction of race and ethnicity in the Caribbean (Look Lai 1998; Moore 1995; Alleyne 2005; Samaroo 2006). It continues to be featured in the continuous reworkings of the cultural behaviours of the majority and minority ethnic groups within the region, a phenomenon referred to as cross-breeding or creolization. Cultural cohesion may turn out to be both an asset and a liability. It may hold homogenous groups together, or it may ignore or play down the social worth of some groups.

In the government-led movements to independence across the region, the various ethnic groups were able to establish themselves in constitutionally articulated positions of "equal rights and freedoms for all". Despite subsequent identity struggles, groups were able to establish themselves in the spheres of education, labour, politics, culture and economics. Equal opportunities, however, do not necessarily translate into equal accomplishments, and the various groups made claims, counterclaims and contestations within a context of colour, wealth and power differentials. In the process, this demonstrated a reluctance to let go of erstwhile values or those that were counterproductive to the development of a Caribbean identity. Gradually cultural norms prescribing mating, dating, and procreation began to emerge and were tested. But it was the intertwining of ethnic, cultural, political and economic activities which produced a hybrid cultural milieu that would present challenges for forging a West Indian identity (Paul 2007).

Economic Dynamism

This is best reflected in the way groups react to essential commodities, as when the supply of food, goods and services fails to meet their expectations and the questions of choice, maximum satisfaction and distribution assume primacy (Stanfield 1990). It sets in motion an economic dynamic interconnectedness among spending practices, savings, income and labour issues, as illustrated by Shone (2001). Extra-regional factors in the Caribbean tend to drive up the prices of food, and tourism and agriculture-based economies are more seriously affected than national resources. This leads to the marginalization of some groups who have grown dependent on these industries. The resultant struggles to cope with rising costs of living and a penchant for ostentatious living causes Caribbean people to spend more and borrow more, seek salary increases and remain dependent on foreign assistance. At the same time, it has also set the stage for certain groups to increase their stature by demonstrating their ability to easily access high-priced, foreign-produced glamorous commodities. However, the ultimate decision with respect to these issues lies with politicians (Carruthers and Kim 2011), whose actions always invariably carry a social cost that tends to link ethnicity with social class.

Religious Dynamism

The various ethnic groups which came to the Caribbean by force and free will were accompanied by their belief systems. Some, despite being torn away from their homelands and exposed to new religious teachings, adjusted their culture. But their erstwhile or traditional beliefs were quietly maintained even as they participated in the practices of their new religions – Presbyterian, Moravian, Methodist and Catholic (see Patterson 1964). Many of these religions expanded, and indigenous religious beliefs were relegated to a lesser status, negatively labelled, and peripheralized. In some instances, the emergence of new religious beliefs found expression in culture, race and class. Interestingly, West Indians have used religion as a way of defining themselves, but this expression does not readily come to the fore in the larger social arena. However, at times they point to achievements of their own nationals in sports and literature, taking pride in comparing the significance of these achievements with the sizes of their countries. Still, these measures do not count for much in alleviating the pain of searching for the elusive West Indian identity.

Sociodynamic Theory versus Competing Paradigms

Post-independence societal formations were adequately captured in M.G Smith's (1965) Plural Society thesis. Then the economic emphasis on prevailing definitions of development, the economic dependency of the region and the economic thrust highlighted by Lewis's *Industrialization by Invitation* (1950), the poverty perspective of George Beckford (1999) and the subsequent plantation economy thesis (Best 1968) and Levitt and Best (1975) produced a movement that gained currency as these elements came to be seen as viable tools in emphasizing the way forward. But these failed to capture the vital nexus of relationship that existed across sectors of the economy and at different levels, all of which were oddly intertwined. Moreover, they did not adequately capture the centrality of interactions across institutions and how these filtered and affected individuals operating at various ethnic, political and social levels.

In very useful ways, however, *Plantation Theory* explained how economic and other factors are consequent upon our own historical legacy and, at the same time, highlighted the centrality of economic issues (Bolland 2002). However, Creolization theory prioritizes and shows how hybridity is reflected in the Caribbean cultural milieu without explaining, for example, how interactions of ethnicity and class combine to shape and reshape expressions of cross-breeding. And plural theory is basically descriptive of cultural processes without explaining intersections with race, ethnicity, religion, social class and gender. It is a classificatory scheme (Craig 1982; Bolland 2002) which does not account for the range of differences that exist within the region.

In a nutshell, sociodynamic theory suggests that ethnicity, culture, education and religion, as well as the economy, intersect to produce changes in the political, economic and social domains to trump identity formations. Identity, therefore, in the context of cultural cohesion, becomes invariably subjective and personal, whereas other social factors are not accorded primacy except in instances where there is a need to treat them opportunistically across the various groups or communities whenever specific circumstances targeting one group arise. As a result of living and tolerating our lives within the vicissitudes of ethnicity, religion and economy, our people find themselves between thesis and antithesis, forming and transforming (Said 2000), acting and counteracting, and, in the process, missing the opportunity of enjoying the benefits that a cohesive multicultural society offers.

Several contemporary identity theories have focused on the existence of a sense of self which shapes individual behaviours in different situations, while others, such as social identity theory and affect control theory stress that situations "draw out" certain identities and influence meanings for different individuals (Owens, Robinson and L. Smith-Lovin 2010). The question is this: Why hasn't this led to a groundswell of behaviours and attitudes that could have been expected to coalesce around the formation of a West Indian identity? The answer lies in the bifurcation of the developmental patterns that are confusing and disengaging to the national psyche. These economic philosophies are sometimes native, sometimes metropolitan, sometimes European, sometimes all of these. And this tends to minimize what little national pride exists. But, more importantly, the thrust of these philosophies does little to pull the competing strands of ethnicity towards a common economic and developmental whole.

We postulate that the nature of the configuration and reconfiguration of sociodynamism appears within a negotiated space where ethnicity, pluralism, multiculturalism, economics and politics interface from time to time to give meaning to culture and identity. It tends to focus on stabilizing, or at least adjusting, to ethnic, class and religious differences and threatening to reshape the structures that have alienated individuals. At the same time, it does not ignore the experiences of colonialism and how these feed into all the aforementioned. Presumably, these same factors could have negotiated their way to the formation of a West Indian identity. For example, Williams (1991) outlined the struggles of the Guyanese to establish a national culture while they were being pulled by ethnic, gender, racial, religious and social class identities. Lazarus-Black (1994) documented the interactional dynamic between legitimate acts and illegal encounters that unfolded in the family courts of Antigua and Barbuda. Deosaran (1993) commented on the interactional forces that required a more dynamic methodology to understand how politics, sociology and psychology underpinned the build-up to the Muslim Uprising in Trinidad. And there are many examples of these issues that are thrown up by sociodynamic intersections – some minor, some major (figure 3.1).

Conclusion

Despite our historical legacy, Caribbean people from time to time reflect a sense of identity. This is seen in how we view other ethnicities, how we perceive

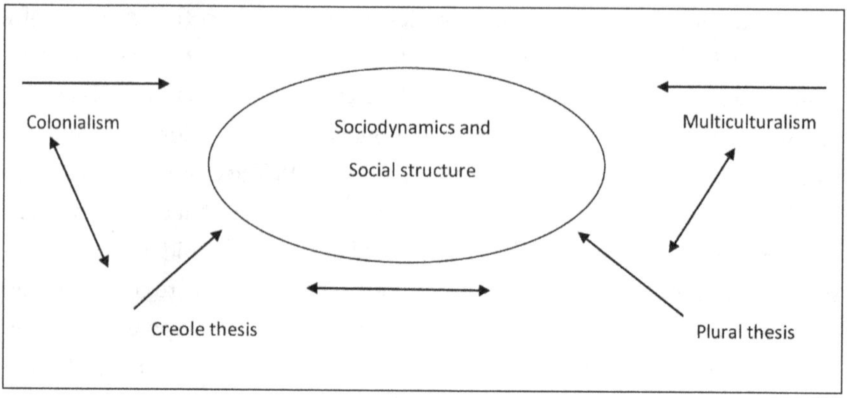

Figure 3.1. Sociodynamic interaction with a negotiated interactedness

governments' interests, how we partake in each others' celebrations, and how we interpret the influence or hold that "other" groups have on the economy. Within this constantly changing mix of political, economic, religious and cultural factors, Caribbean life continues to evolve. Both inside and outside these domains, ethnic, educational and occupational opportunities have also been a cause for concern. In this regard, it is difficult to separate the macro effect from the micro effect on identity formation.

They are intertwined. We therefore argue that Caribbean identity formation is held captive at different levels and in different dimensions in our quest for a Caribbean identity. Each individual in the Caribbean has an "identity" that is simultaneously ethnic, cultural, educational and gendered, as well as political, social and religious. These are individually and collectively manifested at the organizational, community, national and regional levels, depending on the changing manifestations and "significance" of events that gain the attention of various groups from time to time. Organizations and institutions conveniently shift their support or preference for certain groups that are associated with certain cultural, religious or political affiliations.

Given the aforementioned state of affairs, we posit that on any one island, and across the region, one would find transactional Caribbean identities which may be tied to interactional vagaries of multiculturalism (Burke 2003). For example, one might encounter single-identity fragmentized community groups alongside cohesive and highly influential ones and ethnic minorities alongside and intertwined with multiple culturally driven ones. The lesson to be learned is that Caribbean identity still remains at the formation stage (which so far has acted as a constraint to any likelihood of open conflict). This situation must first and foremost be interpreted and addressed by focusing on its interpersonal and intersectional cleavages. This suggests that the seeds of a multicultural West Indian identity lie in the very factors that hinder its full development. We conclude by suggesting that the prevailing challenges in the search for a Caribbean identity rest with our inability to manage our macro and micro social complexities.

Our "identity" lies in our indigeneity, which consists of those things that we have created for ourselves within the region – how we speak, work, make music, dance, worship and celebrate. This is further reinforced by our creativity and achievements past, present and future in various sectors of the Caribbean economy and at different levels of societal functioning. Such multiculturally manifested creativity will remain the major resource that will always be required for simultaneously debunking our colonial legacy, continuing our identity formation and heralding and crystallizing hitherto untapped dimensions of regional integration. But the process still needs to be structured and shaped and be all-inclusive before we can incrementally add value to its core.

References

Aiyejina, F., and P. Morgan. 2006. *Caribbean Literature in a Global Context*. San Juan: Lexicon.

Alleyne, M. 2005. *Construction and Representation of Race and Ethnicity in the Caribbean and the Wider World*. Kingston: University of the West Indies Press.

Bailey, B., E. Leo-Rhynie and C. Barrow. 2001. *Gender: A Caribbean Multidisciplinary Perspective*. Kingston: Ian Randle.

Barrow, C. 1995. *Family in the Caribbean: Themes and Perspectives*. Kingston: Ian Randle.

Baugh, E. 2006. *Another Life*. Boulder: Lynne Rienner.

Beckford, G. 1999. *Persistent Poverty: Underdevelopment in Plantation Economies of the Third World*. Kingston: University of the West Indies Press.

Best, L. 1968. Outlines of a Model of Pure Plantation Economy. *Social and Economic Research* 17: 283–24.

Best, L., and K. Levitt. 2009. *Essays on the Theory of Plantation Economy: A Historical and Institutional Approach to Caribbean Economic Development*. Kingston: University of the West Indies Press.

Bhabha, H.K. 2004. *Location of Culture*. London: Routledge.

Bolland, O.N. 2002. Creolization and Creole Societies. In *Questioning Creole: Creolization Discourses in Caribbean Culture*, edited by V.A. Shepherd and G.L. Richards, 15–46. Kingston: Ian Randle Publishers.

Brathwaite, E. 2005. *The Development of Creole Society in Jamaica, 1770–1820*. Kingston: Ian Randle.

Bryan, P. 1996. The Creolization of Chinese Community in Jamaica. In *Ethnic Minorities in Caribbean Society,* edited by R. Reddock, 173–271. St Augustine, Trinidad and Tobago: Institute of Social and Economic Research.

Burke, P.J. 2003. Relationships among Multiple Identities: Advances in Identity Theory and Research. In *Advances in Identity Theory and Research*, edited by P.J. Burke et al., 195–214. New York: Kluwer Academic.

Carruthers, B.G., and J. Kim. 2011. The Sociology of Finance. *Annual Review of Sociology* 37: 239–59.

Clarke, L. 2004. *Eyeing de Word: Love Poem for Ettylene*. Mount Hope, Trinidad and Tobago: Paria.

Craig, S. 1982. *Contemporary Caribbean: A Sociological Reader*. Maracas.

Dabydeen, D. 2005. *The Intended*. Leeds: Peepal Tree.

Deosaran, R. 1993. *A Society under Siege: A Study of Political Confusion and Legal Mysticism*. St Augustine, Trinidad and Tobago: ANSA McAL Psychological Research Centre.

Dhondy, F. 2001. *C.L.R. James: A Life*. New York: Pantheon.

Dupuy, A. 2001. The New World Order, Globalization and Caribbean Politics. In *New Caribbean Thought,* edited by B. Meeks and F. Lindahl, 521–36. Kingston: University of the West Indies Press.

Elder, J.D. 1968. *From Congo Drum to Steel Band*. Kingston: University of the West Indies Press.

Fox, D. 1996. *Cultural DNA*. Kingston: University of the West Indies Press.

Garner, S. 2008. *Ethnicity, Class and Gender: Guyana, 1838–1985*. Kingston: Ian Randle.

Gray, O. 2004. *Demeaned but Empowered: The Social Power of the Urban Poor*. Kingston: University of the West Indies Press.

Grosfoguel, R. 1999. "Cultural Racism" and Colonial Caribbean Migrants in Core Zones of the Capitalist World-Economy. *Review* (Fernand Braudel Center) 4: 409–34.

Hall, S. 2001. Negotiating Caribbean Identities. In *New Caribbean Thought: A Reader,* edited by B. Meeks and F. Lindahl, 24–39. Kingston: University of the West Indies Press.

Heron, M.P. 2001. *Occupational Attainment of Caribbean Immigrants in the United States, Canada, and England*. El Paso, TX: LFB Scholarly Publishing.

Hodder, R. 2011. *Emotional Bureaucracy*. Piscataway, NJ: Transaction.

King, B., and D. Walcott. 2000. *A Caribbean Life*. Oxford: Oxford University Press.

La Guerre, J. 1974. *Calcutta to Caroni: The East Indians of Trinidad*. New York: Longman.

Lamming, G. 1996. Beckford and the Predicaments of Culture. In *The Critical Tradition of Caribbean Political Economy: The Legacy of George Beckford,* edited by K. Levitt and M. Witter, 19–28. Kingston: Ian Randle.

Lazarus-Black, M. 1994. *Legitimate Acts and Illegal Encounters: Law and Society in Antigua and Barbuda*. Washington, DC: Smithsonian Institution Press.
Levitt, K., and L. Best. 1975. *Pure Plantation Economy.* St Augustine, Trinidad and Tobago: Institute of International Relations, University of the West Indies.
Lewis, A.W. 1950. *Industrialization by Development in the Caribbean*. West Drayton, Middlesex: Penguin.
Lewis, G. 2004. *Growth of the Modern West Indies*. Kingston: Ian Randle.
Look Lai, W. 1998. *Chinese in the West Indies*. Kingston: University of the West Indies Press.
———. 2006. *Essays on the Chinese Diaspora in the Caribbean*. St Augustine, Trinidad and Tobago: University of the West Indies History Department.
Manuel, P. 1989. *Caribbean Currents*. Philadelphia: Temple University Press.
———. 2006. *Caribbean Currents: Caribbean Music from Rumba to Reggae*. Kingston: Ian Randle.
Meeks, B. 2000. *Narratives of Resistance: Jamaica, Trinidad, the Caribbean*. Kingston: University of the West Indies Press.
Moore, D. 1995. *Origins and Development of Racial Ideology in Trinidad: The Black View of the East Indian*. Tunapuna, Trinidad and Tobago: Chakra.
Morgan, P. 2009. Bordering on the Transgressive: (Re)constructing Cultural Identities in Indo-Caribbean Fictions. In *Beyond Borders: Cross-culturalism and the Caribbean Canon*, edited by J. Rahim and B. Lalla, 192–216. Kingston: University of the West Indies Press.
Naipaul, V.S. 1969. *The Mimic Men*. Harmondsworth, Middlesex: Penguin.
———. 1973. *In a Free State*. London: Andre Deutsch.
———. 1987. *Enigma of Arrival*. London: Penguin.
Nettleford, R. 1993. *Inward Stretch, Outward Reach: A Voice from the Caribbean*. London: Macmillan.
———. 2003. *Caribbean Cultural Identity: An Essay in Cultural Dynamics*. Kingston: Ian Randle.
Offe, C. 2006. Political Disaffection as an Outcome of Institutional Practices? Some Post-Tocquevillean Speculations in Political Disaffection in Contemporary Democracies in Social Capital Institutions and Politics. In *Political Disaffection in Contemporary Democracies: Social Capital, Institutions and Politics*, edited by M. Joreal and R. Montero, 23–45. New York: Routledge.
Owens, T., D.T. Robinson and L. Smith-Lovin. 2010. Three Faces of Identity. *Annual Sociological Review* 36: 477–99.
Patterson, O. 1964. *The Sociology of Slavery: An Analysis of the Origins, Development and Structure of Negro Slave Society in Jamaica*. London: MacGibbon and Kee.
Paul, A. 2007. *Caribbean Culture: Soundings on Kamau Brathwaite*. Kingston: University of the West Indies Press.
Premdas, R. 2007. *Trinidad and Tobago: Ethnic Conflict, Inequality and Public Sector Governance*. New York: Palgrave.
Puri, S. 2004. *The Caribbean Postcolonial: Social Equality, Post-nationalism and Cultural Hybridity*. New York: Palgrave Macmillan.
Ramchand, K. 2004. *The West Indian Novel and Its Background*. Kingston: Ian Randle.

Reddock, R., and C. Barrow. 2001. *Caribbean Sociology: Introductory Readings*. Kingston: Ian Randle.

Rohlehr, G. 2004. *A Scuffling of Islands: Essays on Calypso*. San Juan: Lexicon Trinidad.

Ryan, S. 2009. *Eric Williams: The Myth and the Man*. Kingston: University of the West Indies Press.

Said, E. 2000. *Reflections on Exile*. Cambridge, MA: Harvard University Press.

Samaroo, B. 2006. Indian Connection: The Influence of Indian Thought and Ideas on East Indians in the Caribbean. In *India in the Caribbean,* edited by D. Dabydeen and B. Samaroo, 43–59. London: Hansib.

Sankatsing, G. 2001. Social Sciences as a Victim of Its Own Descriptive: The English- and Dutch-Speaking Caribbean. In *Caribbean Sociology: Introductory Readings,* edited by R. Reddock and C. Barrow, 56–83. Kingston: Ian Randle.

Shone, R. 2001. *An Introduction to Economic Dynamics*. Cambridge: Cambridge University Press.

Smith, M.G. 1965. *Plural Society in the British West Indies*. Berkeley: University of California Press.

Stanfield, J.R. 1990. Karl Polanyi and Contemporary Economic Thought. In *The Life and Work of Karl Polanyi: A Celebration,* edited by K. Polanyi Levitt, 195–207. Montreal: Black Rose.

Taylor, K. 2011. *How Caribbean Political Leaders Successfully Managed needed Economic, Entrepreneurial and Social Adjustments, 1981–1995: The Importance of Understanding All the Factors Affecting Change*. New York: Edwin Mellen.

Thomas, K. 2012. *The Demographic Profile of Black Caribbean Immigrants in the United States*. Washington, DC: Migration Policy Institute. www.migrationpolicy.org/pubs/cbi- caribbeanmigration.pdf.

Trent, J.S., and R.V. Freidenberg. 2008. *Political Campaign Communication: Principles and Practices*. Lanham, MD: Rowman and Littlefield.

Walcott, D. 1974. The Caribbean: Culture or Mimicry? *Journal of Interamerican Studies and World Affairs* 16 (1): 3–13. www.jstor.org/stable/174997.

Williams, B.F. 1991. *Stains on My Name, War in My Veins: Guyana and the Politics of Cultural Struggle*. Durham, NC: Duke University Press.

Williams, E. 1979. *Caribbean Man: Address of the Political Leader of the PNM, 21st Annual Convention – September 29, 1979*. Port of Spain: People's National Movement.

CHAPTER 4

Caribbean Foreign Policies in the Twenty-First Century: From Activism to Improvisation in Diplomacy

Jacqueline A. Braveboy-Wagner

Since the 1990s the world has witnessed some truly dramatic events which have focused the attention of international relations scholars on the unpredictability of their field: these include the end of the Cold War; the heightening of global interdependence (globalization); the eruption of vicious civil wars in the Balkans and Africa; the attack on the World Trade Center in New York on 11 September 2001; the drawn-out wars in Afghanistan and Iraq; the Arab Spring and its aftermath; and the battle against Al Qaeda and the Islamic State. The rise of China, as well as India, a newly nationalistic Russia and (with obvious setbacks) Brazil has generated intense speculation about the decline of American dominance and the rise of the "rest", now countered to some degree by the articulation of an "America First" foreign policy by US president Donald Trump. Real estate bubbles have boomed and burst; a deep recession slowed growth in traditional and emerging markets between 2008 and 2012, with effects felt through at least 2015; and the optimism about a liberal, more peaceful, post–Cold War world in which states could concentrate on societal ills such as poverty alleviation, eliminating hunger and the other social goals approved by the United Nations has faded for many, replaced in their minds by a sober perspective tinged with anxieties about terrorism, economic malaise and the deleterious effects of climate change.

Foreign policymaking in such a variable environment has been difficult for all states, let alone very small countries like those of the Caribbean. The lone superpower, the United States, itself has gone from what former secretary of state Henry Kissinger called a foreign policy based on "a series of ad hoc decisions intended to satisfy various domestic constituencies . . . as if the United States needed no long-range foreign policy at all and could confine itself to a case-by-case response to challenges as they arise" (Kissinger 2001, 19) to producing instead a number of specific plans and doctrines. From a diplomacy dubbed "transformational" by former secretary of state Condoleeza Rice – that is, one calling for more public diplomacy and for diplomats who are too often barricaded in fortified embassies to move closer to the streets (US Department of State 2006) – the United States has moved to a more cautious approach based on the acknowledgement that the neoconservative ideal of forcing democracy did not work and that US and Western diplomats often really do need those fortified barriers.

Small developing states can be forgiven for exhibiting even more confusion and uncertainty about the world, given their lack of resources, relatively inferior intelligence and information capabilities, and the constraints of having to conform to great power dictates. The Caribbean small states, long operating with one eye on the hemispheric superpower, have often seemed to be just trying to survive in a difficult world, though with some luck and resources, some states, Cuba for example, have managed to "punch above their weight" to some degree.[1] Given their limitations, overall, it is remarkable that they have found a way to manage their relations with larger neighbors such as Venezuela and with their traditional partners the United States, Canada and Europe while seeking diversification towards other partners. Indeed, they have survived the many global changes despite the limitations of small and very small size. Borrowing from Kishore Mahbubani's likening of Singapore's joining the UN Security Council to suddenly jumping on a moving train and scrambling into the last compartment (quoted in Chong 2016, 402), the Caribbean states can be said to occupy the last compartments of a very crowded train that is moving fast and often lurching so badly that those in the back can barely stand. So it would be quite unfair to expect these countries to show much innovation in their foreign policies.

On the other hand, because in developing countries the link between foreign and domestic policy is so close, with the prime motivation of both being development, foreign policy should be seen as one aspect of public policy. It is geared towards complementing domestic policies and focused on enhancing the well-being of populations. Unfortunately, in the Caribbean few governments have fully appreciated the role of foreign policy in realizing their domestic goals; hence, good foreign policy planning is rare.

Going back to the concept of states as passengers on a train, the last-compartment dilemma of small-sized states[2] tends to lead to the resurrection of an age-old question: Do they really have the capacity to devise independent foreign policies? In the past, scholars said that regardless of what small-state governments *think* they are doing, their actions are too circumscribed by the environment and by the demands of the larger powers to really be considered independent. Alternatively and more simply put, very small states lack the resources and heft to be heard or have any impact on the international system. But this assertion that they lack a sufficient "sovereignty arsenal" (Lewis 1976, 229), while perhaps appropriate in the 1960s, is far less valid today. Yes, small states still generally occupy the lower rungs of the global ladder, but in a globalized world, the distribution of power is more diffuse than before, with a rising number of mid-level powers and even some small powers gaining influence. Likewise, governments have more strategic tools of influence at their disposal – soft power as well as hard (Nye 2002), easier access to information and communication and the ability to tap the networks of non-state and transnational actors as allies in support of jointly agreed goals. Moreover, even in the rigid environment of the 1960s and 1970s, leaders made choices that were not necessarily conformist. The Third World's political experimentation and collective bargaining in the 1970s were clearly illustrative. Today the counter-liberal and post-liberal policies of Latin America in the first decade of the 2000s, not to mention the continued presence of more extreme "resisters" such as Iran and North Korea, show that the locus of decision-making lies in the political elites, not just in the regional or international system. This has been revealed in various comparative analyses of the foreign policies of small states (see, for example, Hey 2003). Of course whether governments or states are able to effectively take advantage of opportunities and *manage* their foreign policies effectively is the heart of the question.

In the following pages I review some key aspects of the foreign policies of the small Caribbean nations in the twenty-first century. To organize my discussion, I use as a benchmark for comparison the 1970s, which I describe as an *activist* period in Caribbean foreign policy. The questions asked are these: Have the foreign policies of the twenty-first century continued that activism, or are they instead less coherent? What policies have these states devised to meet the complex challenges of this era? How effective have they been in managing their interaction with the region and the world?

Before moving on, I must provide a quick note about scope. As is known, the very definition of the Caribbean is a contested one, with the region's states sometimes divided by culture, sometimes by history (older Hispanic states and Haiti versus the newer English-speaking states and Suriname), sometimes by size, sometimes by organizational designations (Eastern Caribbean states, Caribbean Community states, Association of Caribbean States, Caribbean Basin states) and other categories that depend on contextual interests (for a discussion of Caribbean "spaces and places", see Braveboy-Wagner 2014). In this chapter I define the Caribbean as including any independent state between and including Belize in the north (in Central America) and Guyana and Suriname in the south; these three continental states are integral members of CARICOM, the main integration arrangement in the Caribbean. In my discussion of foreign policy I focus on general patterns only. While it would be ideal to analyze each and every state separately because foreign policy remains in many ways a nationalist activity, it would be unrealistic to attempt that in the limited space of one short chapter. Indeed I pay the most attention to CARICOM: when CARICOM is mentioned, it refers *either* to the integration grouping as a whole or to fourteen of the fifteen independent states that are members of that grouping. (The fifteenth, Montserrat, is not fully independent and therefore not responsible for its foreign affairs.)[3] Within CARICOM, I also pay the most attention to Trinidad and Tobago, which has the responsibility for security affairs within CARICOM and is also the most industrialized state. I mention the older Caribbean states – Cuba and Haiti in particular – in specific contexts. I am totally aware that I cannot do justice here to any one state, so the goal is rather to give the reader an *overview* of developments and highlight a few interesting events and cases.

Background

The Benchmark Era: 1970s Activism

Since I am starting from the point of view that the late 1960s into the 1970s was a period of activist diplomacy, it is appropriate to first discuss this period briefly. This is not to imply that the international relations of the region started then, of course: as is quite well known, the Caribbean's colorful history includes having been fought over by the Dutch, Spanish, French and English both for the islands' strategic (military) value and for their economic value as suppliers of that once-precious commodity, sugar. But in terms of foreign policy (which is conducted by independent states), it was at their independence in the nineteenth century that the older islands – Cuba, Haiti and the Dominican Republic – assumed technical responsibility for their foreign affairs. However, as is well known, that independence was compromised by the intrusion of successive US governments. US interventions were rationalized during the nineteenth and twentieth centuries as necessary to preserve order and fiscal responsibility in the region, and the pattern of pseudoindependent foreign policies was not broken until the Cuban revolution brought a volte-face in US–Cuban relations. Even today, Haiti's continued reliance on US political assistance in times of crisis serves as a legacy of the long US occupation between 1915 and 1934; similarly, the Dominican Republic's unwavering close relations with the United States also reflects the bond cemented during a lengthy occupation between 1916 and 1924.[4]

During the Cold War, Cuba stood at first as the lone Caribbean or Latin American socialist outpost, whereas the nearby Dominican Republic and Haiti continued to solidify their relations with the United States and the West. They were joined in their pro-West orientation by the first English-speaking Caribbean states to become independent in the 1960s – Jamaica, Trinidad and Tobago and later, Barbados – which all retained close relations with their former metropole, Britain, and gradually acceded to US dominance over the years. Guyana, which became independent in 1966, offered up a more mixed bag of strategies, retaining Western linkages but also moving fairly quickly to adopt what it termed "cooperative socialism".

Why can this period be deemed one of foreign policy activism in the Caribbean? The 1970s are well known as the heyday of Third World activism in international affairs. Having achieved their independence, many African and Asian states sought new ways to engage the world. Specifically, they sought to diversify their foreign relations in an attempt to reduce their dependence on their former "mother countries". In this effort, creative bilateral, regional and multilateral strategies were devised. For example, they sought to strengthen South-South solidarity in the United Nations and the Non-Aligned Movement, to extract themselves from the East-West rivalry and to focus instead on global as well as domestic economic reforms. They pressed hard for the decolonization of the remaining colonies, and they spoke out loudly against neocolonialism, imperialism and racialism, especially apartheid. Most (but not all) Caribbean states realized that benefits could be had by joining in the activities of the assertive African and Asian states. In retrospect, despite some errors caused by ultranationalist exuberance (in both Michael Manley's socialistic Jamaica and, in particular, the People's Revolutionary Government in Grenada), this period was undoubtedly the heyday of the English-speaking Caribbean nations in foreign affairs, matching the heyday of the Third World.

The strategies adopted by these countries were nationalist, ideological, developmental and diplomatic. Such strategies have been elaborated elsewhere (see Braveboy-Wagner 2007), but they mainly involved, to varying degrees, first, the diversification of linkages (to Latin America, to Japan and China, to the Eastern Bloc, to Asia and Africa), and second, proactive, or at least regularized, participation in multilateral forums, chief among these the United Nations and the Non-Aligned Movement.[5] In reaching out to Latin America, the English-speaking Caribbean countries joined the Organization of American States (OAS), which today may seem quite a mainstream strategy but at the time was quite innovative. It must be remembered that many of the organization's existing members were antipathetic to the inclusion of a host of small English-speaking states which still retained a British monarchical system. But, once accepted, these states were able to promote a more Caribbeanist agenda, including a successful push for repeal of the charter's clause excluding Belize and Guyana because of their border disputes with Guatemala and Venezuela. Indeed, their membership was also incidentally beneficial to the other small Latin Caribbean states as well as the Central Americans who were at the time inadequately represented in the key offices of the organization.

An important economic strategy that was promoted by the non-aligned countries and supported by the progressive UN economic agencies was the deepening of regionalism, primarily as a way to expand market size. And indeed this era also began as a good one for Caribbean regionalism when the core English-speaking countries adopted the Caribbean Free Trade Area in 1967 and moved to CARICOM in 1973. CARICOM remains one of the most durable integration movements in the global south, notwithstanding its disjointed progress. CARICOM cooperation deepened up to 1975, particularly in functional areas. Unfortunately, however, ideological and economic differences led to the arrangement's stagnation after that date, which continued through the early 1980s.

Still in the economic sphere, this was the time when CARICOM states joined with African and Pacific states in negotiating their first preferential trade accord (the Lomé Convention) with the European Community in the wake of Britain's entry into that body. This ACP (African, Caribbean and Pacific) alliance has endured over the decades, despite major changes in the European economic regime. Similar accords with the United States (in the form of the Caribbean Basin Initiative or Caribbean Basin Economic Recovery Act) and with Canada (CARIBCAN) were negotiated, too, though later, in the early 1980s, and in the context of heightened security concerns at the time of ideological dissension in the region.

With all this and more happening, embassies as well as ministries of foreign affairs were kept busy. The busiest Caribbean embassies and missions were located in Washington, Ottawa, London and Brussels. Smaller Caribbean states could hardly be expected to maintain many missions, but, to cope with their responsibilities as they became independent in the late 1970s (1983 for St Kitts and Nevis), the Eastern Caribbean nations experimented with maintaining joint missions in some places and joint financial arrangements in others. (For the UN missions, Commonwealth financing was successfully sought.)

Overall, diplomacy in this era was relatively activist. It is worth noting, however, that without the willing and ambitious leadership of the era – that of Eric Williams, Errol Barrow, Michael Manley in Jamaica, L.F.S. Burnham, John Compton, Robert Bradshaw and other memorable statesmen – this would not have been the case. These Caribbean leaders did not seem to see "smallness" as total weakness, and they played major roles in their countries' foreign policies.

Not surprisingly, diplomats in the region recall this era as one of growth in and respect for the foreign ministries. After independence the ministries of foreign affairs in the newer countries had begun as small bureaucracies, in most cases led by prime ministers themselves and closely tied to that office. During the 1970s more sophisticated arrangements were established: there was the necessary separation from the prime minister's office, rudimentary bureaucracies became more functionally differentiated and professionalized and more talented personnel were hired as the services (or, in cases where there was no separate foreign service, the designated bureaus within the civil service) became an attractive option for university graduates. This does not mean that foreign policy operations were *prioritized;* as is the case around the world, politicians and the population at large do not usually rank the foreign ministry on the same level of importance as ministries or departments of finance, trade and social welfare (Hill 2003, 76–82). Those other ministries are seen as more aligned with development needs. Indeed, with that in mind, in the 1980s many Caribbean foreign ministries began to incorporate foreign trade and other economic priorities in their portfolios.[6] In sum, in the 1970s the pattern and direction of Caribbean foreign policies were not hard to discern.

Before moving on to the 1990s, in which new foreign policy patterns emerged, a few words should be said about the 1980s. This decade is rightly viewed as the "lost decade" in Latin America, when major countries, having borrowed heavily to fund balance-of-payments deficits, found themselves unable to repay their debts, especially given rising interest rates. Similar problems plagued the Caribbean nations, and by the end of the 1970s a new round of high oil prices contributed to a global slowdown and eventual recession.

The nationalistic economic policies adopted in the 1970s gave way to economic liberalization and, in many cases, structural adjustment programmes mandated by the International Monetary Fund. Jamaica, for example, at one point had borrowed 360 times its quota from the fund (Braveboy-Wagner 1986, 335). Given this economic deterioration, progress in regional integration stalled, despite renewed commitments by Caribbean heads of government. (CARICOM was already stressed by the ideological polarization that came to a head during the US–Eastern Caribbean military intervention in Grenada in 1983.) As for foreign policy, although the trends of the 1970s continued (certainly including the efforts at trade partner diversification as well as the [re]negotiation of preferential accords), nationalist approaches in the region and in the Third World replaced much of the rhetoric of South-South solidarity.

The 1990s and 2000s witnessed a great deal of change in the world. Since small states' foreign policies are inherently reactive (which is not the same as compliant) to regional and global events, it is hardly surprising that changes would have had to be made to adapt to the new challenges and complexities. In the next section I explore what adaptations, if any, were made in the 1990s and 2000s.

1990s Ad Hoc Economic Diplomacy

I see the period of the 1990s as one in which traditional foreign policymaking declined and choices were made to refocus diplomacy in an economic direction. However, in the uncertain global environment that followed the end of the Cold War, policymakers adopted an ad hoc approach, responding to external stimuli as they presented themselves.

With the exact shape of the global world order unclear, confronted by the challenges of liberalization and globalization, the Caribbean states needed to refresh their foreign policies, primarily to deal with their loss of political leverage in a world of only one superpower. In practice, this would mean having to work that much harder to secure economic as well as security assistance, a situation that worsened as donors turned their attention not only to the needs of the former Soviet satellites but also to new trouble spots that arose in the Middle East and Africa. Added to this was the challenge of preparing for a world of intense trade competition, a challenge aggravated by the near-total dependence of many of the smaller Caribbean countries on revenues from the special preferential trade programmes mentioned earlier. Indeed, since the late 1980s, even the more economically resilient countries (such as oil-producing Trinidad and Tobago) had been suffering from the effects of the already cited global recession.

Immediately after the Cold War ended, the main focus of the Caribbean states – indeed, of the United States and much of the world[7] – was on adapting to the inexorable spread of liberalization. Foreign policy became more closely linked with public policy as a whole, in the service of development. To be sure, it is difficult to identify a general vision in foreign policy when the outlines of the new world order are not very clear, except for the certainty of heightened liberalization and globalization. With economics at the global center stage, the rise of bilateralism and the rapid decline in importance of supportive Third World coalitions, two basic approaches to diplomacy in the Caribbean region emerged. First, states which felt that they could compete in the new environment because of their abundance of resources and/or level of industrialization were rather optimistic about seizing new opportunities. But second, those which, like the small Eastern Caribbean states, were dependent on trade preferences – especially from a newly consolidated European Union – were preoccupied with defending the status quo. The first position was articulated well by Trinidad and Tobago's prime minister at the time, who asked:

> If our new economic activities must be stimulated on the basis of export-led growth, I ask the question, will everyone succeed? Will the

> world have the capacity to absorb the result of export-led policies in all developing countries and in developed countries? The answer, to my mind, is no. Therefore, it means that some countries will succeed and some will not. . . . It is the early bird which will catch the fattest worm. (Manning 1997)

In this spirit, with the United States offering a new plan to encourage Latin American and Caribbean free trade and investment (that is, the Enterprise for the Americas Initiative), Trinidad and Tobago, along with Jamaica, let it be known that they were ready to negotiate bilateral free trade agreements with the United States. The United States was, however, more interested in promoting a hemispheric free trade arrangement (the Free Trade Area of the Americas) and, as a result, a collective CARICOM approach was developed.

At the same time, a second approach emerged, this time on the defensive side, with the region plunged into negotiations on two fronts: on "NAFTA parity" to offset Mexican advantages in the wake of the negotiation of the North American Free Trade Agreement and on negotiations with the European Union, which were particularly important for the smaller Eastern Caribbean states concerned about being marginalized in the new competitive international environment. With respect to the latter, the region first engaged in an unforgettable battle with Central American banana producers, who complained to the World Trade Organization that the European Union's preferential regime was inconsistent with global free trade rules. The Caribbean states then moved on to fight for the renewal and expansion of preferential arrangements under the Lomé Accords, even while being informed that these would eventually be phased out.

Clearly, then, with opportunities to possibly seize as well as positions to defend, it was understandable that governments of this era should focus intensely on their economic survival. Indeed, the region's governments, some officially in their statements and others not, adopted a "new diplomacy" centered on export promotion and commercial relations but with not entirely welcome consequences for diplomacy:

> The adoption of a "commercial" foreign policy is characterized by: the downgrading in some places of the foreign office and concomitant upgrading of technical departments (finance, economy); greater policy

> consultation with the national and regional business sectors (although the depth and quality of such consultations are as yet debatable); reorientation of the work of missions abroad to focus on economic issues such as export and investment promotion; and greater policy emphasis on economic issues. (Braveboy-Wagner 1995, 20)

In the end, negotiations and lobbying facilitated the expansion of US preferences under the Caribbean Basin Trade Promotion Act of 2000, and the fourth Lomé Accord was extended in 1995.[8] It should be said that the success of this economic diplomacy was represented by developments at the regional level, where a negotiating machinery office was established in 1997 to handle trade talks. Although this particular office was at the time a separate unit from CARICOM's secretariat, it later (2009) became the Office of Trade Negotiations within CARICOM.

Integration affairs is one of the portfolios of the foreign ministries of CARICOM member states, so it is an integral dimension of foreign economic policy. One can cite several promising initiatives taken at the regional level at this time which were in accord with the new, open regionalism trend spreading worldwide: as their counterparts were doing in Africa and Latin America, CARICOM states moved to revive the lagging integration movement, largely adhering to suggestions proffered in a commissioned report which tapped the views of a broad cross-section of the region's population. They sought not only to deepen but also to widen the movement. As a result, they expanded the membership to include non-English-speaking Suriname in 1994 and Haiti in 1997. Moreover, they established a free trade agreement with Cuba, granted observer status to Mexico, Colombia and Venezuela (1990), and signed trade agreements with Venezuela and Colombia (1992 and 1994), with the Dominican Republic in 1998 and with Costa Rica in 2004. Add to this the formation of the wider (Greater Caribbean) Association of Caribbean States in 1994, an initiative credited to the core English-speaking states, and it is reasonable to conclude that this particular period was notable for creative regionalism.

On the bilateral side, however, it is notable that during the 1990s the Caribbean states, including Cuba and the Dominican Republic, made strides in expanding their economic cooperation with Asia, especially Japan, but also China (in the case of countries which recognized the People's Republic), India and some Southeast Asian countries. This was a time when it was common to read of special delegations of businesspersons and government officials making exploratory visits to East Asia. Tourism from Asia picked up as a result (especially for Jamaica), and regular CARICOM-Japan meetings were initiated. Japanese investments in Jamaican coffee, in fisheries in the Eastern Caribbean, and in the oil industry in Trinidad and Tobago were examples of relatively successful foreign economic outreach. In fact, imports from Japan to CARICOM rose tenfold in the 1990s and early 2000s, and China began to be a significant exporter to the region as well (Braveboy-Wagner 2007, 112). Of course, China later went on to surpass Japan in trade with and investment in the region.

In the case of Cuba, that Caribbean country entered into a difficult period after the Cold War, having been abruptly cut off by its Soviet benefactor. Cuba did not choose to liberalize politically, but it instead shaped its foreign policy to ensure its economic survival by seeking out new partners in Europe and Latin America. Notably, the Caribbean region was one of its prime targets for cooperation: in 1993 the Cuba-CARICOM Commission was established to explore areas of joint collaboration; trade and investment cooperation agreements were established in 2000 and 2001.

Guyana, however, *did* liberalize politically, under a new government led by still-Marxist Cheddi Jagan after the first free elections since 1964.[9] Jagan became an unlikely liberalizer, although he did not lose his individualism, as seen in his tenacious commitment to a social development model and his energetic promotion within the international community of his ideas for a New Global Human Order. Still, Guyana sought foreign investment and aid from traditional sources which had been deprioritized in earlier times. As a low-income country, Guyana was able to access such new funding as that provided by the International Monetary Fund to heavily indebted poor countries. By cleverly committing itself to a low-carbon development model, it was also able to gain ready access to environmental financing.

Although economic diplomacy was the order of the day in the 1990s, it would be incorrect to assume that some security issues did not preoccupy the region as well. CARICOM countries assisted in peacekeeping after an attempted coup in Trinidad and Tobago in 1990. The perennial problem of drug trafficking intensified as the decade progressed, and there was some stir in the region when the United States requested that countries sign ship-rider agreements permitting US agents on local patrol vessels. Jamaica resisted on sovereignty grounds and eventually was satisfied through the receipt of various concessions. A change in US immigration law in 1996, requiring the deportation of non-citizens convicted of misdemeanors and felonies that merit more than a year in prison, led to a large number of "criminal deportees" being returned to their countries of origin, however tenuous their social links to these states. Into the 2000s, diplomats and government officials registered complaints about the deportations without producing any real effect on US policy, although some US states (California, for example) have independently moved to change the labelling of some crimes to reduce deportations.

But the most pressing political problem of the 1990s was a prolonged crisis in Haiti. Liberalization had also arrived in Haiti when the dictator Jean-Claude Duvalier was overthrown in 1986. After a period of instability, Haiti held its first free elections, but the euphoria evaporated when President Jean-Bertrand Aristide was overthrown less than a year later. Years of international efforts finally resulted in the return of Aristide in 1994, via US and UN intervention. CARICOM states participated in the post-crisis peacekeeping, and their personnel played essential roles in the UN/OAS human rights mission which operated in Haiti during and after the crisis. This security activism was unusual for a group that had traditionally tended to avoid intervening in conflicts in the neighborhood. (Haiti continued to be unstable, however, in the 2000s.)

In sum, responding to being buffeted by global changes, particularly at the economic level, Caribbean states in the 1990s proclaimed an intense focus on economic diplomacy as their central strategy, even though certain events in the security sphere could not be ignored and also demanded a response. Drumming up investment and trade was prioritized as a mandate for diplomatic missions, and traditional diplomatic skills and priorities were downgraded in favor of economic and financial skills, economic ministries, personnel and specialized negotiators working from the new regional office. Since comprehensive planning did not appear to be a priority at a time when focused responses to fixed and specific problems were required (in both the economic and security arenas), I designate the 1990s as a decade of ad hoc approaches in foreign policy.

The Twenty-First Century: Improvised Foreign Policies

By the beginning of the 2000s, even in the United States, the limits of 1990s economic diplomacy were becoming clear as the country's wars and efforts to democratize the Middle East took center stage. These limits were reflected in Kissinger's call for a return to long-range foreign policy planning after the optimism of the post–Cold War, when triumphant Americans had assumed that US moral values would prevail worldwide, that economic globalization had made military concerns irrelevant and that the pursuit of economic self-interest would bring about global reconciliation and democracy (Kissinger 2001, 19–20, 29–30).

Notwithstanding the obvious differences between the superpower's twenty-first-century challenges and those of the small Caribbean states, Kissinger's critique includes several points of interest to a region so reactive to world events. These states had obviously "bought into" the idea that democracy and economic liberalization would be durable models in the Caribbean and Latin America, as in the world. Moreover, they had bought into a particular type of economic model, without questioning its relevance or sustainability in the region. Thus the turn to the left in Latin America and the erosion of democracy in nearby Venezuela were not anticipated. Likewise, Caribbean states were forced to react to the events of 9/11, but the lack of widespread popular discussion of the Iraq war reflected a lack of awareness of the long-term implications of Middle East events for even the small states of the globe. As a result, in the 2000s foreign policy planning, if indeed "planning" can be discerned, has taken on a tinge of improvisation, along with the continuing ad hoc reaction to external events that characterized the 1990s. A few illustrative cases are elaborated below.

Terrorism

The twenty-first century brought with it a number of pressing security issues which required rapid foreign policy as well as domestic policy decisions, but none more than the rise of Islam-related extremism. The first major event occurred on September 11, 2001, when about a hundred Caribbean immigrants died in the destruction of the World Trade Center. Over the next few years, the United States sought to protect its interests by asking other nations to toughen their security policies: in the Caribbean, immigration controls had to be tightened, machine-readable passports introduced and greater airline and port scrutiny put in place, and the financing of terrorism added to the purview of the Caribbean Financial Action Task Force, which until then had focused primarily on money laundering.[10] Other states, including the United Kingdom and Canada, also toughened their laws and introduced more stringent scrutiny and visa requirements for Caribbean nationals.

The second major event was the outbreak of turmoil in the Middle East. At first the US invasion of Iraq in 2003 seemed remote from the region, but in the wake of the popular revolts of the "Arab Spring", the activities of the Islamic State in Iraq spread to Syria and beyond, bringing a new global emphasis on countering terrorism. The call by ISIS (the Islamic State in Iraq and Syria) or ISIL (the Islamic State in the Levant) for help from foreign fighters has reverberated surprisingly strongly in the region, with a significant number of Caribbean nationals heading for the Middle East, an estimated 150 in 2015 (Mosendz 2015; *Jamaica Observer* 2016). Given older (unproven) rumors of al-Qaeda links to the Muslimeen in Trinidad and Tobago (Marajh 2004), the alleged travel on a Caribbean passport of a Saudi operative, Guyanese nationals' involvement in a plot to blow up John F. Kennedy International Airport in New York, as well as occasional suspicion surrounding various groups and persons in Trinidad and Tobago and Venezuela, the allure of ISIS came as an add-on to increasing awareness that the region could not escape the repercussions of terrorism. Caribbean participation in terrorist activities has posed a major headache for domestic security agencies pressed both at home and internationally to be more proactive. Worries about the reintegration of those returning from their jihadist pursuits have engendered unusual popular discussion of options.

In this national security sphere, foreign policy personnel have specific roles. Foreign ministries and ministers have had to do damage control to the images of their countries. They have had to assure their larger partners that robust counterterrorism measures are being adopted. They have had to attend to consular arrangements when suspects have been arrested or families stranded. Most importantly, foreign ministers have had to work closely with their national security counterparts at home and abroad in developing strategies in this area, piggybacking on collaboration already in place on the older security issue of drug trafficking. (In this regard, the Caribbean Basin Security Initiative, a joint collaboration with the United States formed in 2009, has provided a channel for consultation, along with the regional platform, the Implementation Agency for Crime and Security, originally put in place to deal with security for the Cricket World Cup in 2007.)

Apart from the practical foreign policy involvement mentioned, one of the more proactive strategies taken in the region occurred when Jamaica and

Trinidad and Tobago opted to be listed as cosponsors of a UN Security Council resolution shepherded by US president Barack Obama in 2014 requesting that countries take action to prevent the flow of persons and financing to the Islamic State (see UNSC resolution 2179 [2014]; other Caribbean countries joined in support of the vote, even though they were not cosponsors). This serious decision, however, appears to have been undertaken in both countries in a manner that illustrates the improvisational nature of decision-making in the 2000s, particularly the second decade. The decision appeared to have been made quite quickly by the prime ministers and their closest advisers. The result was that in Trinidad and Tobago, complaints erupted that neither the cabinet nor parliament had been consulted. The political opposition accused the prime minister (questionably so) of bringing unwarranted Islamic State attention to the country and thereby making the country more vulnerable (*Trinidad Express* 2014; *Trinidad Guardian* 2014). In Jamaica, the vote came as a total surprise as well, and the prime minister was accused of not consulting or even publicizing the decision, leaving the society completely uninformed (*Jamaica Observer* 2014). While every foreign policy or national security decision need not pass the test of popularity with a wide range of actors, in a world in which information from alternative sources other than the government is widely accessible, this was a good example of an important decision, with significant state and societal ramifications, that was made as a quick response to a US push for support. Public anxiety would have been relieved by a more open public diplomacy. Indeed, since then, publics have remained anxious and unclear about governments' plans for the reintegration of ISIS families.

The Situation in Venezuela

Except for Haiti, which has for much of the 2000s experienced government instability, including the second exile of President Aristide in 2004 and subsequent changes of prime ministers and legislative-executive tensions, the Caribbean states have enjoyed political liberalization and stability in the 2000s, even though this does not mean that good governance has prevailed; in almost every country, corruption has been increasing. As they embarked on the search for economic sustainability in the 1990s, they also began to deepen their relations with oil-rich Venezuela, in particular benefiting from the PetroCaribe programme, under which Venezuela extended concessional financing to Caribbean and Central American countries. Warm relations were maintained with the populist Bolivarian socialist government of Hugo Chávez, even though Chávez initiated an anti-US policy that placed states allied with Venezuela at risk of losing their good relationships with the United States. When US officials expressed premature support for an opposition coup against the Venezuelan government in 2002, the Caribbean countries waited out the crisis, with most remaining loyal to Chávez. Fortunately, after the embarrassment of having appeared to support an overthrow that lasted a mere four days, the United States returned to its preoccupation with the Middle East and a possible pivot to Asia, resolving to also basically wait out the Bolivarian experiment. This meant that the Caribbean countries could continue their ties without having to worry about repercussions from the United States. Venezuela, however, continued to be a major irritant to the United States, which over the years reduced its diplomatic presence, placed sanctions on key individuals and declared the state to be a threat to US national security.

With the death of Chávez in 2013 and the rise to power of former vice president Nicolás Maduro, Venezuela entered into a period of heightened authoritarianism and economic deterioration, the latter hastened by the steep decline in oil prices since 2014. High inflation, food shortages, rising poverty and continual popular protests against Maduro's rule intensified in 2014–16. The official Venezuelan opposition won a majority in the legislature in December 2015 and worked on an effort to recall Maduro. But in 2017 Maduro replaced the legislative assembly with one packed with loyalists, after holding a referendum which, held in an atmosphere of violence, supported the initative.

The deepening of the Venezuelan crisis presented a challenge for foreign policy analysts in general who needed to think about at least the following: first, given the soured state of relations between the region's two important trade and aid partners, Venezuela and the United States, what diplomatic stances should the region adopt? Second, with oil prices falling in the past few years, what would be the impact on Venezuela's petrodiplomacy? (Indeed, Venezuela has reduced its level of support for PetroCaribe recipients.) Third, any societal deterioration in Venezuela has the potential to destabilize neighboring countries, in this case Trinidad and Tobago in particular (as happened even in the 1960s, when antigovernment guerrillas engaged in some activities affecting Trinidad). What plans could be put in place in anticipation of adverse consequences? As the crisis deepened, Venezuelans sought refuge in Trinidad and Tobago and travelled in fairly large numbers by boat to nearby Trinidad to find basic essentials. In response, that island nation sold emergency supplies to Venezuela after an urgent request was made by Maduro, and also tried to ignore the crisis by continuing to move forward in operationalizing earlier agreements to collaborate in the exploration of several marine gas fields. Trinidad and Tobago's position was that the situation in Venezuela was a domestic crisis not necessitating external intervention. As for the other Caribbean states, they expressed diplomatic support for Venezuela presumably for instrumental reasons as well as a certain ideological sympathy grounded in a mix of anti-imperialism and small state wariness of intervention. CARICOM has a history of not intervening in regional disputes under the guise of non-interference. The one exception to this support has been CARICOM's firm opposition to Venezuela's renewed push to assert its claim to the Essequibo region of Guyana, where potentially large marine deposits of oil have been discovered (Miroff 2015).

As the Venezuelan standoff between Maduro and the opposition worsened and violence escalated in 2017, the OAS, led by an increasingly assertive secretary-general, Luis Almagro, sought to condemn and isolate Venezuela. Available avenues included invoking the organization's democratic charter (resisted by most member states), holding a meeting of Consultation of Foreign Ministers (the body in charge of dealing with threats to the peace), or suspending Venezuela. CARICOM states opposed all these initiatives. But while most Latin American states began to coalesce over time in their disapproval of Maduro, a split in CARICOM was deep enough that in May, the prime minister of St Vincent and the Grenadines, a stalwart supporter of Maduro, sent a letter to his fellow heads of government warning against attempts by "powerful" nations to divide the group in order to pursue "regime change" in Venezuela. In the letter, he implied that some CARICOM states were being lured into supporting "fair weather friends" (at the time the CARICOM dissenters included St Lucia, Guyana, Jamaica and the Bahamas).[11]

Division in CARICOM is, unfortunately, not unusual but the more intense the conflict, the more the grouping tends to move toward disarray. In this case the Vincentian prime minister's position (largely reflected as well in a surprisingly public statement by Trinidad and Tobago's prime minister; see Boodram 2017) and the neutralist position of the dissenters appeared to have been ironed out by July when, at their annual meeting, CARICOM heads took a measured approach, reaffirming the members' commitment to democracy and non-intervention, calling for dialogue by the factions within Venezuela, and importantly, offering their good offices to facilitate this dialogue (CARICOM 2017). Unfortunately, the group's lack of earlier coordination and seeming passivity in the face of deteriorating conditions in Venezuela has probably precluded any successful mediation at this stage. As of mid-2017, the Venezuelan government remains uninterested in working with the opposition.

Cuba

The same lack of anticipatory and coherent planning has been the case with respect to Cuba, despite the region's long familiarity with that country. The Caribbean states, including the Dominican Republic and Haiti, have developed relatively robust trade and aid relations with Cuba; work well with Cuba in organizations including CARICOM, the Association of Caribbean States, the newer Community of Latin American and Caribbean States and the Latin American and Caribbean group at the United Nations; and have long supported Cuba's goal to have the US embargo removed. Moreover, Cuba has a history of collaborative exchanges with other Caribbean states in areas such as tourism and health. All the Caribbean countries have an ambassadorial presence in Havana. Despite these close links, however, the region appears to have done very little planning with regard to the eventual liberalization of Cuba, except in one area: tourism. The region's governments cannot be criticized for being caught offguard when Raúl Castro and US President Barack Obama simultaneously announced their decision to work toward normalizing diplomatic relations in December 2014. Negotiations were a well-kept secret. But now that Cuba and the United States have reopened their embassies, the region needs to go beyond welcoming the rapprochement and prepare for the future. As Cuba pursues its own interests further afield (and without consulting its neighbors), will it deepen its relations with the north at the expense of collaboration with its region, and how can the region's interests with both partners best be preserved? For, notwithstanding President Trump's relatively minor reversal of policies toward Cuba, Cuba has already been cooperating well in security and technical areas with the United States, and further exchanges can be expected with increasing economic liberalization and new leadership in Cuba in 2018.

Foreign Economic Policies in the 2000s

Given the prominence of economic diplomacy in the 1990s, the 2000s has seen a real decline in the enthusiasm for using foreign policy as a platform and tool for seeking opportunities in globalization (or countering it). The decline is largely attributable to the limitation of choices due to the global recession that began in the north in 2008. Most Caribbean countries have been experiencing a prolonged economic malaise in the second decade of the twenty-first century. Even before the recession of 2008, few countries other than oil- and gas-producing Trinidad and Tobago were thriving economically. As the recession wore on, many countries found their market shares reduced, their aid diminished and no other recourse available than turning to the International Monetary Fund.

The global economic downturn was foreseeable to economists to some degree, given the excessive global stock market exuberance, the exposure to bad debt of the large banks in the north at the time, inflated housing costs and other economic problems. Yet the bursting of the bubble caught the United States and Europe relatively unprepared. Initially, the problems in Europe and the United States did not affect growth in the rising states – Brazil, Russia, India and China – as well as many other smaller economies. But inevitably the slowdown became a global one, especially after China's growth slowed. The plunge in oil prices in 2014 slowed growth further in the oil-producing states, including Trinidad and Tobago.

Once the recession hit the Caribbean, few options presented themselves to most states; hence it was acceptable for decisions to be improvised. The smaller islands of the Eastern Caribbean faced the most economic uncertainty, given the phasing out of trade preferences with the European Union, an Economic Partnership Agreement having been signed in 2008 with the European Union committing the Caribbean countries to fully liberalized trade in twenty-five years. The decision by Britain in 2016 to exit the European Union has surely added more uncertainty to trade and aid planning throughout the region.

With prices for primary products low and international crackdowns making offshore financial centres less profitable, few other alternatives for economic diplomacy have recommended themselves, although St Kitts and Nevis, for one, has managed to progress well on the basis of a somewhat controversial citizenship-by-investment programme.[12] Given the economic problems of the small economies, which contributed as well to the stagnation of CARICOM, aside from accessing the International Monetary Fund, one regional option available was to join the Bolivarian Alternative for the Americas (ALBA), the Venezuela-led institution which was created as an alternative to the neoliberal Free Trade Area of the Americas. While providing access to generous funding, ALBA membership also brought with it some risk, as has already been described. (Note that St Kitts and Nevis and Grenada joined ALBA only in 2014.) Interestingly, in 2014 the United States announced its own "energy security" initiative for the Caribbean – surely an attempt to woo the region away from a floundering Venezuela.

One bright area for all the Caribbean states has been the partnership established with China. Like other states of the global south, the Caribbean states have encouraged Chinese investment in construction and other industries and have increased their trade with China considerably. Table 4.1 shows the truly remarkable increase in trade between 1995 and 2016.

The emergence of China has generated exceptional interest among scholars of international relations, who have spent much time theorizing about China's commitment to a "peaceful rise/development", its challenges to the current superpower, its new non-conditional model of development assistance, the pros and cons of its special relationship with Africa and much more.[13] Having worked to secure a dominant role in Asia and an exceptional role in Africa, China also reached out to Latin America in the 2000s. Its presence has been increasing in the small states of the Caribbean, not only in trade but also through visits by diplomatic and military officials, including a visit by President Xi Jinping himself to Trinidad and Tobago in 2013. But while China has certainly grown in influence in the region, serving as a counterweight to the United States, China's role in trade and aid is still small by comparison with the role of the United States as the traditional partner. The imbalance in China's trade with the region is also widening. Moreover, as welcome as Chinese aid and investment is to countries seeking "easy" loans, Chinese policies have already raised concerns in Africa (with implications for the Caribbean) about a potentially new form of colonization, about environmental problems, about the exclusive use of Chinese labor on many projects and about weak linkages or even negative linkages in investment to the local economies. With China still heavily focused on building its "New Silk Road" via its Belt and Road initiative in Asia, its attention to the small states of the Caribbean may be limited and highly specific. One positive consideration, however, is that Chinese activity does help draw US attention back to the region.

Table 4.1. China's Trade with Caribbean Countries, 1995 and 2015 (US$'000)

	Exports		Imports	
Country	**1995**	**2015**	**1995**	**2015**
Antigua and Barbuda	2,007	54,021.3	60	339 (2013)[a]
Bahamas	3,456	1,586,188.2	11,651	24,365.2
Barbados	1,319	65,336.6	13 (1999)	18,529.6
Belize	1,402	80,078.5	258 (1997)	1,786.1
Cuba	146,326	1,884,177.5	213,554	330,656.1
Dominica	37,164	34,064.9	16 (1996)	654.1
Dominican Republic	38,067	1,559,822.9	19	211,766.1
Grenada	133	12,546.3	14 (1998)	32(2013)[a]
Guyana	5,405	160,996.4	38 (1996)	49,373.2
Haiti	5,528	436,884.2	55	10,676.7
Jamaica	21,501	630,291.4	4,318	31,174.3
St Kitts and Nevis	27	13,424.8	14 (2001)	337.9
St Lucia	199	21,281.6	2 (2000)	68.6
St Vincent and the Grenadines	1,705	39,537.7	258 (1997)	49.3
Suriname	5,212	202,207.2	2,110	50,841.2
Trinidad and Tobago	9,626	481,805.5	961 (1996)	39,251.6[b]

Source: UNCTADSTAT, the World Statistical Database merchandise trade matrix created by the United Nations Conference on Trade and Development, http://unctadstat.unctad.org/.

Note: Belize, the Dominican Republic, Haiti, St Kitts and Nevis, St Lucia, and St Vincent maintain diplomatic relations with Taiwan even though there is some smaller trade listed with the People's Republic of China.

[a]Imports for these countries peaked in 2013 with trade with Taiwan significantly more important in 2014 and 2015.

[b]Imports from Trinidad and Tobago were much higher, $119,502,000 in 2013.

As in the 1990s, finance and trade personnel are largely responsible for foreign economic policies. In the second decade of the 2000s, the unfortunate trend has continued whereby foreign offices and embassies, hampered by lower government resources, have been less involved than they could or should be in trade outreach. Meanwhile, the reliance on the more technical ministries tends to foster a disaggregated approach aimed at responding to immediate specific challenges.

Institutional Performance

The Caribbean states have a history of being proactive in international organizations, including the United Nations, the OAS, the Non-Aligned Movement and Latin American organizations. Indeed, this institutional area has been the unquestioned domain of the foreign ministries inasmuch as post–Cold War leaders and their advisers have often displayed some scepticism about the benefits of multilateralism. Continuity rather than improvisation is therefore to be expected in this sphere, and in fact, the Caribbean continues to hold its own institutionally, displaying a high level of participation in key organizations. In the 2000s, a perusal of UN records (available at www.un.org) shows, however, that larger states of the region (Haiti excepted) have been less well represented than before in terms of office holding in the General Assembly and Economic and Social Council. On the other hand, the smaller states have assumed a somewhat larger presence, notably St Lucia and Antigua and Barbuda.[14] In addition, the region's states have developed a reputation in certain areas, in particular environmental matters (since at least the 1994 conference on small island developing states held in Barbados), as well as the newer focus on the prevention of non-communicable diseases. With respect to the former, it is notable that the leaders of Cuba, the Dominican Republic, the Bahamas, and all the Eastern Caribbean islands attended the important Paris Climate Change (Conference of Parties 21) meeting in December 2015 and that all Caribbean countries signed the Paris Accord, with all except Cuba, the Dominican Republic, Haiti, Jamaica, Suriname and Trinidad and Tobago ratifying it by 2016.

On the other hand, some major decisions on institutional matters, generally decisions that hinge on leadership or governmental preferences rather than bureaucratic standard operating procedures, still create undue political tension because of uncoordinated regional planning. For example, in 2015 the region was divided over candidates to head two important groupings, the ACP group and the Commonwealth, continuing a pattern in the 2000s of lack of cohesion on office-holding decisions.[15] Another example was the effort by Trinidad and Tobago, with the support of CARICOM, to gain the headquarters of the secretariat of the Small Arms Treaty approved by the United Nations in 2013. There was no consistent follow-up either by the country or by CARICOM, and Trinidad was eliminated as a candidate early on. Finally, one might add here the lack of follow-up to CARICOM's seemingly bolder-than-usual decision, taken in 2013, to halt negotiations on the Dominican Republic's membership in CARICOM after the Dominican Republic passed a law depriving a large percentage of its Haitian population of citizenship. The community's leaders condemned this violation of human rights and declared that they would review their relations with the Dominican Republic in the CARIFORUM (the Caribbean's arm of the ACP) and in the Community of Latin American and Caribbean States. Instead they ended up continuing to do business as usual with the Dominican Republic. (The Dominican Republic later passed a naturalization law, but many persons of Haitian heritage did not have the required documents to register and gain citizenship.)

The Caribbean's attention, however, appears to be more firmly fixed on Latin American institutions in the 2000s. Apart from ALBA (with the liabilities of joining already described), they have joined two prominent new groupings, the Community of Latin American and Caribbean States and the Union of South American Nations, both groupings that reflected Latin America's leftward turn. The Community of Latin American and Caribbean States was envisaged as an alternative to the OAS amid rising tensions in US–Latin American relations after a military coup in Honduras in 2009 against the left-leaning Manual Zelaya. The coup had been condemned by most regional states, but not by the United States. The Community of Latin American and Caribbean States was launched in 2011 and has quickly become the premier organization for regional political cooperation. The Union of South American Nations includes Guyana and Suriname and focuses on a post-liberal approach to regionalism that includes adequate attention to social development. Both organizations were supported largely by then-left leaning Brazil as well as Venezuela. While it is still unclear just what the Caribbean states have been able to contribute to these groupings other than generic diplomatic support, joining them has to be seen as a nod to geopolitical realities that link them to Latin America, as well as a move away from dependence on the United States and an embrace of a more progressive Latin American agenda. But now that the trend toward the left has faded in Latin American – with Brazil's Lula da Silva indicted for corruption, his successor, Dilma Rousseff, removed from office for the same reason, Argentina's Cristina Kirchner replaced by the conservative Mauricio Macri, and Venezuela in crisis – it may be more difficult for the Caribbean members to leverage their diplomatic support for more tangible benefits. Indeed, changing politics in Latin America as a whole suggest the need for robust, well-developed foreign policies in order to anticipate change.

Assessment

The discussion above does not do justice to the wide scope of Caribbean foreign policy and the changes, in the United States and Britain in particular, which have impacted the region's foreign policy planning and decisions. Moreover, it should be said that there have been *successes* in Caribbean foreign policy in the second decade of the 2000s. For example, the region successfully planned and hosted the Cricket World Cup in 2007. Trinidad and Tobago hosted the Fifth Summit of the Americas and the Commonwealth Heads of Government Meeting in 2009 (although there was significant public outcry over the expense). Between 2009 and 2016, visits to the region were made by a number of world leaders, including US president Barack Obama (who visited Trinidad and Tobago, Jamaica and Cuba, meeting also with CARICOM leaders in the case of the first two), Japan's prime minister Shinzo Abe (who met with CARICOM leaders in Trinidad and Tobago), US vice president Joe Biden (visiting the Dominican Republic and Trinidad and Tobago), China's Xi Jinping (who met with CARICOM leaders in Trinidad and Tobago) and Nigeria's Goodluck Jonathan (who visited Jamaica and Trinidad and Tobago). Numerous other delegations have visited in search of trade and investment collaboration. Still, the argument here is that the Caribbean region as a whole has not projected itself internationally as well as it did in the 1970s and has thus missed the opportunity to showcase its strengths. In this era of "soft power" (Joseph Nye's term for exerting influence through attraction [Nye 2002]), the region and some individual states have made strides in promoting their sports, music and culture, as well as relative stability and natural beauty, but have been less proactive in leveraging these into a foreign policy brand. Singapore, for example, promotes itself as a rational and efficient country (Chong 2016), Bhutan promotes itself as a happy place to international audiences via the catchy Global

Happiness Index (taken up also by the United Arab Emirates), Asian countries as a whole promote what they deem Asian values and the "Asian way" of mediating disputes, Thailand developed "CEO diplomacy" and Qatar uses no particular phrases but promotes itself as a proactive regional mediator (Mansour 2016). In the twenty-first century, Cuba is the one state that comes close to having a specialty in foreign policy: medical diplomacy (Cassells 2016). Other states appear uninterested in establishing unique or creative foreign policies, preferring policies that are ad hoc reactions to events as they happen.

Of course, foreign policy bureaucrats are continuing to manage the day-to-day activities of diplomacy, regardless of changes in government or what the public thinks, largely left to operate on their own while other administrative units – finance, energy, security and social – conduct more vigorous business abroad. But this disjointed approach makes it difficult for foreign policy personnel to know and promote the country's true aims and goals effectively. The place of foreign policy within overarching public policy remains unclear.

Ironically, in the 2000s progress has been made in the larger CARICOM countries in actually formulating "grand" visions for national development in which foreign policy naturally could and should play a role. To focus briefly on two of these initiatives, Jamaica's Vision 2030 Plan was put in place in 2009 and provides a vision for Jamaica to become a developed country and "the place of choice to live, work, raise families, and do business". However, apart from the encouragement it gives to foreign economic linkages and diaspora involvement, the plan is unclear as to exactly where foreign policy fits (for the plan and relevant updates, see the Jamaica Planning Institute's website at www.vision2030.gov.jm/National-Development-Plan). In Trinidad and Tobago, a Vision2020 plan was launched in 2002 which similarly sought to guide the country toward developed-country status. Going further, the country initiated a specific foreign policy review in 2007, which produced a strategic vision and plan for the sector. However, with a change in government in 2010, Vision2020 was abandoned in favor of shorter-term planning.

The common practice in the region has been for the executive to conduct foreign policy in a personal fashion, aggravating this unpredictable ad hoc approach to foreign policy. Consultation with relevant stakeholders in foreign policy, including non-governmental organizations, is not the norm, and the public comes into (remote) contact with foreign policy only when a summit is hosted or a dignitary visits. Embassies abroad are valued more for their consular roles (providing visas, giving help to nationals abroad) than for their role in projecting and protecting the country's interests. Public input into foreign policy is not encouraged. Debates on foreign policy are largely absent from the newspapers and television and even social media, except when a controversy erupts. Public diplomacy hardly exists. Often foreign policy is equated with some contentious issue in the regional integration movement, and there is a sense in some circles that small countries need not look beyond their regions.

Sustainability is not just an economic attribute but a matter of policy as well. It can be applied to foreign policy. While "improv" diplomacy has its place as a reaction to the unusual and unexpected, it is not "good" diplomacy. Instead, a commitment to more comprehensive planning in foreign policy would allow small Caribbean states to anticipate events and devise *rational* responses based on historical, developmental criteria that do not change with every external or domestic permutation. Sustainability would be further promoted if, in the interest of democracy and openness, governments were more inclusive in foreign policy decision-making, ensuring that relevant standing parliamentary committees are given adequate information to allow for their input, that proper coordination is mandated across relevant ministries and that, wherever possible, non-governmental stakeholders sit at the table. In a similar vein, outreach to the public at large would help sustain support for well-executed and rational foreign policies. Imagine, for example, if business sectors and publics were formally polled for their perspective on Venezuela or Cuba. While final decisions cannot be made on this basis, at least publics would feel somewhat invested in foreign policy.

In terms of the *craft* of diplomacy, around the world foreign services have tried to inject new technical and technological skills into their operations in order to keep up with modern demands. The Caribbean is no exception. But none of this is sustainable without the support of governments. It is not necessarily financial support that is key: diplomats around the world are used to doing more with less. Rather, Caribbean governments need to provide a supportive political *environment* for the work of diplomats; this support does not seem to be strong in 2017 when financial resources are scarce. Overall, the aim of governments should be to convert what may be seen as an unpredictable external environment into a somewhat predictable one, one in which developmental public policies, including foreign policies, can be sustained over the medium and longer term.

Notes

1. For a sense of how some small states do this, see Braveboy-Wagner (2010) as well as part 3 of Braveboy-Wagner (2016), in which the diplomatic strategies of Cuba, Qatar, Senegal and Singapore are elaborated.
2. In this chapter I am referring to small size when I say "small". There is a good deal of debate about small states, both definitional and theoretical. "Small" has often been conflated with "weak", and "small" has often simply meant "any power that is not one of the traditional great powers". I criticize this in Braveboy-Wagner (2010). See also Rothstein (1968), East (1973) and Hey (2003), among others.
3. The fourteen states are Antigua and Barbuda, Bahamas, Barbados, Belize, Dominica, Grenada, Guyana, Haiti, Jamaica, St Kitts and Nevis, St Lucia, St Vincent and the Grenadines, Suriname, and Trinidad and Tobago.
4. For a good background on the Caribbean, see Hillman and D'Agostino (2009), including the chapter on international relations by Braveboy-Wagner, 161–89.
5. Countries that did not join the Non-Aligned Movement by the end of the Cold War were Dominica, the Dominican Republic, Haiti, St Kitts and Nevis, and St Vincent. They were able to join with the end of global ideological rivalry.
6. For much more on this, see Braveboy-Wagner (1989, 2007).
7. In the United States, President Bill Clinton noted in his inauguration address in 1992: "We will make the economic security of our nation a primary goal of our foreign policy" (quoted in Braveboy-Wagner [1995, 20]). He proceeded to seek fast-track authority for the North American Free Trade Agreement and to vigorously support Asian and Pacific trade integration.
8. In the 1990s preferences in rum were phased out and the sugar regime was renegotiated several times to conform to the rules. The Caribbean established its regional negotiation machinery in 1997 to facilitate further negotiations on free trade with Europe, Canada and the United States.
9. Liberalization occurred in the Dominican Republic as well, with the country's strongman president, Joaquín Balaguer, finally leaving in 1996 amid popular protests about vote tampering in the election of 1994.
10. This is a regional grouping of the Financial Action Task Force of the Organization for Economic Co-operation and Development, which began operations in 1996. The Financial Action Task Force had pressed for each country to establish financial intelligence units to counter money laundering, and indeed the new concerns of the 2000s accelerated the formation of these in the Caribbean.
11. Ralph Gonsalves's letter was leaked to the public. A link to it is available at https://barbadosunderground.wordpress.com/2017/05/15/prime-minister-ralph-gonzales-letter-to-hogs-leaked/. See also *Caribbean360* (2017).
12. The citizenship programme has been abused by a number of high-profile foreigners, including Teodoro Nguema Obiang, son of the president of Equatorial Guinea. See, for example, *Caribbean News Now* (2014).
13. Among prominent works on China see, among many, Womack (2010), Shirk (2008), Brautigam (2010) and Shambaugh (2013).

14. Antigua and Barbuda held the presidency of the former, assuming the presidency of the General Assembly in 2013, only the third Caribbean state to do so (although it should be noted that the presidency ended badly, with allegations of corruption being pursued in court in New York). See *Guardian* 2015.
15. A notable case was the divisions on the election of a new OAS secretary-general in 2005 (Belize and St Vincent and the Grenadines committed to the Mexican candidate initially before Chilean Miguel Insulza won).

References

Boodram, Kim. 2017. "OAS Head Must Step Down, Says Rowley". *Trinidad Express*, 1 June. http://www.trinidadexpress.com/20170601/news/oas-head-must-step-down-says-rowley.

Brautigam, Deborah. 2010. *The Dragon's Gift: The Real Story of China in Africa*. Oxford: Oxford University Press.

Braveboy-Wagner, Jacqueline A. 1986. *Interpreting the Third World: Politics, Economics and Social Issues*. New York: Praeger.

———. 1989. *The Caribbean in World Affairs: The Foreign Policies of the English-Speaking States*. Boulder: Westview.

———. 1995. *Caribbean Diplomacy*. New York: Caribbean Diaspora Press, Caribbean Research Center, Medgar Evers College and City University of New York.

———. 2007. *Small States in Global Affairs: The Foreign Policies of the Caribbean Community (CARICOM)*. New York: Palgrave Macmillan.

———. 2010. Opportunities and Limitations of the Exercise of Foreign Policy Power by a Very Small State: The Case of Trinidad and Tobago. *Cambridge Review of International Affairs* 23 (3) (September): 407–27.

———. 2014. Spaces and Places: How Geopolitics Has Impacted Caribbean International Relations and Foreign Policy. Paper presented at the International Studies Association Annual Convention, Toronto, March.

———, ed. 2016. *Diplomatic Strategies of Nations in the Global South: The Search for Leadership*. New York: Palgrave Macmillan.

Caribbean360. 2017. We've Got Your Back: CARICOM Defies Pressure and Stands with Venezuela. 19 May. http://www.caribbean360.com/news/weve-got-back-caricom-defies-pressure-stands-venezuela.

Caribbean News Now. 2014. St-Kitts-Nevis Economic Citizens Split $22.5 Million Corruption Payout. 10 June. www.caribbeannewsnow.com/topstory-St-Kitts-Nevis-economic-citizen-split-$22.5-million-corruption-payout-21504.html.

Caribbean Community (CARICOM). 2017. Communique. 38th Regular Meeting of the Conference of Heads of Government. 4–6 July. http://caricom.org/cochog/view/communique-thirty-eighth-caricom-heads-of-government-meeting.

Cassells, E. 2016. Cuba: Still Punching Above Its Weight. In *Diplomatic Strategies of Nations in the Global South: The Search for Leadership*, edited by J. Braveboy-Wagner, 319–44. New York: Palgrave Macmillan.

Chong, A. 2016. The Diplomacy of Singapore: Rationality and Pitfalls. In *Diplomatic Strategies of Nations in the Global South: The Search for Leadership,* edited by J. Braveboy-Wagner, 393–424. New York: Palgrave Macmillan.

East, M. 1973. Size and Foreign Policy Behavior: A Test of Two Models. *Policy Sciences* 4 (4): 491–509.

Guardian (UK). 2015. Antiguan Ex-President of UN General Assembly Faces $1m Corruption Charges. 6 October. www.theguardian.com/world/2015/oct/06/antiguan-ex-president-un-general-assembly-faces-corruption-charges.

Hey, Jeanne K. 2003. *Small States in World Politics: Explaining Foreign Policy Behavior.* Boulder: Lynne Rienner.

Hill, C. 2003. *The Changing Politics of Foreign Policy.* New York: Palgrave Macmillan.

Hillman, Richard S., and Thomas J. D'Agostino, eds. 2009. *Understanding the Contemporary Caribbean.* Boulder: Lynne Rienner.

Jamaica Observer. 2014. Jamaica Co-Sponsors ISIS Resolution: Opposition Blasts Government on Non-Disclosure of UN Participation. October 9. www.jamaicaobserver.com/latestnews/Jamaica-co-sponsors-ISIS-resolution.

Jamaica Observer. 2016. "Top US General Warns About ISIS Fighters in the Caribbean". 6 January. http://www.jamaicaobserver.com/news/Top-US-general-warns-about-ISIS-fighters-in-the-Caribbean.

Kissinger, H. 2001. *Does America Need a Foreign Policy? Toward a Diplomacy for the 21st Century.* New York: Simon and Schuster.

Lewis, Vaughan A. 1976. The Commonwealth Caribbean and Self-Determination in the International System. In *Size, Self-Determination, and International Relations: The Caribbean,* edited by Vaughan A. Lewis, 227–47. Mona, Jamaica: Institute for Social and Economic Research.

Manning, Patrick A.M. 1997. A Policy Vision for the Region. In *Caribbean Public Policy: Regional, Cultural, and Socioeconomic Issues for the Twentieth Century,* edited by Jacqueline Anne Braveboy-Wagner and Dennis J. Gayle, 223–28. Boulder: Westview.

Mansour, I. 2016. Qatar's Global Activism: Pursuing Global Ambition in the Midst of Domestic and Aregional Transitions. In *Diplomatic Strategies of Nations in the Global South: The Search for Leadership,* edited by J. Braveboy-Wagner, 344–70. New York: Palgrave Macmillan.

Marajh, Camini. 2004. "US on Jammat Trail". *Trinidad and Tobago Express,* 15 August (archived).

Miroff, Nick. 2015. Taking Land from Guyana Might Be the One Thing All Venezuelans Can Agree On. *Washington Post,* 16 July. www.washingtonpost.com/news/worldviews/wp/2015/07/16/something-venezuelans-can-all-agree-on-taking-land-from-guyana/.

Mossendz, Polly. 2015. "General Warns of ISIS Fighters Entering US Through Caribbean". *Newsweek,* 13 March. http://www.newsweek.com/general-warns-isis-fighters-entering-us-through-caribbean-313807.

Nye, J. 2002. Hard and Soft Power in American Foreign Policy. In *The Paradox of Hard Power,* edited by J. Nye, 4–17. New York: Oxford University Press.

Rothstein, Robert L. 1968. *Alliances and Small Powers*. New York: Columbia University Press.

Shambaugh, D. 2013. *China Goes Global*. Oxford: Oxford University Press.

Shirk, Susan L. 2008. *China: Fragile Superpower*. New York: Oxford University Press.

Trinidad Express. 2014. Govt Misrepresenting PNM Position on ISIS. 3 October. www.trinidadexpress.com/news/Govt-misrepresenting-PNMs-position-on-ISIS-278089101.html.

Trinidad Guardian. 2014. Rowley Clears Air on ISIS Comment. 6 October. www.guardian.co.tt/news/2014-10-06/rowley-clears-air-isis-comment.

US Department of State. 2006. Transformational Diplomacy: Remarks of Secretary Condoleeza Rice at Georgetown University. 18 January. http://2001-2009.state.gov/secretary/rm/2006/59306.htm.

Womack, Brantly, ed. 2010. *China's Rise in Historical Perspective*. Lanham, MD: Rowman and Littlefield.

Part 2

Economic Policies for Sustainable Growth

CHAPTER 5

The Post-Independence Performance of Caribbean Economies: The Centrality of Economic Policy Choices

Dave Seerattan

The small, open nature of all CARICOM countries means that the international economic environment in many respects drives the performance of these economies. This general economic feature does not, however, do justice to the tremendous heterogeneity inherent in this group of countries. This is highlighted by the fact that the group includes two countries, one with very high (the Bahamas) and one with the lowest (Haiti) per capita income in the Western Hemisphere. The region also includes countries with credit ratings which range from selective default to investment grade, countries whose economies vary from commodity-based to ones dominated by the services sector and a country with high scores on the Human Development Index (Barbados), as well as countries which rank among the lowest (Haiti) on this index. This inherent diversity, which is reflected in large differences in economic performance over time,[1] is driven by factors such as initial factor endowment, productivity and business competitiveness, policy choices over time, strategic economic diversification, political and social stability and vulnerability.[2]

These factors invariably affect the competitiveness and economic performance of the region. Some of the most important factors affecting the competitiveness of the Caribbean include low productivity, especially that of labour; small market size; low investment in research and development; a relatively underdeveloped institutional framework to support business development; strategic mistakes by governments and major corporations and a sometimes convoluted business environment.

Very importantly also, competitiveness is increasingly based on knowledge and information rather than on traditional factor accumulation. The quality of the research, education and training systems, which are often underdeveloped in the region or inappropriately structured, therefore has to be upgraded to meet the demands of the new economic realities. Moreover, the increasing plethora of international economic, industrial and business standards now impacting Caribbean countries' ability to participate and compete in global markets means that they now have to modernize and restructure their business processes and policy frameworks to consolidate and improve their growth prospects.

The International Economic Environment

The international economic environment facing Caribbean countries since independence has been difficult, as it is for most small, open, developing countries with undiversified economic structures, limited factor endowment and susceptibility to the vagaries of international commodity and financial markets. This difficult environment was to an extent mitigated by preferential trade agreements and the relative protection offered by the CARICOM arrangements. When these preferential arrangements were found to be in contravention of World Trade Organization rules, it signaled the beginning of the end of these arrangements. CARICOM also provided some level of protection, but the asymmetric impact of this arrangement meant that larger, more efficient countries benefited the most and led some to question the usefulness of CARICOM, especially to smaller members. The well-known governance issues at the secretariat level and the related problems with implementation of CARICOM decisions did not help the perception that the CARICOM arrangement had not realized its full potential to act as a mechanism to ease the challenges of the Caribbean's insertion into the global economy.

The gradual erosion of preferential arrangements and the problems with the CARICOM arrangement meant that to maintain their economic viability Caribbean countries had to make significant structural economic changes over a very short period of time. In less than a decade (1990–2000), Eastern Caribbean Countries moved from agriculture-based economies to ones based on services, mostly tourism, with some contribution from financial services. In other Caribbean countries, a similar process had started earlier as agriculture gave way to services and light manufacturing, with only Trinidad and Tobago having a significant heavy industrial sector based on oil and gas. Over this period there were significant swings in economic growth, employment and trade balances.

The international economic environment facing the Caribbean became more complicated in the post-2008 era. The 2007–8 international financial and economic crisis weakened Caribbean economies already facing serious challenges in areas such as fiscal sustainability, weak international competitiveness and slow growth. Global economic growth in the post-crisis era is expected to remain uneven and relatively muted for the near to medium term (table 5.1).

Table 5.1. Real Global Economic Growth, 2013–2019 (Per Cent)

World/Region	2013	2014	2015	2016	2017	2018	2019
World	3.3	3.4	3.1	3.6	3.8	3.9	4.0
Developed Countries	1.1	1.8	2.0	2.2	2.2	2.2	2.0
Euro Area	−0.3	0.9	1.5	1.6	1.7	1.6	1.6
Emerging and Developing Countries	5.0	4.6	4.0	4.5	4.9	5.1	5.2
Emerging and Developing Asia	2.2	1.0	−2.7	0.5	2.0	2.4	2.5
Emerging and Developing Europe	7.0	6.8	6.5	6.4	6.3	6.4	6.5
Latin America and the Caribbean	2.9	2.8	3.0	3.0	3.4	3.3	3.3

Source: International Monetary Fund, World Economic Outlook Database, October 2015.
Note: Data for 2016 to 2019 are based on projections made in 2015.

In this environment, exchange-rate instability among the major currencies is expected to feature prominently. In the near future, the US dollar is likely to continue its rise relative to other major currencies, which means we will see appreciating trends for currencies pegged to the US dollar. This would also serve to reinforce the current trend of falling commodity prices, which are generally quoted in US dollars. The resulting volatility in exchange rates would also lead to a more difficult environment for foreign investment and trade. Rising interest rates in the United States as its economy improves also set the stage for increased interest-rate risks and the associated volatility in capital flows.

These developments suggest that the global economy is likely to be characterized now and in the near future by significant disparities in growth performance, lower and more volatile commodity prices and more volatile exchange and interest rates, with the associated volatility in capital flows. These exchange-rate developments are likely to drive appreciating trends among developing countries pegged to the US dollar, which could put them at a competitive disadvantage, especially in situations in which their levels of international competitiveness have already been weak.

Given existing vulnerabilities in terms of the fiscal accounts and international competitiveness, the region is likely to face serious challenges to its economic stability in the medium term. In this uncertain environment, Caribbean countries will need to build their resilience by sticking to a disciplined policy framework, especially on their fiscal accounts. They will also need to intensify efforts at structural reforms to address long-standing systemic issues which reduce efficiency and international competitiveness in the face of significant real appreciation of exchange rates in the region, driven by international currency developments.

Caribbean Economic Performance

The average economic growth performance of Caribbean countries has been moderately successful over the past five decades. Over this period the region has undergone tremendous change in terms of a general move away from dependence on agriculture to more service-based economies, the regions' greater integration into the global economy and the attendant increased vulnerability to external shocks and increased competition from more efficient producers. Over the period 1960–2014, the rate of growth of the Caribbean economies as a group has been consistently better than that of Latin America, with the growth of per capita gross domestic product (GDP) in the Caribbean averaging 2.37 per cent compared to 1.71 per cent in Latin America but lower than the 5.28 per cent recorded by the more dynamic economies in the East Asia and Pacific (EAP) region. One problem for growth in the Caribbean has been that it is driven more by consumption and less by net exports and investment relative to the EAP region. This has implications for the sustainability and improvement of the growth trajectory in the Caribbean. Growth in net exports, in particular, has been a platform on which the robust growth in the EAP region has been built.

Another worrying trend has been the increasing disparity in growth over time between the Caribbean economies and high-performance economies such as those in the EAP region. For example, although the Caribbean performed better than the EAP region on a per capita basis in the 1960s, this region surpassed the Caribbean in the 1970s, and the gap in performance has widened consistently since then, moving from a gap of 1.1 per cent in the 1970s to 6.16 per cent in the first fourteen years of the twenty-first century (table 5.2). This suggests that in terms of fundamentals such as productivity, innovation and competition, Caribbean countries have not kept pace with the more dynamic extra-regional economies and, more worryingly, may have regressed in these areas over time. The Region's ability to maintain its record of growth and development may therefore be at risk.

The issue of the trends in productivity and efficiency in the Caribbean over time can be evaluated in the growth accounting framework, which decomposes overall growth. In this framework growth is attributed to increases in factor inputs (labour and capital) and a residual called total factor productivity (TFP), which is thought to represent increases in productivity and technical progress.[3] Utilizing this methodology, a report by the World Bank (2005) highlighted the decline in productivity in the 1990s, which may partially explain the slowdown in growth in that period. In particular, using the Solow method to estimate TFP, it was found that productivity declined from 2.06 in the 1980s to 1.09 in the 1990s. The report also suggests that the growth in capital and labour in the 1990s was more significant for growth relative to productivity than it was for growth in the 1980s (see table 5.3).

This pattern was generally repeated when one looks at individual countries in the Caribbean as countries which had increases in TFP between the 1980s and the 1990s, such as Trinidad and Tobago and Guyana, experienced higher growth rates, while countries which recorded a deterioration in TFP in the 1990s, such as Jamaica and the Eastern Caribbean Currency Area countries, recorded slower growth. Estimates of TFP for the Caribbean countries from 2000 and beyond indicate that TFP continues to be lower in the Caribbean generally and in some Caribbean countries in particular compared to their Asian counterparts (Sosa, Tsounta and Kim 2013). Sosa Tsounta and Kim (2013) also

Table 5.2. Per Capita GDP Growth in Caribbean Forum Member Countries, 1960–2014 (Per Cent)

	Years					
Country/Region	**1960s**	**1970s**	**1980s**	**1990s**	**2000s**	**1960–2014**
Antigua and Barbuda	NA	NA	6.30	2.20	0.96	3.15
Bahamas	5.40	0.04	1.60	−0.20	−0.75	1.22
Barbados	6.00	3.00	1.90	0.50	0.70	2.42
Belize	2.20	4.40	2.80	3.50	1.59	2.90
Dominica	NA	NA	6.30	2.40	1.70	3.47
Dominican Republic	1.60	5.40	1.50	2.80	3.38	2.94
Grenada	NA	NA	4.70	2.70	1.61	3.00
Guyana	1.30	0.90	−2.50	4.50	2.62	1.36
Haiti	−1.30	1.80	−1.50	−3.20	−0.36	−0.91
Jamaica	2.70	−0.20	0.20	0.60	0.30	0.72
St Kitts and Nevis	NA	NA	6.50	3.90	1.32	3.91
St Lucia	NA	NA	4.30	3.30	0.40	2.67
St Vincent and the Grenadines	−0.20	17.70	4.80	3.00	2.21	5.50
Suriname	NA	2.70	−1.70	0.40	3.34	1.19
Trinidad and Tobago	3.50	3.50	−2.50	2.20	4.13	2.17
Caribbean	2.30	3.90	2.20	1.90	1.54	2.37
Latin America and Caribbean	2.40	3.30	−0.20	1.20	1.83	1.71
East Asia and Pacific (EAP)	1.80	5.00	5.70	6.20	7.70	5.28
Caribbean Growth Gap to EAP	−0.50	1.10	3.50	4.30	6.16	2.91

Sources: World Bank, *A Time to Choose: Caribbean Development in the 21st Century*, 2005; World Bank, World Development Indicators, 2016; author's calculations.

indicated that the gap in growth performance between the high-performance economies in Emerging Asia and Latin American and Caribbean countries can also be explained in part by the far superior TFP in the Asian countries.

The main factors driving this decline in productivity have been identified as the increase in unproductive public investments, large investments in low-productivity traditional agriculture sectors such as sugar and bananas and the channelling of significant investments to maturing sectors such as tourism (World Bank 2005).

Table 5.3. Growth Decomposition for Latin America and the Caribbean, 1980s and 1990s

Region	Growth Component	1980s	1990s
Caribbean	GDP	3.06	2.61
	Labor	0.90	0.96
	Capital	0.79	1.08
	TFP	2.06	1.09
Latin America	GDP	1.37	3.50
	Labor	1.67	1.64
	Capital	0.96	1.32
	TFP	−1.43	0.64

Source: World Bank, *A Time to Choose: Caribbean Development in the 21st Century*, 2005.
Notes: GDP, gross domestic product; TFP, total factor productivity.

This link between growth and productivity in the Caribbean also seems to be supported by the fact that the aggregate level of investments also does not seem to be a problem. Overall investment in the Caribbean has been quite high in the recent past. Total investment has been about 30 per cent of GDP since 1990, with private investment at 20 per cent of GDP and foreign direct investment about 6 per cent of GDP (World Bank 2005). Foreign direct investment is an important barometer of the thinking of private investors as to the competitiveness of particular sectors. The fact that foreign direct investment flows to the Caribbean are concentrated in the mining, tourism and agriculture subsectors in some countries suggests that the region has only a few internationally competitive sectors.

Private-Sector Entrepreneurial Capacity

The entrepreneurial capacity in the Caribbean has long been recognized as a constraint on economic growth and development in the region. In fact, as far back as 1973 Sir Arthur Lewis, in his capacity as president of the Caribbean Development Bank, in his statement to the board of governors of the bank at their meeting in Jamaica, in relation to the prospects for the tourism and manufacturing sectors, stated: "The missing factor in both these cases is business entrepreneurship in which our region is notoriously weak. This is not a factor which the Bank can of itself supply. Moreover, no community can suddenly be endowed with adequate native entrepreneurial capacity. The growth of this element is a long-term phenomenon, requiring cultural changes of a kind that are slow and not always obvious" (Lewis 1973).

In that statement Lewis also expanded on the factors which encourage entrepreneurial activity. He indicated that culture has a big part to play in the development of entrepreneurial activity, since culture either celebrates or negates certain qualities and practices necessary for innovation and entrepreneurial activity. A culture that celebrates business acumen, innovation and saving will normally be able to sustain entrepreneurial activity. He identified the general requirements for success in any field as a desire to achieve, self-confidence, strong self-discipline, an ability to learn, self-criticism, a willingness to innovate and preferably also support from a closely knit family which stands together behind its individual members. He went on to identify additional factors which are specific to success in business and entrepreneurship. These include the following:

1. A willingness to save and invest in the expansion of one's business with a long-term view.
2. A willingness to make decisions.
3. A strong respect for the contracts into which one enters so that one has the reputation for paying one's debts when due, for delivery on or before the delivery date and for adhering to the stipulated quantities and qualities.
4. A sense of oneself as a servant, which causes one to seek to please. Applied to one's customers, this leads to courtesy, reliability and innovation, which are the bases of continued and expanding patronage. Applied to one's staff, it leads to good personnel relations, high morale and high productivity. This is one of the most difficult requirements for Third World countries.

Lewis outlined some strategies which have been used to address our deficiencies in these areas, such as the establishment of business schools; institutions to support business and entrepreneurship, such as small business development agencies and development banks; and protected markets for a variety of products. He argues that these strategies though helpful does not deal with the central problem. He argued:

> In fact none of the current techniques comes to grips with the basic problem. To be a good businessman one needs to know something about business management and to have access to credit, but above all one needs to have the right personality: our deficiencies lie here rather than in the colleges, in the law, or in the banking system. Personality is formed on one's mother's knee. One's image of the kind of person one wishes to be is absorbed from one's culture, as one grows up. We shall not be well endowed with business types until our society learns to appreciate the business-like personality, and absorbs this appreciation into the cultural framework of boyhood, girlhood and adolescence.

These sentiments are as relevant today as they were then, with efforts to promote business development and entrepreneurship being an important part of government policy in all Caribbean countries and with significant help from multilateral financial institutions. These efforts have produced a range of special-purpose institutions, such as business development agencies and development banks, in virtually all territories. In spite of these efforts, the capacity for entrepreneurial activity is still not well developed in many countries in the Caribbean. Some countries appear, however, to have been more successful than others, with countries such as Trinidad and Tobago, Barbados, and Jamaica appearing to have had more success in this area. In these countries successful indigenous businesses have grown out of family-based entrepreneurial activity and have emerged as large enterprises, in some cases comparable to foreign-based multinational corporations and state enterprises.

The fact that most of these indigenous enterprises evolved out of families seems to lend credence to the view that entrepreneurial activity is heavily dependent on culture and that the propensity for entrepreneurship is something that is a learned or socialized behavioral pattern. The policy solutions that are adopted to enhance our entrepreneurial capacity therefore need to pay attention to this reality. Efforts to create a more business-friendly environment should also take on board these realities, since we have weaknesses in this area also.

The Ease of Doing Business in the Caribbean

Using the indicators from the World Bank's *Doing Business* report (2015),[4] we can see that the region did not perform well relative to some of the more successful economies in terms of the general business environment (table 5.4). This is not surprising given that businessmen in the region have always complained about the number of national bureaucratic processes, standards and rules they must endure to conduct business in national jurisdictions, which is of course multiplied when attempting to do business across borders (see CARICOM Secretariat 2006). They complain that these bureaucratic processes are unnecessarily complicated, with different parts of the processes often controlled by multiple different, poorly staffed agencies. This results in convoluted and lengthy processes for business activities which require approvals or assistance from the state. Businessmen also complain about a lack of transparency and about inconsistency in the application of standards and rules.

The Caribbean region did poorly in terms of enforcing contracts, resolving insolvency, registering property, paying taxes and getting credit.[5] Very importantly, the region generally did poorly in terms of protecting minority investors and trade across borders. This implies that the legal or administrative frameworks in the areas of contract enforcement, business closure and property registration need to be simplified. Often, even if the legal frameworks for these activities are clear and well developed, the problem lies in the fact that the government agencies charged with administering these processes are poorly financed and staffed.

These processes are therefore time-consuming and unnecessarily lengthy. The problem of accessing financing, at least for normal investment and working capital needs, does not seem to be a major one and was not flagged as a binding constraint by large firms that were surveyed by the CARICOM Secretariat in December 2009.[6] The development of a regional financial market based on large regional financial institutions, particularly from Trinidad and Tobago, has made the financing of large projects easier. The development of a nascent regional bond market has also helped in this regard. Nevertheless, for very large projects requiring hard currency, syndicated lending involving large international financial institutions would still normally have to be used.

Some of the major challenges for these large firms are therefore the bureaucratic hurdles and the variety of different national rules, regulations and standards they must deal with when conducting business across the region. The specific issues that were flagged by large firms as being important in this area include the need for transparency and predictability in the application of rules and standards. Other important needs in terms of the operating environment

Table 5.4. The Business Environment in Caribbean Community Countries, 2015

Economy	EDB	SB	DP	GE	RP	GC	PI	PT	TAB	EC	RE
Antigua and Barbuda	89	102	30	17	141	151	35	159	89	76	114
Bahamas	97	95	92	50	179	131	141	31	63	125	60
Barbados	106	94	147	118	144	116	177	92	38	160	26
Belize	118	148	69	54	120	160	169	61	91	170	71
Dominica	97	63	43	53	149	131	87	94	88	148	121
Grenada	126	80	40	77	128	131	141	106	51	144	189
Guyana	123	99	38	155	103	165	135	115	82	71	150
Haiti	180	188	132	94	175	171	187	142	142	89	189
Jamaica	58	20	26	111	126	12	71	147	115	117	59
St Kitts and Nevis	121	87	16	10	170	151	87	137	67	116	189
St Lucia	100	72	39	23	132	151	141	69	122	145	100
St Vincent and the Grenadines	103	80	35	8	155	151	71	93	45	101	189
Suriname	162	181	79	69	178	171	171	71	106	184	130
Trinidad and Tobago	79	71	113	21	159	36	62	113	76	180	66
Costa Rica	83	118	52	46	47	89	181	121	47	129	89
Dominican Republic	84	113	96	119	82	89	83	80	24	73	158
Malaysia	18	13	28	27	75	23	5	32	11	29	36
Mauritius	28	29	117	41	98	36	28	13	17	44	43
Singapore	1	6	2	11	24	17	3	5	1	1	19

Source: World Bank, *Doing Business*, 2015.

Notes: EDB, ease of doing business; SB, starting a business; DP, dealing with construction permits; GE, getting electricity; RP, registering property; GC, getting credit; PI, protesting minority investors; PT, paying taxes; TAB, trading across borders; EC, enforcing contracts; RE, resolving insolvency.

for business in the region included the simplification and standardization of custom procedures, speedier customs clearance and the standardization of non-tariff standards such as labelling requirements and sanitary and phyto-sanitary standards. The large firms surveyed also indicated that harmonization of legislation, especially in terms of company laws and financial regulation, the licensing regime and intellectual property rights, needed to be expedited. The removal of restrictions on rights of establishment with the creation of the CARICOM Single Market and Economy, as well as the expected implementation of the CARICOM Investment Code, should go some way towards addressing these problems.

The economic performance of the Caribbean economies has therefore been driven over the past fifty years by the traditional factor endowment and the global or regional system in which they operated as very small, highly open and vulnerable economies. Entrepreneurial activity has also come to be recognized as one of the most important determinants of growth, with this intangible predisposition dependent on the culture and the mores and values of a particular society. Growth in the region is, however, increasingly driven by productivity, innovation and competitiveness, which are, in turn, dependent on the business environment and, very importantly, on the policy regime over time. Problems related to the appropriate policy mix have been and continue to be some of the most serious factors hampering stable growth in the region and therefore the area. The region needs to devote more time and resources to these problems in the future.

The Challenge of Finding the Right Policy Mix

The underdeveloped nature of many Caribbean economies and their small sizes mean that the state has played and will play for the foreseeable future a disproportionately large role in these economies. This implies that the effectiveness of government policy has significant implications for the performance of an economy. The effectiveness of fiscal policy in particular has proven to be critical to stable economic growth and development in the region. In this regard, the region has not done well in this area, as is evident from the huge fiscal and debt sustainability problems in almost all Caribbean countries. Additionally, the region faces huge challenges in terms of productivity and international competitiveness.

In the immediate post-independence period most countries in the region adopted an interventionist and state-driven approach to development. The approach began to change in the early 1990s with the increasing adoption of liberalization as a policy framework. In this framework, the private sector was supposed to be the main engine of growth, with the state playing a supporting role. In spite of this paradigm shift, however, problems with fiscal management and the challenges related to small size meant that government expenditure relative to the size of an economy continued to rise, leading to problems of fiscal and debt sustainability. This problem with fiscal management was driven in large part by a number of factors, such as inefficient public expenditure programmes, underdeveloped tax systems, a pro-cyclical fiscal policy stance and a susceptibility to external shocks.

Many of these expenditure problems often reflected the general lack of a culture that sought to get "value for money". This was compounded by an under-developed tax system in many countries, caused mainly by a tax base that was small due to a small and undiversified economic structure which was compounded by underdeveloped tax systems. These problems led to rising sovereign debt burdens in the region, which in turn fed back into increased government expenditure as debt servicing became increasingly onerous. Very importantly, this dynamic was entrenched by the fact that fiscal policy tended to be pro-cyclical, which meant adequate buffers were not built up during periods of robust growth.

The highly open nature of these economies, where such a high proportion of domestic consumption and investment was based on imports, also meant that any fiscal imbalance was almost immediately reflected in balance-of-payments problems. This is evident from the fact that for much of the period since independence many of the countries in the region have experienced the "twin deficit" phenomenon. The external imbalances caused by fiscal deficits reinforced a more serious structural weakness – that of low and decreasing international competitiveness.

The problem with international competitiveness is often reflected in poor terms of trade and the attendant problems for the current account of the balance payments. Poor terms of trade resulted from a situation in which countries depended on primary commodity exports while importing more expensive manufactured and industrial products. This dynamic changed a little as countries transitioned to service-based economies and as commodity prices rose. The growing problem of a loss of market share in the important tourism industry, a lack of significant progress on diversification, and the continued dependence on expensive imported products for consumption and industry meant that weakness in the external accounts remained a feature of Caribbean economies. This situation reflects the relative lack of progress on structural reforms to make these economies more competitive in traditional markets, as well as to develop and exploit new products and markets.

Finding the right policy mix to drive improvements in fiscal management and external competitiveness has so far eluded most Caribbean countries. Recent improvements in fiscal management, often driven by structural adjustment programmes financed by the International Monetary Fund, have helped correct domestic imbalances, but the very complicated efforts to promote external competitiveness have not yet brought the kind of improvement that is required. The private sector in many of the region's countries is still mostly engaged in sectors that consume rather than produce foreign exchange. The continued development of the productive capacity of countries and the redirection of business activity away from consumption-based domestic retail enterprises to internationally competitive export industry have not produced the kind of progress that is needed to put the Caribbean on a more stable economic trajectory. How to entrench a more prudent approach to fiscal management underpinned by a culture of "value for money" in the public sector and accelerate the structural policy reforms needed to expand and broaden the productive capacity of economies in the region remains the most pressing policy dilemmas faced by the Caribbean.

Conclusions and Policy Implications

Economic performance in the Caribbean since independence has been significantly affected by problems with productivity and efficiency, a lack of sufficient entrepreneurial capacity, a convoluted and underdeveloped business environment and inappropriate policy regimes. The first three factors are all generally related in some way to small size. In the Caribbean these structural weaknesses have, however, been accentuated over time by inappropriate policy regimes. This is an important point, because many other small, open, developing countries such as Singapore, Mauritius and Costa Rica, with many of the same structural weaknesses as Caribbean countries, have managed to achieve better economic outcomes by developing strong institutional, governance and policy frameworks, which have increased their resilience to shocks (Olson, Sarna and Swamy 2000). The well-known macroeconomic vulnerabilities in the Caribbean, such as high and unsustainable public debt, high and persistent fiscal and balance-of-payments deficits, high levels of unemployment and low growth rates can be attenuated by putting in place more effective institutional, governance and policy regimes. This strategy can help Caribbean countries to successfully exploit the opportunities arising from integration into the global economy while limiting the risks associated with such integration.

Maintaining the status quo is not a viable strategy, since it would imply worsening fiscal and debt problems, further erosion in international competitiveness and chronically low growth, with the attendant problems of high levels of unemployment and poverty. A study by the World Bank (2005) projected that improving the policy frameworks of the region's economies can generate significant improvements in the median growth rate in the Caribbean, with most of the improvements coming from reduction in the size of governments as measured by the ratio of government consumption to GDP, with countries which have relatively larger government burdens registering the biggest growth improvements from the reduction. Policy action would also need to target improvements in productivity and diversification, which would require significant improvement in the business environment.

Policy Implications

Public-Sector Management

The demand for public services in the Caribbean will tend to be higher given the small sizes of these economies and the competitive political environment.[7] The minimum size of a state that is required to provide the basic level of public services has been an issue that has not attracted the attention it deserves in the region.[8] Escalation in the number of international forums in which the region's countries participate has also put increasing pressures on small states which may not have the economic mass to support the complex underlying apparatus.[9] In this context, small open economies are more predisposed to developing imbalances in their fiscal accounts and therefore have to be relatively more fiscally prudent than their larger counterparts.

The general practice of policymakers in the region of exercising more *forbearance* rather than using *preemptive action* in their fiscal consolidation efforts has to change. In most instances countries in need of economic adjustment have opted to put it off until there was little or no option, usually in the context of a structural adjustment programme under the auspices of the International Monetary Fund. This perspective is informed by the political sensitivity of fiscal policy and the general unpopularity of fiscal consolidation, especially during periods of robust growth. This has led to a situation in which fiscal policy is generally *pro-cyclical* and fiscal consolidation is generally implemented in periods when aggregate demand and growth are weak. The more difficult policy decisions therefore tend to be taken when the economy is in a precarious state, precisely when it is very costly to do so.[10] To counter this dynamic, the authorities must build a level of counter-cyclicality into their fiscal policy stance and be more proactive in dealing with problems at the earliest stages, when the scale and cost of adjustments is relatively small.

More generally, improvements in this area would involve reorienting the state to deliver good governance by increasing the efficiency of government expenditure programmes by developing a culture of "value for money" in the public sector. This must involve the rationalization of the state enterprise sector, which may include privatization, as well as closure in some cases. It must also involve the more frequent use of public-private partnerships in the provision of public goods and services. Additionally, regional cooperation in the provision of trade and diplomatic services has the potential to reduce costs related to the terms on which countries interface with the international community.

Productivity and International Competitiveness

The key to success, however, is to be competitive in the production of goods and services for the home and export markets. International competitiveness is driven by firms, and it is firms that carry out international trade and investments, not countries, so the competitiveness of firms is the most important ingredient for successful cross-border activity. Nevertheless, competitiveness at a country level is also important since it provides a better environment in which businesses can thrive.[11] The drives to make firms more competitive and to create more business-friendly environments are therefore the two most important planks on which more competitive regional economies would be built.

In this regard, firm size has emerged as one of the most important bases for the enhancement of firms' competitiveness.[12] Size is important, since only when a large critical mass is achieved do firms have the requisite human, financial and technological resources to compete effectively outside of their home markets. It is only after this critical mass is achieved that the search for more cross-border opportunities becomes systematic rather that occasional and opportunistic.

The policy framework for the facilitation of this process of enlargement is therefore central to the drive to have more competitive firms in the Caribbean. At the regional level, the creation of a larger market space through the establishment of the CARICOM Single Market and Economy was central to this growth. The sustenance and widening of this process are therefore factors critical to the continued growth of large firms in the region.

Nevertheless, these efforts are unlikely to be sufficient in the future. The fact that the saturation of home markets was one of the main factors driving the expansion into the regional market implies that at some point the regional market would also become saturated, since this market is still small by international standards. This is going to be more of an issue for some sectors, such as the financial sector, than for others. Firms in these sectors must therefore begin shifting their focus and begin preparing for the inevitable expansion into extra-regional markets. Some firms have already made headway in this area.

Additionally, there needs to be an increased focus on improving productivity in mature industries such as tourism. There also needs to be an increased focus on diversification away from some of the sectors that traditionally drove growth but may now be experiencing challenges with international competitiveness into sectors that have more growth potential. This involves rationalizing mature sectors to weed out entities which are no longer competitive and need subsidies to survive and encouraging new investments and the adoption of best practices.

Conclusion

The adjustment in policy regimes required to address the serious problems facing Caribbean countries would require political will and political consensus in all jurisdictions. The competitive political systems that characterize the Caribbean, however, sometimes lead to perverse incentives to avoid making hard decisions, especially on the fiscal front. Political competition also tends to frustrate political consensus on key issues, which makes progress on adjustment slow and difficult. The region cannot afford the luxury of adjusting at this pace. Therefore, the adjustment in the policy regime I have detailed would be possible only if accompanied by political reforms that maintain democratic traditions but reduce perverse incentives for inaction and divisiveness.

Notes

1. This decline in average growth performance has been underpinned by huge disparities in growth across countries, with the gap between the best and worst growth performance being 7.30 per cent in the 1960s and 6.61 per cent in the first ten years of the twenty-first century.
2. This refers to vulnerability to natural disasters and weakness in the external accounts.
3. This methodology has its weaknesses, which are detailed in Felipe (1999), 1–41.
4. The *Doing Business* report ranks 183 countries on a range of attributes important to successful business operations.
5. The latest (2016) *Doing Business* report shows that Jamaica has made significant progress in terms of resolving insolvency, paying taxes and getting credit. Significant progress was also made in the area of dealing with construction permits and starting businesses.
6. This is due in large part to their financial strength and established relationships with financial institutions, but small firms do have many challenges in this area.
7. Small states tend to have relatively bigger governments (see Remmer 2010).
8. Part of the problem relates to the lack of sufficient data availability about the sizes of very small economies.
9. This problem has also affected large industrialized countries since the 1960s (see Mussa and Masson 1995).
10. See Mercer-Blackman and Seerattan (2014).
11. See Bernal (2006).
12. There is also a voluminous literature that confirms that size is positively related to export success. Additionally, the size factor is particularly important in industrial activity. There are instances in which small firms have become internationally competitive, but these are exceptions to the rule.

References

Bernal, R. 2006. Nano-Firms, Regional Integration and International Competitiveness: The Experience and Dilemma of the CSME. In *Production Integration in CARICOM from Theory to Action*, edited by K. Hall and D. Benn, 90–115. Kingston: Ian Randle.

CARICOM (Caribbean Community) Secretariat. 2006. *Caribbean Trade and Investment Report 2005*. http://archive.caricom.org/jsp/community/regional_issues/CTIR2005/EXECUTIVE%20SUMMARY%20CTIR%202005.pdf.

Felipe, J. 1999. Total Factor Productivity Growth in East Asia: A Critical Survey. *Journal of Development Studies* 35 (4): 1–41.

Lewis, A. 1973. The Shortage of Entrepreneurship. Statement made at the Caribbean Development Bank for the 3rd Annual Board of Governors Meeting, Jamaica, 26 April 1973.

Mercer-Blackman, V., and D. Seerattan. 2014. To Cut or Not to Cut: Does the Caribbean Follow the Advice of Multilaterals? Policy Brief No. 214, Inter-American Development Bank, New York, March 2014.

Mussa, M., and P. Masson. 1995. Long-Term Tendencies in Budget Deficits and Debt. Working Paper No. 128, International Monetary Fund, December 2015.

Olson, M., N. Sarna and A. Swamy, A. 2000. Governance and Growth: A Simple Hypothesis Explaining Cross-Country Differences in Productivity Growth. *Public Choice* 102 (3–4): 341–64.

Remmer, K. 2010. Why Do Small States Have Big Governments? *European Political Science Review* 2 (1): 49–71.

Sosa, S., E. Tsounta and H. Kim. 2013. Is the Growth Momentum in Latin America Sustainable? Working Paper No. 109, International Monetary Fund, May.

World Bank. 2005. *A Time to Choose: Caribbean Development in the 21st Century.* https://openknowledge.worldbank.org/bitstream/handle/10986/10330/342080ENGLISH0Jun05173EN.pdf?sequence=1&isAllowed=y.

CHAPTER 6

Central American Common Market and Caribbean Community Trade Policy and Competitiveness on the European Union Market

Anthony Peter Gonzales

The objective of this chapter is to determine the state of trade policy reform and trade competitiveness of the Central American Common Market (CACM) and CARICOM countries[1] in the context of the Economic Partnership Agreement (EPA)[2] and the recently concluded agreement between the twenty-eight countries of the European Union on the one hand and Central America and Panama on the other (the EU-Central America Association Agreement, or EU-CAAA).[3] The EU market, where the CACM and CARICOM countries compete in a range of sensitive products, is considered an appropriate arena in which to measure their competitiveness in this post-preference world.

Both CACM and CARICOM countries, parties to these trade agreements with the European Union, need to take advantage of the trade opportunities they offer. The latter will depend essentially on their ability to compete in the EU market under more intense competition. The EPA and EU-CAAA both anticipate this condition of growing competition and seek to spur certain trade reforms in these developing countries to make them more competitive.

The trade competitiveness approach used in this study underscores the positive aspects of greater trade openness and trade liberalization backed by sound macroeconomic and structural interventions that strengthen policies and institutions at all levels. It will be argued, therefore, that the economies that have been pursuing greater openness since before the trade agreements with the European Union will be the better performers on the EU market. In this light, a comparison of the CARICOM and CACM countries' products is made to assess trade openness, competitiveness and trade performance on the EU market, which is the second largest for both of them.

Another important aim is to identify the products for which comparative advantage has been gained or lost among the products in which these countries directly compete. Some comparative advantage work has been done for individual countries (not necessarily with the European Union in all cases), as, for example, Lewis and Webster (2001); Lorde, Alleyne and Francis (2010); and Sinanan and Hosein (2012) for CARICOM, and the Centre for Economic Policy Research (2012) and Osterlof (2011) for the CACM, but a comparison between the two regions in competing products has not been undertaken.

Trade Policy and Growth: An Analytical Overview

The early literature of outward- versus inward-looking trade policies and their impact on growth and development set the context for a debate on trade policy that has remained relatively inconclusive up to today. Models of effective rates of (trade) protection (ERP) were used to show that if the rate of effective protection was higher on tradables than on non-tradables there would be a bias against tradables, and the impact on growth and development would be less than if there was a neutral ERP policy. A positive bias in favour of exports to counter certain market failures and difficulties in accessing foreign markets was even advanced at times.

The previous arguments were used to support an export-oriented trade policy approach over one of import substitution. With the failure of import substitution and the infant industry argument as a growth approach, anti–free trade proponents placed more emphasis on strategic trade policy where a degree of temporary protection was considered important in nurturing export industries. The role the state could play in providing support in the form of tariff protection, subsidies and so on until these industries can compete was also underscored. Rodrik (1992), for instance, in examining the export boom in Taiwan and Korea in the 1960s, stressed the role of the exchange rate and export subsidies rather than the reduction of trade barriers. Rodrik and Rodríguez (2000) further reinforced this position by highlighting the importance of institutions in determining success in trade liberalization.

The strategic approach appeared to have its most relevance in the case of the development of complex technological goods as opposed to low-tech goods, since the accumulation of knowledge, innovation and learning by doing over a period of time require some degree of initial protection. The Asian experience was used to demonstrate empirically how this approach was used and how outward orientation has a stronger long-term development impact even though the process and channels used to create that outward orientation were never conclusively proven.

In the context of moving to an innovation economy, New Growth Theories (Romer 1986; Lucas 1988; Grossman and Helpman 1991) relaxed the classical assumption of constant returns to scale and used instead more realistic assumptions as increasing returns to scale and imperfect competition. As a result, the importance of human capital and research and development was emphasized and trade policy was respecified.

Trade policy was seen as a double-edged sword in the sense that it was good for knowledge spillovers, but the competition from a widening set of imported differentiated goods would not make local research and development profitable. The latter would lead to a case in which the country would specialize in primary production and standardized manufacturing goods (Grossman and Helpman 1991), though it would still have a higher growth rate than if it engaged less in trade. A case was made for subsidizing export industries, which were seen as having more growth potential than import-substituting ones since they had greater spillover effects in more advanced goods. Export promotion also facilitated greater technology acquisition, even in related industries.

In the Grossman and Helpman endogenous growth theory, there was a larger role for state policy in the forms of tax credits, subsidies to research and development and production for export, and tariffs. This observation received some empirical support at the micro level in small developing countries, particularly regarding public policy towards research and development (Anatol 2011). The extent of trade barriers to promote growth, however, has remained unclear in this theorizing. In general, it would appear that advocates of an endogenous approach would argue for low selective temporary barriers, as the international spillover effect is still critical for growth.

In summary, the theoretical debate does not give clear guidelines as to the best channel to use to open a particular economy and how that channel can be best supported by macroeconomic and institutional changes. In general it would appear that a correctly valued exchange rate, fiscal moderation and institutional development accompanied by structural interventions, particularly in education, health, infrastructure and capital markets, can best support a trade policy of opening if innovation is not the goal. If the latter becomes the objective, stronger state interventions appear to be required to back a policy of export orientation.

Trade Policy, Country Size and Growth

The theoretical discussion mentioned above has generally tended to discount the factor of size. Where such a discussion has occurred, the assumption, either implicit or explicit, was that small size implies a greater reliance on trade openness and international competition to increase factor productivity, exports and growth. Market size was largely equated with country size, and the international market was seen as essential for achieving economies of scale in production.

Smith (1986) saw small market size as limiting specialization. Today, in endogenous growth theory market size is regarded as critical for positive externalities derived from accumulating human capital and creating knowledge (Romer 1986; Lucas 1988; and Grossman and Helpman 1991).

Spolaore and Wacziarg (2005) and Alesina, Spolaore and Wacziarg (2005), dissatisfied with the performance of population, gross domestic product (GDP) and land area as measures of country size in growth regressions, used a model of country formation to determine the equilibrium size of a country. Trade openness was considered an endogenous variable (Spolaore and Wacziarg 2005).

Alesina, Spolaore and Wacziarg (2005) suggested that no significant relationship between market size and country size would exist in a world of completely free trade. They concluded that in the latter world, changing borders would have no effect on economic efficiency and productivity. They were, however, quick to recognize that even crossing borders without explicit trade restrictions does indeed involve an economic cost in that doing business within a country is less costly than doing it across borders. It is well known that the border in a world of free trade still has an effect which could be related to culture and other differences.

Alesina, Spolaore and Wacziarg (2005) thus argued that some correlation between a country's size and its market size could be observed even when explicit trade barriers were removed, and this led them to suggest that trade policy is important. In the context of free trade, therefore, small countries can grow and develop better by accumulating market size through trade openness.

Trade openness is therefore perceived as being optimal for small countries, especially those not plagued by heterogeneity, and the relevant concept of scale is market size as measured by a combination of country size and trade openness. This contribution emphasizes the role of trade opening in that a small country is not really a small economy when looked at from this angle of market size. A good example is Singapore, whose ratio of exports to GDP is over 180 per cent for a population of 5.3 million. As compared to the CARICOM and CACM countries, Singapore cannot be regarded as a small economy even though, by measures of land area and population, the country is regarded as small.

Size, Openness and Growth: Empirical Evidence

Trade openness and growth have been strongly associated in the post-war world, whether assessed in terms of the reduction of trade barriers or of ratios of trade to GDP. One of the most extensive pieces of work on the subject came from Edwards (1998). Using a sample of ninety-three countries, he demonstrated that, out of nine indicators of trade policy openness, eight were strongly related to total factor productivity growth.[4] In a cross-country model, Wacziarg (2001) showed that an increase in the ratio of trade to GDP due to the reduction/removal of trade barriers is connected positively to growth.

Rodrik and Rodríguez (2000), while expressing little confidence in cross-country empirical analysis, nevertheless argued that trade openness covered inappropriate policies such as protectionism, which was associated with other policies with a negative effect on growth. Many of those responding to the latter position suggest that evidence remains in favor of a positive impact of openness on growth, as the vast majority of indicators of openness show this.

Alesina, Spolaore and Wacziarg (2005) used the ratio of imports plus exports to GDP, measured in US dollars in terms of purchasing power parity, to assess real openness as well as the same ratio in nominal terms. Taking a sample median of countries (above and below 6.7 million inhabitants), they found correlations between country size (population) and growth conditional on openness that was greater or lower than the sample medians for both measures.

Openness and growth for small countries (those with fewer than 6.7 million inhabitants) had a much higher correlation than for large countries. Similarly, the correlation between country size and growth is low for open countries and much higher for closed ones. The authors concluded that there was enough evidence to suggest that openness and country size are substitutes and that, as openness increases, the correlation between country size and growth falls.

Trade Liberalization in the CARICOM and CACM Economies

The process of trade liberalization in CARICOM and the CACM started in the late 1980s and early 1990s and was certainly marked by the Uruguay Round from 1986 to 1994.[5] The CARICOM countries, with the exception of Haiti, set an average bound rate of 100 per cent for agriculture and 50 per cent for non-agriculture. With the exception of Suriname and Barbados, the CARICOM countries have 100 per cent or nearly 100 per cent bindings. The CARICOM overall average bound rate is 50.2 per cent (table 6.1). The CACM countries, with the exception of Guatemala, all have 100 per cent bindings and a lower average bound rate of 38.1 per cent (table 6.2). As regards applied rates, and using non-agriculture, in which liberalization is generally faster, the average figures for the CARICOM and CACM countries are 8.2 per cent and 6 per cent, respectively. The CACM countries, on average, therefore have lower applied rates.[6]

In examining trade restrictions in CARICOM, Finger, Ng and Soloaga (1998) noted that in these countries tariffs were relatively high compared to post–Uruguay Round applied rates in Latin America and East Asia. It was also noted that many agricultural goods were set aside for state trading and that exchange controls remained in place in many of the countries. Some quantitative restrictions and non-automatic licensing requirements were also applied by many of the countries, particularly to most food products and to beverages.

Using a trade restrictions index covering the average tariff and adjusting for the incidence of non-tariff barriers, a comparison was made between the CARICOM countries and those of Central and Latin America. CARICOM, on average, was more restrictive than either Central America or South America. The trade regimes in CARICOM were thus characterized as similar to those in

Table 6.1. Caribbean Community Bound Duties in the World Trade Organization for All Products, 2015: Coverage and Average Duty

Country	Binding Coverage (Per Cent)	Simple Average (Per Cent)	Standard Deviation
Antigua and Barbuda	97.9	58.7	20.9
Barbados	57.6	81.0	26.2
Belize	98.0	58.2	17.9
Dominica	96.9	58.6	23.0
Grenada	100.0	56.6	20.2
Guyana	100.0	56.7	17.0
Haiti	89.2	17.6	9.3
Jamaica	100.0	49.8	24.5
St Kitts and Nevis	97.9	75.9	17.8
St Lucia	99.6	61.9	26.9
St Vincent and the Grenadines	99.5	62.4	27.3
Suriname	26.3	18.5	9.2
Trinidad and Tobago	100.0	55.7	19.8

Source: WTO Consolidated Tariff Schedule database.

Note: The Bahamas is not included because it is not a WTO member.

Table 6.2. Central American Common Market Bound Duties in the World Trade Organization for All Products, 2015: Coverage and Average Duty

Country	Binding Coverage (Per Cent)	Simple Average (Per Cent)	Standard Deviation
Costa Rica	100.0	42.6	12.9
El Salvador	100.0	36.6	12.0
Guatemala	34.6	36.9	29.9
Honduras	100.0	32.5	6.9
Nicaragua	100.0	41.7	7.6

Source: WTO Consolidated Tariff Schedule database.

Latin America before the reforms of the 1980s and 1990s. Even worse, it was argued that the policies in place had no inherent consistency and were a product of ad hoc actions of the past. The social costs of these policies were high. Even in 2009, while there had been some noteworthy tariff reduction, especially in Trinidad and Tobago, the Dominican Republic and Jamaica, tariff dispersion remained a problem, and it was seen that further reduction of tariffs as well as more uniformity were needed in some of the countries (WB/OAS 2009).

In terms of reciprocal liberalization, the first major effort on the part of CARICOM came with the EPA. However, with the exception of Trinidad and Tobago, the degree of liberalization achieved by the CARICOM countries remains questionable when compared to that of the Dominican Republic (DR) under the EPA and the pace and depth of liberalization attained by the CACM countries and the DR under the CAFTA/DR free trade agreement (FTA) with the United States. In the EPA, the exclusion rate was 6 per cent for Trinidad and Tobago as compared to twice that level for Jamaica, with 22 per cent and 18 per cent, respectively, for Barbados and Guyana and up to an average of 30 per cent for the CARICOM less-developed countries.[7]

Over the past two decades the CACM countries have actively pursued FTAs.[8] Apart from regional FTAs, they made significant progress in adopting the FTA between the United States and a group comprising the Dominican Republic and Central American countries such as Costa Rica, El Salvador, Guatemala, Honduras, and Nicaragua (CAFTA-DR)[9] – and in the signing, in June 2012, of an association agreement with the European Union. The latter agreement will eliminate tariffs for manufactured goods and fisheries, with complete liberalization at the end of the phase-out period of generally ten years. For 4 per cent of products this phase-out will last fifteen years. Tariffs on key agricultural products will largely be eliminated. Under the CARIFORUM–EU EPA, in addition to the high rates of exclusion, 26 per cent of tariff lines will not be liberalized until after fifteen to twenty-five years. Under CAFTA-DR, a larger percentage of tariffs will be eliminated by all countries in ten years, even after much more significant immediate liberalization.

In terms of unilateral, multilateral and bilateral reciprocal liberalization, the CACM countries have been outpacing those in CARICOM. This policy of liberalization is reflected in trade openness, where, in terms of exports of goods and services to GDP, the CACM countries have been increasing their ratios from the early 1990s (1991–1995) to 2014.[10] The CARICOM countries, on the other hand, with one or two exceptions, have been experiencing a decline in this ratio on average (table 6.3).

Table 6.3. Ratio of Exports of Caribbean Community and CACM Goods and Services to GDP, 1991–2014

Region/Country	Exports/ GDP Ratio	Exports/ GDP Ratio	Exports/ GDP Ratio	Exports/ GDP Ratio
Caribbean Community	Ave 1991–1995	Ave 2000–2004	Ave 2008–2012	Ave 2011–2014
Antigua and Barbuda	85.2	59.1	45.1	46
Bahamas	50.8	42.5	46.7	44
Barbados	56.0	40.8	45.3	38
Belize	49.8	52.1	61.1	61
Dominica	50.2	37.8	35.8	35
Grenada	44.6	35.5	24.9	26
Guyana	111.4	93.9	n.a.	54
Haiti	8.8	13.7	13.2	18
Jamaica	52.2	35.6	39.7	31
St Kitts and Nevis	57.0	35.3	33.7	37
St Lucia	68.0	48.7	39.9	45
St Vincent and the Grenadines	51.8	39.1	31.0	26
Suriname	26.0	21.6	n.a.	n.a.
Trinidad and Tobago	45.4	54.6	65.2	54
Central American Common Market	Ave 1991–1995	Ave 2000–2004	Ave 2008–2012	Ave 2011–2014
Costa Rica	35.8	45.1	40.1	36
El Salvador	18.8	26.7	25.9	27
Guatemala	18.2	25.5	25.2	26
Honduras	37.2	54.1	47.7	49
Nicaragua	18.8	20.3	36.2	43

Source: World Bank, World DataBank.

Note: n.a. = not available.

It is not my intention at this point to seek a full explanation as to why the pace of liberalization is faster in the CACM countries. Suffice it to say that according to the theoretical discussion, the smaller the country in terms of size (population), the greater the need for trade liberalization and openness to build market size. One would expect that the CARICOM countries, which are smaller in size than those in Central America, would have pursued trade liberalization with more vigour as a result. This has not been the case, however, and maybe the role of macroeconomic balance and intuitional capability have had some effect here.

In the case of Jamaica, Hudson (2003), for instance, justified the slowing down of the pace of liberalization for balance-of-payments reasons. Intuitively it is difficult to accept that a region which by and large over the last thirty years has had a stronger record of institutional building as compared to the CACM (Costa Rica being the exception) should find itself lagging in terms of a more open trade policy. However, some argue that fiscal imbalances and high debt overhang are reducing the scope for many CARICOM countries to engage in faster trade liberalization (WB/OAS 2009).

Liberalization and Competition on the EU Market

In light of the previous discussion, it is of interest to examine how the CARICOM and CACM regions compete on a foreign market. The EU market represents a good case study, because both regions have now signed FTAs with the European Union and compete strongly in some basic sensitive goods for which CARICOM enjoyed special non-reciprocal trade preferences beyond the Generalized System of Preferences (GSP)[11] over the CACM for a long time under the Lome and Cotonou agreements before the EPA, while the CACM was confined to the EU GSP Plus[12] before the EU-CAAA.

While the difference in market access terms was significant and highlighted especially for goods such as bananas, rum, rice and sugar, it was not negligible in many others, such as shrimps, ethyl alcohol, T-shirts, sauces, arrowroot, vegetables, men's and boys' trousers, communion wafers, palm hearts, plants, oranges, orange juice, fruits, tires, tuna and others.

Under the EU-CAAA, 70 per cent of existing CACM exports will be duty-free on the entry into force of the agreement, as well as 92.1 per cent of all tariff lines. On another 3.1 per cent of these lines, tariffs will be reduced to zero in three to ten years, and 0.9 per cent of these lines will have duty-free access within tariff rate quotas. But 3.8 per cent have been excluded from any tariff reduction.[13] Most of the tariffs for manufactured goods and products of fisheries are eliminated, with complete liberalization to take place at the end of the phase-out period, which will be ten years for most products, with the period for about 4 per cent going up to fifteen years and after.

For agricultural goods, tariffs will be reduced or eliminated with the exception of those for some sensitive products. Immediate duty-free access has been granted to the majority of them, and tariff reductions will take place in phase-outs of three, five, seven and ten years. Duty-free tariff quotas were established for some sensitive products, while quotas for certain other products were created with or without tariff reduction outside the duty-free quotas. These applied to mainly sensitive products such as meat, beef, rice, sugar, rum, sweet corn, garlic, manioc starch and mushrooms.[14] With respect to the latter, Rueda-Junquera (2010) points out that the traditional agricultural products which presented the biggest difficulties in the negotiation were bananas, meat, sugar and rice, as they were in direct conflict with the Common Agricultural Policy of the European Union and the special protocols which the European Union has with the ACP group. Examples of particularly sensitive products relevant to CARICOM are sugar, rum, bananas and rice, for which increased quotas were granted.

As regards other tropical fruits, such as pineapples and melons, among others, their duty-free status under the special GSP Plus was maintained. Ad valorem duties were also suspended, as well as specific duties in cases in which there were no ad valorem duties. In cases in which there were both an ad valorem duty and a specific duty, the ad valorem duty was suspended. From 1 July 2005, the European Union applied this regime to the Central American countries.

Before the EU-CAAA, the EU weighted-average applied tariffs facing the CACM countries (given existing trade flows) were around 9 per cent for agricultural and food items. The agreement takes this down to 4.7 per cent (CEPR 2012). For other products, current weighted-average applied tariffs (given current trade flows) are zero. EU imports from Central America are concentrated in agricultural and food products.

The EPA, except for a short transition in rice and sugar, provided unlimited duty-free access for all items. All quotas and duties have been removed, along with specific levies.

The recently signed EU-CAAA should now confer an improved preferential status on the CACM countries. In the area of tropical products, where the CACM countries have not been enjoying special preferences in the European Union, the agreement provides a major boost to CACM exporters. In general, therefore, the difference in preferential treatment received by the CARICOM countries in agricultural goods under the Cotonou Agreement and later the EPA, as compared to that accorded to the CACM countries under the EU GSP Plus and now the EU-CAAA, will now be significantly reduced.

CACM and CARICOM Trade Competitiveness on the EU Market: Some Evidence

Methodology

Balassa (1965) revealed comparative advantage (RCA) index is generally employed to measure comparative advantage in world and specific markets. Formally, the index can be presented for two regions and one particular market, as follows:

$$\mathrm{RCA}_{ai} = (E_{aik}/E_{wik})/(E_{aiw}/E_{wi}), \tag{1}$$

where

aik = Region a exports of good i to market k,

E = Exports,

wik = total world (w) exports of good i to market k,

aiw = Region a exports of good i to world market w and

wi = total world (w) exports of good i.

The RCA_{ai} compares the share of Region' a's good i in market k with a's share of the same good in total world exports. The index reveals that Region a has a comparative disadvantage in good i with respect to world exporters if $0 < \mathrm{RCA}_{ai} < 1$, while it has a comparative advantage in good i if $\mathrm{RCA}_{ai} > 1$. In other words, when $\mathrm{RCA}_{ai} > 1$, then $(E_{aik}/E_{wik}) > (E_{aiw}/E_{wi})$ and Region' a's share of good i in market k is greater than the same good's share of world exports.

The change in RCA for Region a in good i in market k from period t to period $t + 1$ is given by

$$\Delta\mathrm{RCA}_{ai} = (\mathrm{RCA}_{ai,t+1} - \mathrm{RCA}_{ai,t})/\mathrm{RCA}_{ai,t} \tag{2}$$

where

$RCA_{ai,t}$ = RCA value in period t for good i and

$RCA_{ai,t+1}$ = RCA value in period $t + 1$ for good i.

For the second region, Region *b*, the RCA index and its change would be similar, as follows:

$$RCA_{bi} = (E_{bik}/E_{wik})/(E_{biw}/E_{wi}) \text{ and} \quad (3)$$

$$\Delta RCA_{bi} = (RCA_{bi,t+1} - RCA_{bi,t})/RCA_{bi,t}. \quad (4)$$

In assessing the performance of Region *a* over its rival Region *b* in good *i*, the rival revealed comparative advantage (RRCA) could be stated in logarithmic form as follows, as derived from equations 1 and 3:

$RRCA_{ab} = ln\ (E_{aik}/E_{ak})/(E_{bik}/E_{bk})$ where *ak* and *bk* represent respectively Regions' *a* and *b* total exports to market *k*. (5)

$RRCA_{ab} > 0$ means that Region *a* has a comparative advantage in market *k* over Region *b* in good *i*. The opposite is the case if $RRCA_{ab} < 0$.

Since RCA provides a measure at a point in time and it is useful to know how changes occur over time, it is important to assess comparative advantage variation, which customarily has been estimated by ΔRCA (Yeats 1992; Havrila and Gunawardana 2003). A higher ΔRCA_{ai} at time $t + 1$ than at time t implies that Region *a* has increased its comparative advantage in good *i*, while a lower ΔRCA_{ai} implies the opposite.

Concern has been expressed that a change in the RCA index would not reflect the state of comparative advantage based on export specialization in a particular market if the sizes of the markets change in a disproportionate way (Cai and Leung 2008).[15] Since RCA, as seen in equation 1, reflects the proportion between the share in market *k* and the share in the world market *w*, when markets change in sizes between times *t* and *t* + 1, a country cannot maintain its RCA the same in all markets. Correction for changes in the sizes of markets is needed in order to distil the changes in comparative advantage based on specialization.

One method for making this correction is to determine what a country's RCA in a particular market would be in time *t* + 1 if it kept its comparative position in time *t*. A country's market share reflects its degree of dominance in a market and can be broken down into the size advantage shown in its total export capacity as compared to those of other countries and its comparative advantage, which would indicate its export structure as compared to those of other countries. RCA measures directly the total change in dominance in the market, and market share variation attributable to structural comparative change in a country's export specialization needs to be separated out. This change in structural comparative advantage between t and $t + 1$ could be shown by taking the difference between the actual RCA in time $t + 1$ from an estimated benchmark RCA in time $t + 1$.[16]

Let Region a's share in market k for good i be stated as $s_{aik} = (E_{aik}/E_{wik})$ and its share in the world market for good i as $s_{aiw} = (E_{aiw}/E_{wi})$. Then RCA_{aik} could be stated as $\frac{s_{aik}}{s_{aiw}}$. Assuming no change in comparative advantage between time t and time $t + 1$, a's share in market k in time $t + 1$ could be stated hypothetically as $\hat{s}_{aik,t+1}$. The change in size in market k would be measured by $\hat{s}_{aik,t+1} - s_{aik,t}$.

As an RCA index is the share in market k divided by the share in market w, if $\frac{\hat{s}_{aik,t+1}}{\hat{s}_{aiw,t+1}} = \frac{s_{aik,t}}{s_{aiw,t}}$, it means that there has been no change in comparative advantage, as the region's market share in each of the two markets would have grown at an equal rate. Rearranging this formulation, $\frac{\hat{s}_{aik,t+1}}{s_{aik,t}} = \frac{\hat{s}_{aiw,t+1}}{s_{aiw,t}} = g$, where g would be the same growth rate in each market.

If Region a had kept its comparative advantage between time t and time $t +$ 1, its share in market k could be stated as

$$\hat{s}_{aik,t+1} = g s_{aik,t}, \tag{6}$$

and the corresponding estimated exports ($\hat{\text{E}}$) without any change in comparative advantage would be

$$\hat{\text{E}}_{k,t+1} = g s_{aik,t} E_{k,t+1}. \tag{7}$$

Since the sum of Region a's benchmark exports of good i in each k market should be consistent with its actual total exports, then

$$\Sigma_k \hat{\text{E}}_{k,t+1} = E_{ai,t+1}. \tag{8}$$

Through a series of algebraic manipulations, the following equation can be derived:[17]

$$R\hat{C}A_{aik,t+1} = \beta \text{RCA}_{aik,t} \tag{9}$$

where

$$\beta = \frac{1 + g_w}{1 + \Sigma_k c_{aik,t} g_k},$$

in which $g_w = (E_{t+1} - E_t)/E_t$ represents the average growth rate of the total world exports of all goods between time t and time $t + 1$, g_k is the growth rate of world exports to each market k of good i and c_{aik} is the share of Region's a exports of good i to a particular market k in its total exports of i. The revealed comparative advantage variation (RCAV) based on export specialization can then be stated in the following way:

$$\mathrm{RCA}V_{aik,t+1} = \mathrm{RCA}_{aik,t+1} - R\hat{C}A_{aik,t+1} = \mathrm{RCA}_{aik,t+1} - \beta\mathrm{RCA}_{aik,t}. \quad (10)$$

If $\mathrm{RCA}V_{aik}$ is positive, Region a has increased its structural comparative advantage in market k in good i; the larger the index, the greater the comparative advantage gain. A negative index would yield the opposite result. $\mathrm{RCA}V_{aik}$ therefore measures structural market share variation of the region in market k normalized by its world market share. This measure should facilitate cross-country comparisons of export structural changes. If a region has a higher RCAV index in a market than another region it means that its exports are more focused on that market than are those of the other region.

Data

The present analysis is done for two regions, the CACM and CARICOM, based on the annual time-series data on EU-28 imports sourced from United Nations Comtrade database. In terms of exports to the European Union for 2011–13, all 5,381 six-digit products in the harmonized system tariff code universe were compared, and thirty-five competing products, based on a cutoff value of US$1 million, were identified.[18] Twenty-one of these products enjoyed special trade preferences for CARICOM under the Cotonou Agreement and were considered sensitive. They have been the target of preference erosion in the World Trade Organization Doha negotiations. Due to data constraints, three products were dropped. They are tunas, all commodities and skipjack.

Eight of these thirty-five competing products, sugar, all commodities, bananas, rock lobster, ethyl alcohol, shrimps, light petroleum oils and T-shirts, are among the top thirty of all CARICOM exports to the European Union. For the CACM, twelve of these products are among the top thirty of all their export products to the European Union. They are coffee, bananas, medical instruments, tunas, ethyl alcohol, shrimps, artificial body parts, T-shirts, fruits, plants, sugar and rum. The latter CACM products rank much higher in value in the overall CACM top thirty products.

Two periods selected for dynamic comparison are 2007–09 and 2011–13, using data on exports and average time periods to smooth the impacts of transitory shocks on countries' exports.[19]

Results

Four indices are computed for each region. They are *RCA* in (1), ΔRCA in (2), *RRCA* in (5), and *RCAV* in (10). Balassa revealed comparative advantage measures in RCA (1), *ΔRCA* in (2) and RRCA (5) are used to assess dominance in the market while RCAV (10) is employed to examine a region's degree of specialization in one product as compared to the other region and the world average specialization in the product.[20]

For the period 2011–13, products in which CARICOM had an *RCA* > 1 and which are generally considered under the Balassa RCA Index as having a comparative advantage on the EU market are sugar, bananas, rock lobster, shrimps, essential oils, arrowroot, vegetables, waste (stainless steel), palm hearts, plants, sweet potatoes and oranges (table 6.4).

According to Hinloopen and van Marrewijk (2001) RCAs > 1 can be classified into four categories: one with comparative disadvantage 0–1 and three categories with comparative advantage weak, 1–2; medium 2–4; and strong, 4 and over. For CARICOM, sugar is the only product that can be considered strong on this basis, with plants and palm hearts in the medium category. Generally, therefore, these products' comparative advantage can be regarded as weak.

In terms of comparative advantage based on export specialization, RCAV increased for sugar, bananas, shrimps, essential oils, arrowroot, vegetables, waste (stainless steel), sweet potatoes, plants and oranges (table 6.4). Declines were recorded for palm hearts and rock lobster. Other products which did not register a comparative advantage (*RCA* < 1) and also had a negative RCAV index were rum, T-shirts, waste (copper), medicaments, orange juice (frozen), medical instruments, waste (aluminium), artificial body parts, paintings, wood articles and orange juice. Similar products with an RCA < 1 but enjoying

Table 6.4. Caribbean Community, Revealed Comparative Advantage Index (RCA), Its Change over the Two Sub-periods (ΔRCA) and Revealed Comparative Advantage Variation Index (RCAV) in the Selected Products, 2007–2013

Product Description	RCA 2007–2009	RCA 2011–2013	ΔRCA (Per Cent)	RCAV
Raw sugar, cane	4.573	5.105	0.116	0.814
Bananas	1.100	1.509	0.372	0.060
Rum and tafia	0.433	0.400	−0.076	−0.065
Light petroleum oils	0.157	0.598	2.810	0.261
Rock lobster	1.551	1.576	0.016	−0.486
Shrimps and prawns	0.816	1.167	0.430	0.299
Undenatured ethyl alcohol	0.120	0.310	1.579	0.208
T-shirts, singlets	0.127	0.077	−0.393	−0.079
Essential oils	1.264	1.229	−0.027	0.071
Cocoa beans	0.550	0.742	0.350	0.237
Sauces and preparations	0.494	0.507	0.025	0.033
Waste, copper	0.853	0.374	−0.562	−0.329
Coffee, not roasted	0.323	0.477	0.477	0.210
Arrowroot	0.502	1.186	1.362	0.478
Medicaments	0.517	0.110	−0.787	−0.508
Vegetables	0.910	1.535	0.686	0.105
Men's/boys' trousers, cotton	0.002	0.089	36.156	0.087
Waste, stainless steel	0.318	1.370	3.307	0.893
Communion wafers	0.078	0.168	1.173	0.093
Palm hearts	1.866	2.290	0.227	−0.244
Plants	1.488	3.009	1.023	1.580
Orange juice, frozen	0.069	0.071	0.028	−0.010
Fruits	0.078	0.309	2.959	0.243
Sweet potatoes	0.817	1.055	0.291	0.508
Oranges	1.125	1.381	0.228	0.033
Pneumatic tires	0.588	0.737	0.252	0.196
Instruments, medical	0.314	0.491	0.565	0.176
Waste, aluminum	0.779	0.289	−0.630	−0.520
Artificial body parts	0.337	0.179	−0.468	−0.118
Paintings	0.378	0.069	−0.816	−0.377
Wood articles	0.351	0.153	−0.566	−0.252
Orange juice	0.182	0.007	−0.959	−0.203

Source: Author's calculations using trade data from ITC Trade Map Database.

a positive RCAV were light petroleum oils, ethyl alcohol, cocoa beans, sauces, fruits, coffee, communion wafers, pneumatic tires, medical instruments and men's and boys' trousers. Twenty-two of the thirty-two products exported by CARICOM and measured by the RCAV did show an enhanced position on the EU market in terms of their export specialization.

In the case of the CACM, products with an RCA > 1 are light petroleum oils, shrimps, ethyl alcohol, essential oils, cocoa beans, arrowroot, palm hearts, plants, orange juice (frozen), and sweet potatoes (table 6.5). In general, the RCA of these products is weak, as only one of them, light petroleum oils, can be classified as having moderate comparative advantage.

Assessed in terms of RCAV, seven of these ten products reflected an improvement based on export specialization. They are light petroleum oils, ethyl alcohol, essential oils, cocoa beans, arrowroot, orange juice (frozen) and sweet potatoes. The three that saw a decline in RCAV are palm hearts, plants and shrimps. Products with RCA < 1 that made an advance on the EU market in terms of RCAV are sugar, rum, sauces, rock lobster, waste (copper), waste (stainless steel), coffee, medicaments, vegetables, men's and boys' trousers, fruits, oranges, pneumatic tires, paintings, wood articles and orange juice.

The rest with RCA < 1 that experienced a decline in RCAV are bananas, T-shirts, communion wafers, medical instruments, waste (aluminium) and artificial body parts. Twenty-six of the thirty-two products exhibited structural comparative advantage based on export specialization with RCAV > 0 (table 6.5).

In general, six products of CARICOM had RCA > 1, ΔRCA > 0, and RCAV > 0 (table 6.6). They are sugar, bananas, shrimps, arrowroot, vegetables, waste (stainless steel) plants, sweet potatoes and oranges, indicating both a size and a specialization advantage. Those that were negative on all three counts are rum, T-shirts, waste (copper), medicaments, waste (aluminium), artificial body parts, paintings, wood articles and orange juice. The latter enjoyed neither a size nor a specialization advantage.

For the CACM, the similar respective categories are light petroleum oils, ethyl alcohol, cocoa beans, arrowroot, orange juice (frozen) and sweet potatoes with all positive results and bananas, T-shirts, communion wafers, waste (aluminium) and artificial body parts with all negative results (see table 6.6).

A comparison between ΔRCA and RCAV reveals that for the CACM about twice the number of products gained a specialization advantage as well as a

Table 6.5. Central American Common Market Revealed Comparative Advantage Index (RCA), Its Change over the Two Sub-periods (ΔRCA) and Revealed Comparative Advantage Variation Index (RCAV) in the Selected Products, 2007–2013

Product Description	RCA 2007–2009	RCA 2011–2013	ΔRCA (Per Cent)	RCAV
Raw sugar, cane	7.536	0.370	−0.951	0.341
Bananas	−0.141	0.909	−7.452	−0.472
Rum and tafia	0.758	0.790	0.042	0.307
Light petroleum oils	2.328	2.385	0.024	0.809
Rock lobster	0.872	0.622	−0.286	0.200
Shrimps and prawns,	−0.123	1.355	−11.987	−0.387
Undenatured ethyl alcohol	1.010	1.150	0.139	0.650
T-shirts, singlets	−0.096	0.141	−2.480	−0.051
Essential oils	−0.057	1.379	−25.365	0.023
Cocoa beans	1.416	1.569	0.108	0.965
Sauces and preparations	1.028	0.027	−0.974	0.015
Waste, copper	0.882	0.469	−0.468	0.262
Coffee, not roasted	−0.024	0.856	−36.759	0.112
Arrowroot	0.981	1.390	0.418	0.392
Medicaments	4.289	0.023	−0.995	0.018
Vegetables	0.568	0.540	−0.049	0.000
Mens/boys trousers, cotton	7.663	0.224	−0.971	0.197
Waste, stainless steel	0.977	0.896	−0.083	0.210
Communion wafers	−0.061	0.011	−1.185	0.000
Palm hearts	−0.238	1.069	−5.489	−0.774
Plants	−0.187	1.448	−8.748	−0.324
Orange juice,frozen	0.832	1.099	0.321	0.384
Fruits	−0.039	0.423	−11.914	0.030
Sweet potatoes	0.949	1.848	0.947	1.186
Oranges	1.073	0.270	−0.749	0.134
Pneumatic tires	2.126	0.188	−0.911	0.135
Instruments, medical	0.021	0.935	43.069	−0.021
Waste , aluminum	−0.223	0.060	−1.268	−0.017
Artificial body parts	−0.321	0.518	−2.615	−0.157
Paintings	1.551	0.599	−0.613	0.321
Wood articles nes	0.672	0.967	0.438	0.168
Orange juice	0.026	0.102	2.913	0.072

Source: Author's calculations using trade data from ITC Trade Map Database.

Table 6.6. Revealed Comparative Advantage Index (RCA), Its Change over the Two Sub-periods (ΔRCA) and Revealed Comparative Advantage Variation Index (RCAV) in the Selected Products, 2011–2013

	Caribbean Community 2011–2013			Central American Common Market 2011–2013		
Product Description	**RCA > 1**	**ΔRCA > 0**	**RCAV > 0**	**RCA > 1**	**ΔRCA > 0**	**RCAV > 0**
Raw sugar, cane	+	+	+			+
Bananas	+	+	+			
Rum and tafia					+	+
Light petroleum oils		+		+	+	+
Rock lobster	+	+				+
Shrimps and prawns	+	+	+	+		
Undenatured ethyl alcohol		+	+	+	+	+
T-shirts, singlets						
Essential oils	+		+	+		+
Cocoa beans		+	+	+	+	+
Sauces and preparations		+	+			+
Waste, copper						+
Coffee, not roasted		+	+			+
Arrowroot	+	+	+	+	+	+
Medicaments						+
Vegetables	+	+	+			+
Men's/boys' trousers, cotton		+	+			+
Waste, stainless steel	+	+	+			+
Communion wafers		+	+			
Palm hearts	+	+		+		
Plants	+	+	+	+		
Orange juice, frozen		+		+	+	+
Fruits		+	+			+
Sweet potatoes	+	+	+	+	+	+
Oranges	+	+	+			+
Pneumatic tires		+	+			+
Instruments, medical		+	+		+	
Waste, aluminum						
Artificial body parts						
Paintings						+
Wood articles					+	+
Orange juice					+	+

Source: Author's calculations from tables 6.4 and 6.5.

Note: + indicates a positive result.

market-size one, while for CARICOM the difference in the numbers is not significant. In comparing the performance of CARICOM vis-à-vis the CACM in each good, the RRCA results largely support the strong growth of comparative advantage for the CACM. There are fifteen cases between the two periods in which CARICOM has shown a decline in RRCA vis-à-vis the CACM over the two periods (table 6.7). They are sugar, rum, rock lobster, essential oils, cocoa beans, sauces, coffee, medicaments, orange juice (frozen), sweet potatoes, oranges, waste (aluminium), paintings, wood articles and orange juice. For eleven of these products, even though their RRCA in 2011–13 was still positive, it was not as high as in 2007–9. They were sugar, rum, rock lobster, essential oils, cocoa beans, sauces, medicaments, sweet potatoes, oranges, waste (aluminium) and paintings.

Twelve other products, however, although their RRCA improved over the two periods, still continued to be negative vis-à-vis the CACM in the later period. They are artificial body parts, medical instruments, pneumatic tires, fruits, orange juice (frozen), palm hearts, men's and boys' trousers, vegetables, T-shirts, ethyl alcohol, shrimps and bananas. In all, therefore, twenty-seven of the thirty-two CARICOM products showed no strong rival comparative advantage. Fifteen of them are among the nineteen very sensitive products examined in this study enjoying a special Cotonou preference for which preference erosion has been a major preoccupation of CARICOM (table 6.7). The other four that were not among the twenty-seven products referred to above are arrowroot, communion wafers, fruits and plants.

If the size of RCAV is taken into account, the CACM had a higher RCAV in rum, rock lobster, cocoa beans, medicaments, orange juice (frozen), sweet potatoes, oranges, waste (aluminium), paintings, wood articles, orange juice, men's and boys' trousers, T-shirts and ethyl alcohol. The latter products, with the exception of wood articles, also appear in the RRCA calculation of the previously mentioned twenty-seven CARICOM products.

CARICOM and the CACM have twenty and twenty-three products, respectively, with a positive RCAV. However, the CACM recorded a higher average RCAV index for all the thirty-two products (.148) as compared to .106 for CARICOM. The CACM also had twelve of its twenty-three products with a positive RCAV score greater than .2 as compared to the seven of the similar respective twenty for CARICOM.

Table 6.7. Rival Revealed Comparative Advantage Index (RRCA), Its Changes over the Two Sub-periods and a Comparison of the Revealed Comparative Advantage Variation Index (RCAV) between the Two Regions in the Selected Products, 2007–2013

Product Description	RRCA 2007–2009 A	RRCA 2011–2013 B	RRCA Difference B–A	Central American Common Market RCAV Minus Caribbean Community RCAV, 2011–2013
Raw sugar, cane	1.824	0.881	−0.944	−0.473
Bananas	−1.028	−0.547	0.482	−0.532
Rum and tafia	0.674	0.521	−0.153	0.372
Light petroleum oils	0.474	1.019	0.546	0.548
Rock lobster	0.826	0.556	−0.269	0.686
Shrimps and prawns	−0.758	−0.385	0.373	−0.686
Undenatured ethyl alcohol	−0.775	−0.444	0.331	0.442
T-shirts, singlets	−0.562	−0.350	0.212	0.028
Essential oils	0.939	0.796	−0.143	−0.047
Cocoa beans	0.667	0.452	−0.216	0.727
Sauces and preparations	1.115	1.002	−0.112	−0.019
Waste, copper	−0.058	0.129	0.187	0.590
Coffee, not roasted	−2.103	−2.146	−0.042	−0.099
Arrowroot	−0.212	0.373	0.585	−0.086
Medicaments	1.056	0.162	−0.894	0.526
Vegetables	−0.647	−0.302	0.346	−0.105
Men's/boys' trousers, cotton	−1.228	−0.166	1.062	0.110
Waste, stainless steel	−0.156	0.437	0.593	−0.684
Communion wafers	0.280	0.585	0.306	−0.093
Palm hearts	−0.615	−0.271	0.344	−0.531
Plants	0.024	0.372	0.348	−1.904
Orange juice, frozen	0.348	−0.250	−0.598	0.394
Fruits	−1.372	−0.426	0.945	−0.213
Sweet potatoes	0.352	0.086	−0.267	0.679
Oranges	0.618	0.313	−0.304	0.101
Pneumatic tires	−0.915	−0.665	0.249	−0.061
Instruments, medical	−2.708	−1.710	0.999	−0.197
Waste, aluminum	0.258	0.206	−0.052	0.503
Artificial body parts	−2.720	−1.607	1.113	−0.040
Paintings	1.566	1.221	−0.345	0.698
Wood articles	−1.006	−1.224	−0.218	0.420
Orange juice	−0.337	−2.443	−2.106	0.275

Source: Author's calculations using trade data from ITC Trade Map Database.

The larger number of positive CACM RCAV indexes would stem largely from a sizeable increase in CACM market share in the European Union, as shown in table 6.8. The CACM had a 50 per cent and over increase for twenty of its thirty-two products as compared to eleven for CARICOM. For products such as sugar, rum, light petroleum oils, rock lobster, cocoa beans, vegetables, men's and boys' trousers, waste (stainless steel), oranges, tires, paintings and orange juice, the average CACM increase was well over 100 per cent. CARICOM, on the other hand generally exhibited stagnation, with a marginal increase or a decline for most of these products. As a test of the latter, the correlation between CACM EU market changes and its RCAV yields a coefficient of .384, which is significant at the 0.05 level. The equivalent figure for CARICOM was –.209, which was not significant.

The positive CACM results were seen even though, as regards market dominance, ΔRCA, CARICOM over the two periods had improvements in twenty-two products as compared to ten for the CACM. A possible explanation for this may be that in a recessionary period in the European Union, since CARICOM was still enjoying some more of the EU preferential market access, it may have fared better in terms of price and demand for its products than the CACM, where such access was not available.

However, the evidence from a look at the other indexes would suggest that there was, over the period 2011–13 as compared to 2007–9, a greater targeting of the EU market on the part of the CACM countries, leading to greater comparative advantage based on export specialization in this market for a wider range of the thirty-two products. Overall, CARICOM total exports declined substantially, with its market share dropping by 30 per cent, while that of the CACM increased by 16 per cent. This occurred even when CARICOM was still enjoying special preferences over the CACM.

This greater EU targeting by the CACM is also borne out to some extent by regressing the world market changes in CARICOM and CACM exports over the two periods on changes in their exports to the EU market (table 6.9). The test shows that there was a higher regression coefficient for CARICOM as compared to the CACM, indicating that relatively more CACM products were diverted from the world market to the EU market.

Table 6.8. Central American Common Market (CACM) and Caribbean Community (CARICOM) Changes in the European Union and World Markets (Per Cent) in the Selected Products, Average 2007–2009 and 2011–2013

	CACM		CARICOM	
Product Description	**Change in EU Market Share**	**Change in World Market Share**	**Change in EU Market Share**	**Change in World Market Share**
All products	16	5	−30	5
Raw sugar, cane	702	−6	−45	−50
Bananas	−9	6	68	22
Rum and tafia	102	15	−14	−7
Light petroleum oils	137	−29	406	33
Rock lobster	243	83	12	10
Shrimps and prawns	5	20	50	5
Undenatured ethyl alcohol	6	−47	38	−47
T-shirts, singlets	−4	6	−5	57
Essential oils	56	66	−32	−30
Cocoa beans	154	5	−6	−31
Sauces and preparations	152	24	18	15
Waste, copper	51	−20	41	222
Coffee, not roasted	7	9	−41	−60
Arrowroot	−17	−58	94	−18
Medicaments	336	−18	−66	59
Vegetables	95	24	162	56
Men's/boys' trousers, cotton	665	−12	5256	44
Waste, stainless steel	658	283	1703	319
Communion wafers	13	20	38	−36
Palm hearts	−42	−24	−22	−37
Plants	−6	15	27	−37
Orange juice, frozen	609	287	9	6
Fruits	−43	−41	203	−23
Sweet potatoes	84	−5	−39	−53
Oranges	175	33	−17	−33
Pneumatic tires	216	1	241	172
Instruments, medical	90	86	1051	636
Waste, aluminum	−30	−10	−62	2
Artificial body parts	109	208	1545	2991
Paintings	280	49	4	468
Wood articles	13	−22	−59	−5
Orange juice	120	−40	−99	−73

Source: Author's calculations using trade data from ITC Trade Map Database.

Table 6.9. Regression Results of Changes in World CARICOM and CACM Exports on Changes in Similar Exports to the European Union, 2007–2013

Region	R^2	Adjusted R^2	Standard Error of the Estimate
Caribbean Common Market	.403	.383	.07001
Caribbean Community	.502	.485	.01551

Source: Author's calculations using trade data from ITC Trade Map Database.

Conclusion

In this chapter I have attempted to highlight through an analytical discussion the importance of market size (country size and trade openness) to economic growth. Trade policy, insofar as it promoted trade openness and widened market size, was shown to be positively related to growth.

Against this background a comparison was made between the CARICOM and the CACM countries regarding the pace of trade liberalization. It was shown that the CARICOM countries lag behind the CACM countries in terms of trade policy opening at the unilateral, multilateral and reciprocal bilateral levels. This was reflected in the CACM's showing of a higher increase in trade openness as measured in terms of exports to GDP as compared to that of CARICOM.

The expectation from the theory was that the CACM would perform better on the EU market, as it has been promoting greater trade openness, and this was shown in terms of the relatively larger number of competing products in which it enjoyed a higher level of competitiveness as compared to CARICOM, which exhibited a significant decline in structural competitive advantage in a large number of products, including many long-standing traditional ones.

The major implication of this finding is that if the CACM countries, without the special access enjoyed by the CARICOM countries, were able to demonstrate this level of competitive performance, we can anticipate that, with the recent application of the EU-CAAA, they will outcompete the CARICOM countries even further, especially in areas of tropical products in which significant market access had been denied them over the years.

In this study, CARICOM's goods performance in sensitive agricultural and agro-processed products on the EU market showed a significant decline in competitiveness. These findings tally with the recent research on CARICOM goods exports to the European Union in general (B&S Europe and Linpico 2014) which showed a major decrease in competitiveness. The latter was particularly noteworthy when compared to the positive performance of the Dominican Republic.

Notes

1. CACM countries in this study are Costa Rica, El Salvador, Guatemala, Honduras and Nicaragua. Panama, which negotiated as part of the CACM and recently joined the CACM, is not included in this discussion. CARICOM includes Antigua and Barbuda, Bahamas, Barbados, Belize, Dominica, Grenada, Guyana, Haiti, Jamaica, Montserrat, St Kitts and Nevis, St Lucia, St Vincent and the Grenadines, Suriname, and Trinidad and Tobago. Haiti and Montserrat are not part of the EPA. Montserrat is not included in this study.
2. The EPA was signed on 15 October 2008 by the European Community and all the members of CARICOM except Guyana, which later signed on 20 October 2008, and Haiti, which requested more time to review the EPA. Haiti has not yet become a signatory to the agreement. The agreement has been provisionally applied since the signing.
3. The agreement was signed in Honduras in June 2012 and includes a provisional application of the trade part, to enter into force unilaterally in the European Union immediately after the European Parliament gave its approval on 11 December 2012. The trade deal has been applied to Guatemala since 1 December 2013; to Honduras and Nicaragua since 1 August 2013; and to Costa Rica and El Salvador since 1 October 2013.
4. For some similar results, see Dollar (1992); Ben-David (1993); and Frankel and Romer (1999).
5. The Uruguay Round was the 8th round of multilateral trade negotiations conducted within the framework of the General Agreement on Tariffs and Trade.
6. It should be noted that the bound rates were set at the end of the Uruguay Round and still exist. The applied rates are those prevailing up to 2011 and 2012 and may have since been changed. These rates can be sourced from the World Trade Organization (WTO).
7. For the individual country schedules, see ODI (2008), table on p. 4.
8. For evidence of this pursuit of FTAs, see Cas, Swiston and Barrot (2012), 8–13.
9. The Dominican Republic–Central America–United States Free Trade Agreement (CAFTA-DR) entered into force for the United States, El Salvador, Guatemala, Honduras, and Nicaragua in 2006, for the Dominican Republic in 2007, and for Costa Rica in 2009.
10. Using indexes of outward orientation, Cas, Swiston and Barrot (2012, 3) noted that a plateau was reached in overall ratios of exports to GDP ratios in the CACM since their peak in the late 1990s, and this did not compare favourably with the ratios of

some similar regions, which were higher and continued to rise. Their export sectors were thus regarded as not well placed to sustain long-term economic growth relative to similar countries in other regions. The plateau mainly applies to Costa Rica, El Salvador and Guatemala, but even in these cases their ratios at the end of 2014 were higher than those of the early 1990s. In relation to CARICOM, only Belize, Haiti, and Trinidad and Tobago ended 2014 with ratios above those they started with in the early 1990s, and in the other cases the deterioration was generally appreciable.

11. The GSP is a non-reciprocal preferential tariff system which departs from the most favoured nation principle of the WTO that obliges WTO member countries to treat the tariffs on imports from all other WTO members equally. It therefore allows WTO member countries to lower tariffs for the developing countries, without also lowering tariffs for rich countries.
12. GSP Plus is a special non-reciprocal preferential tariff scheme from the European Union that goes beyond its standard GSP. It is designed to support vulnerable developing countries in their ratification and implementation of relevant international conventions in the fields of Sustainable Development and Good Governance.
13. Annex II of the EU-CAAA lists excluded products as well as products subject to a slow process of tariff reduction.
14. According to the EU-CAAA, "Appendix 2 includes import tariff-rate quotas for originating goods of Central America under staging category 'Q' in the Schedule of the EU Party. The EU Party shall administer these tariff-rate quotas in accordance with its internal regulations."
15. There are also limitations to the RCA index, some of which are discussed in Vollrath (1991), Yeats (1992), and Greenaway and Milner (1993).
16. For the separation of size advantage from structural comparative advantage, see Cai and Leung (2008).
17. For the derivation, see Cai and Leung (2008) and Cai, Leung and Hishamunda (2009), chap. 3, 13–34.
18. The harmonized system is an international nomenclature for the classification of products adopted by the World Customs Organization. Harmonized System Revision 2002 was used. Rice was not captured, as quantities exported by the CACM were either zero or insignificant because this product was excluded previously under CAP regulations, although exceptions were made for a few CARICOM countries.
19. Data on production instead of exports is considered more appropriate in determining specialization, but this poses enormous data requirements beyond the scope of this exercise. Export supply has been used as a substitute in some studies.
20. The independence of the ΔRCA and RCAV variables was verified by correlating ΔRCA and RCAV. For both regions the coefficient of variation was low, .154 for CACM, with a covariance .694, and .087 for CARICOM, with a covariance of .240.

References

Alesina, A., E. Spolaore and R. Wacziarg. 2005. Trade, Growth and the Size of Countries. In *Handbook of Economic Growth*, edited by P. Aghion and S. Durlauf, 1499–542. Amsterdam: Elsevier B.V.

Anatol, M. 2011. The Scope of Developing a Sustainable Knowledge-Based Industry in Trinidad and Tobago: The Application of Endogenous Growth Model. PhD diss., Institute of International Relations, University of the West Indies, St Augustine, Trinidad and Tobago.

B&S Europe and Linpico. 2014. *Monitoring the Implementation and Results of the CARIFORUM–EU EPA Agreement*. Final Report. European Commission. http://trade.ec.europa.eu/doclib/docs/2014/october/tradoc_152824.pdf.

Balassa, B. 1965. Trade liberalisation and "revealed" comparative advantage. *Manchester School* 33 (2): 99–123.

Ben-David, D. 1993. Equalizing Exchange: Trade Liberalization and Income Convergence. *Quarterly Journal of Economics* 108 (3): 653–79.

Cai, J., and P. Leung. 2008. Towards a More General Measure of Revealed Comparative Advantage Variation. *Applied Economics Letters* 15 (9): 723–26.

Cai, J., P. Leung and N. Hishamunda, N. 2009. Assessment of Comparative Advantage in Aquaculture: Framework and Application on Selected Species in Developing Countries. Technical Paper No. 528. Food and Agriculture Organization of the United Nations, Rome. www.fao.org/docrep/012/i1214e/i1214e.pdf.

Cas, S., A. Swiston and L. Barrot. 2012. Central America, Panama, and the Dominican Republic: Trade Integration and Economic Performance. Working Paper No. 234. Western Hemisphere Department, International Monetary Fund, September 2012. www.imf.org/external/pubs/ft/wp/2012/wp12234.pdf.

CEPR (Centre for Economic Policy Research). 2012. The Economic Impact of the Trade Pillar of the Association Agreement between the European Union and Its Members and Central America. Final Project Report. European Commission DG Trade. http://trade.ec.europa.eu/doclib/docs/2012/september/tradoc_149938.pdf.

Dollar, D. 1992. Outward-Oriented Developing Economies Really Do Grow More Rapidly: Evidence from 95 LDCs, 1976–85. *Economic Development and Cultural Change* 40 (3): 523–44.

Edwards, S. 1998. Openness, Productivity and Growth: What Do We Really Know? *Economic Journal* 108 (447): 383–98.

Finger, M., F. Ng and I. Soloaga. 1998. Trade Policies in the Caribbean Countries: A Look at the Positive Agenda. Paper presented at the World Bank for the Caribbean Group for Cooperation and Economic Development, Washington, DC, 8 June. http://siteresources.worldbank.org/INTTRADERESEARCH/Resources/finger-ng-soloaga_policieslacagenda_dp_june98.pdf.

Frankel, J., and D. Romer. 1999. Does Trade Cause Growth? *American Economic Review* 89 (3): 379–99.

Greenaway, D., and C. Milner. 1993. *Trade and Industrial Policy in Developing Countries: A Manual of Policy Analysis*. London: Macmillan.

Grossman, G., and E. Helpman. 1991. *Innovation and Growth in the Global Economy.* Cambridge, MA: MIT Press.

Havrila, I., and P. Gunawardana. 2003. Analyzing Comparative Advantage and Competitiveness: An Application to Australia's Textile and Clothing Industries. *Australian Economic Papers* 42 (1): 103–17.

Hinloopen, J., and M. Marrewijk. 2001. On the Empirical Distribution of the Balassa Index. *Weltwirtschaftliches Archiv* 137 (1): 1–35.

Hudson, S. 2003. *Trade Liberalization and the Jamaican Economy: Prospects and Effects of Tariff Adjustments.* Kingston: Research Services Department, Bank of Jamaica. http://boj.org.jm/uploads/pdf/papers_pamphlets/papers_pamphlets_trade_liberalization_and_the_jamaican_economy_prospects_and_effects_of_tariffs_adjustments.pdf.

Lewis, D., and A. Webster. 2001. International Trade and Comparative Advantage in the Caribbean: An Empirical Analysis. *Journal of Eastern Caribbean Studies* 26 (1): 45–65.

Lorde, T., A. Alleyne and B. Francis. 2010. An Assessment of Barbados Competitiveness within the EU Market, 1992–2006. *Global Economy Journal* 10 (2): 1–22.

Lucas, R. 1988. On the Mechanics of Economic Development. *Journal of Monetary Economics* 22 (1): 3–42.

ODI (Overseas Development Institute). 2008. *CRNM Note on CARIFORUM Economic Partnership Agreement: What Europe Is Offering Africa: The Pros and Cons of EPAs.* London: Caribbean Regional Negotiating Machinery. www.odi.org/sites/odi.org.uk/files/odi-assets/events-documents/1974.pdf.

Osterlof, D. 2011. *Potenciales impactos del Acuerdo de Asociación entre América Central y la Unión Europea sobre el sector agropecuario de América Central.* Santiago de Chile: Revisión de la literatura, FAO. www.fao.org/docrep/019/as393s/as393s.pdf.

Rodrik, D. 1992. The Limits of Trade Policy Reform in Developing Countries. *Journal of Economic Perspectives* 6 (1): 87–105.

Rodrik, D., and F. Rodríguez. 2000. Trade Policy and Economic Growth: A Skeptic's Guide to the Cross-national Evidence. In *NBER Macroeconomics Annual,* vol. 15, 2001, edited by B. Bernanke and K. Rogoff, 261–325. Cambridge, MA: MIT Press.

Romer, P. 1986. Increasing Returns and Long Run Growth. *Journal of Political Economy* 94 (5): 1002–37.

Rueda-Junquera, F. 2010. *El Acuerdo de Asociación Unión Europea-Centroamérica: Una nueva etapa en las relaciones económicas birregionales.* Burgos, Spain: Universidad de Burgos. https://halshs.archives-ouvertes.fr/halshs-00532785/document.

Sinanan, D., and R. Hosein. 2012. Transition Probability Matrices and Revealed Comparative Advantage Persistence in a Small Hydrocarbon-Based Economy. *West Indian Journal of Engineering* 34 (1–2): 16–29.

Smith, A. 1986. *An Inquiry into the Nature and Causes of the Wealth of Nations.* Harmondsworth, Middlesex: Penguin.

Spolaore, E., and Wacziarg, R. 2005. Borders and Growth. *Journal of Economic Growth* 10 (4): 331–86.

Vollrath, T. 1991. A Theoretical Evaluation of Alternative Trade Intensity Measures of Revealed Comparative Advantage. *Review of World Economics* 127 (2): 265–80.

Wacziarg, R. 2001. Measuring the Dynamic Gains from Trade. *World Bank Economic Review* 15 (3): 393–429.

WB/OAS (World Bank and Organization of American States). 2009. CARICOM: Accelerating Trade Integration – Policy Options for Sustained Growth, Job Creation, and Poverty Reduction. Report No. 30. http://siteresources.worldbank.org/INTLACINSPANISH/Images/CaribeReporte.pdf.

Yeats, A. 1992. What Do Alternative Measures of Comparative Advantage Reveal about the Composition of Developing Counties' Exports? *Indian Economic Review* 27 (2): 139.

CHAPTER 7

Inclusive Growth and CARICOM Economies: Considerations in Developing a Green Growth Framework

Debbie A. Mohammed

Caribbean Community (CARICOM) countries have been impacted in varying degrees by a general lack of competitiveness attributed to a number of factors. Smallness is often cited as a causal factor for problems associated with economies of scale, undiversified production and limited domestic investment. Concentration on a few exportables, often at the low end of the value chain and with declining levels of productivity, suggests a failure or unwillingness at both public- and private-sector levels to mobilize research and development and innovation as transformative tools, not only in boosting industry competitiveness but in developing new, high-value market activities. Exports remain heavily concentrated in resource-intensive sectors which are finite in nature and rely on or are impacted by certain environmental and climatic conditions. These bring to the forefront issues of decline or depletion and environmental degradation and have implications for long-term growth, employment and environmental sustainability.

These export industries, as major contributors to economic growth and public-sector financing, including financing of social programmes, have experienced serious challenges associated with declining output and uncompetitive exports, maturing industries and external competition for foreign investment. These challenges were compounded by the impacts of the global economic downturn and the Eurozone crisis on the region. The CARICOM countries have now recognized that diversification is required to place their economies on a more sustainable growth trajectory. However, diversification can no longer mean shifting from one resource-intensive activity to another. It must take account of the loss of natural assets, including biodiversity, and increasing climate variability and their potential economic and development impacts.

The focus of this chapter is on economic greening as a means of generating more inclusive, sustainable growth, looking specifically at the agriculture and tourism sectors. It recognizes that replacing these major export industries is neither practical nor feasible for CARICOM states since they exhibit some comparative advantage and are major generators of revenue, employment and investment. Instead, an alternative is to introduce green practices to these industries using a range of instruments, including eco-labelling, environmental standards, certification and accreditation and life-cycle analysis, which may provide avenues for CARICOM economies to develop new niche segments or move products and services further along the value chain to capture a share of a global market poised for growth. Several studies have highlighted the growing demand for green goods and services globally, which provides a basis for realigning the tourism and agriculture sectors to capture rents from this potential market segment.

One Massachusetts Institute of Technology study (2011) noted that companies recognize green practices as vital to their competitiveness and profit generation, and sustainability is now a permanent part of 70 per cent of corporate agendas. This supports the Boston Consulting Group's 2009 survey showing that consumers "more systematically purchased green products in 2008 than 2007" and were willing to spend more for such products, despite the recession (BCG 2009). This trend is reinforced by a Deloitte Financial Advisory Services study in 2009, which found that "a significant portion of consumers are now considering social and environmental benefits as part of their calculation of product value and purchasing decisions", which impact what and how companies produce and market goods and services (Deloitte Financial Advisory Services 2009). This trend, according to the Mintel Group (2014), is expected to intensify as "the case for going clean has clear global resonance". A US Department of Commerce report (2010) noted the growth potential of the green sector, with shipments or receipts of green products and services valued between US$371 billion and US$516 billion in 2007 and green jobs employing between

1.8 million and 2.4 million. In developing a green growth framework for both the agriculture and the tourism sectors, the chapter examines the technology, standards and human resource implications for policymakers and decision-makers at the government and firm levels in the Caribbean.

The chapter's first section provides an overview of the region's current economic position in the post-global recessionary period and its attempts at diversification to address declining competitiveness and revenue. It suggests that for diversification attempts to be more impactful and translate to more sustainable, inclusive socioeconomic growth, strategies which invariably will involve ramping up sector activities that increase usage of natural assets must also take account of the potential impacts of such resource-driven initiatives on long-term economic growth and development.

In the chapter's next section it introduces greening as a diversification option for the agriculture and tourism sectors. The concepts of green growth and sustainable development are elaborated as the bases for actionable frameworks for revitalizing major industries within CARICOM countries through the incorporation of green principles and practices. It further examines the current pattern of industry activities, details key features of industry-relevant green practices and identifies major elements than can contribute to greening, including eco-labelling, the development of certification and industry standards and the adaptation of technologies drawing from industry's best practice and country's examples.

The third section examines some of the major inputs required to develop green growth frameworks for agriculture and tourism and the policy implications for both governments and firms in the region. The final section concludes the chapter with specific recommendations that can facilitate the creation of viable green agriculture and tourism sectors specifically and a more sustainable green approach generally in the Caribbean.

CARICOM's Economic Performance in the Post–Economic Recession Period

Although the International Monetary Fund (IMF) estimates that real gross domestic product (GDP) growth in the Caribbean is likely to rebound to around 3 per cent over the medium term, after a cumulative flat performance from 2009 to 2012 (Ramsaran 2016), much of this anticipated growth and its sustainability will depend on the region's ability to move beyond "business as usual" and to understand where in life-cycle analysis its exportables reside and the implications for competitiveness and sustainable, inclusive development, defined in the chapter as the ability of countries to increase economic growth across sectors which results in increased economic well-being, reduction in social inequities and enhanced environmental prudence.

In the post-recession period, several CARICOM countries, which rank among the most tourism-dependent in the world (Fritz-Krockow and Sun 2009), experienced revenue shortfalls as a result of a decline in tourism receipts (figure 7.1), which forced nine countries, among them Belize, Dominica, Grenada and St Lucia, to seek IMF assistance in 2009. Jamaica negotiated a new IMF loan in February 2013 for US$750 million, but this is accompanied by extremely onerous conditionalities, and unless there is a marked improvement in tourism receipts, many of its CARICOM neighbours may be faced with the new National Debt Exchange index introduced by the IMF.

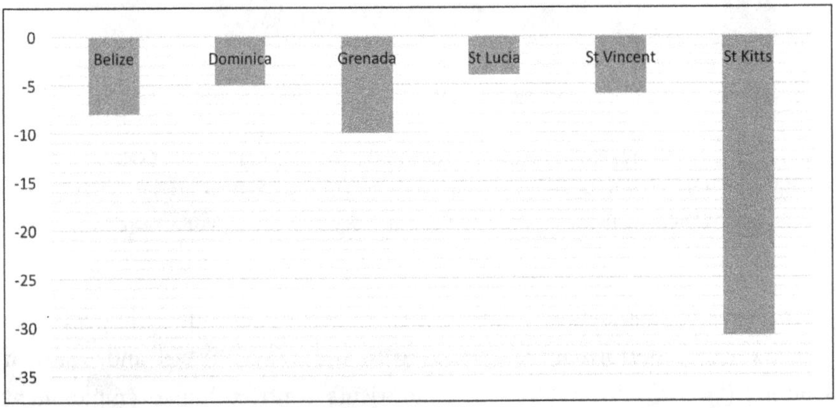

Figure 7.1. Decline in tourism expenditure of select CARICOM countries, 2009–2010
Source: Author's compilation from select CARICOM central banks' reports, 2009–2010.

The direct contribution of tourism and travel to the GDP and employment of four of CARICOM's tourism-dependent countries, Antigua and Barbuda, the Bahamas, Barbados, and St Lucia, before and after the recession, is depicted in figure 7.2. What is evident is the importance of tourism for GDP and employment in these countries, with Barbados and St Lucia seemingly most negatively impacted in the post-recessionary period in terms of contribution to GDP; the former registered 4.2 per cent in 2007, which declined to 12.7 per cent in 2010 and 11.8 per cent in 2012, while the latter experienced a marginal decline from 13.6 per cent in 2007 to 13.3 per cent in 2010, dipping to 12.7 per cent in 2011 (WTTC 2013a). While the other three countries showed a slight recovery over 2013–15, the Barbados economy experienced its seventh consecutive year of stagnation in 2014, due largely to weak performance in tourism coupled with the impact of public-sector layoffs under its fiscal adjustment programme (CDB Annual Report 2014, 7).

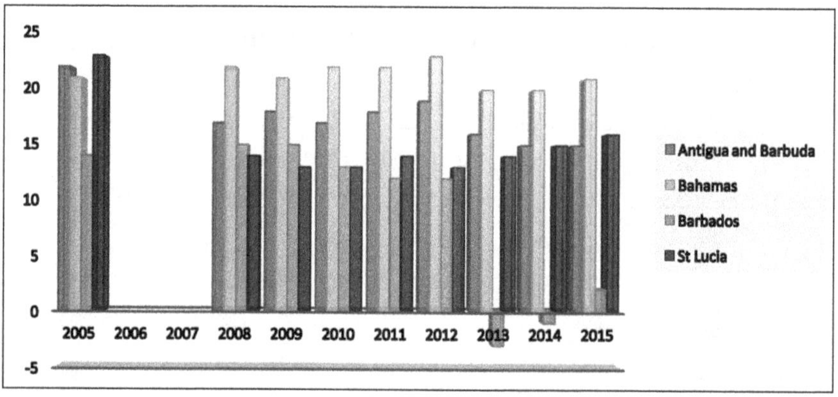

Figure 7.2. Direct contribution (per cent) of travel and tourism to GDP of select CARICOM countries, 2005–2015

Source: WTTC, www.wttc.org/research/economic-impact-research/country-reports/.

In terms of employment, Barbados was the most negatively impacted by this industry's performance. According to the World Travel and Tourism Council (WTTC 2013b), travel and tourism's contribution to employment dropped from 14.5 per cent in 2007 to 12.9 per cent in 2010 and continued this downward trend to 12.0 per cent in both 2011 and 2012, falling to 11 per cent from 2013 to 2015.

The poor performance of this sector was exacerbated by competition from destinations such as Australia, the Mediterranean and Cuba, as well as other tourism-dependent CARICOM countries for already declining tourism receipts. Continued instability within the Eurozone and the United States, which constitute the bulk of its tourist market, saw a reduction of 6.2 per cent in long-stay arrivals. Additionally, the imposition of the UK Air Passenger Duty and a reduced number of flights to the island contributed to this sector's contraction by an estimated 3.5 per cent (Bourse Securities Limited 2013, 1).

The picture was one of cautious optimism for some tourism-dependent countries due to a slight improvement in tourism's contribution to GDP and employment in 2012. Although several countries registered minimal recovery in 2014 due to tourism and construction services, contraction of the Chinese economy in late 2014 and subsequent instability in global markets may negatively impact growth possibilities in 2016 and beyond. Sustainable gains from this industry will require policies and strategies at both governmental and firm levels that protect the inputs for the industry while creating new, differentiated niches to attract different market segments. For both scenarios, it will be necessary to address supply-side issues, particularly in the environmental and natural resource sectors, since this industry is a heavy consumer of water and energy, which can put severe pressures on the limited resources of these small island nations.

Furthermore, green growth and sustainable development are contingent on the use of fragile or finite environmental assets such as seas, coastlines, forests and other ecosystems, all of which are already being negatively impacted by global warming due to climate variability. One report commissioned by the United Nations Development Programme suggests that a sea-level rise of one metre could result in the damage or loss of 149 resorts. Further, damage and rebuilding could cost CARICOM countries US$187 billion by 2080 (McCarthy 2010). The CARICOM Declaration for Climate Action 2015 therefore emphasized that the Caribbean countries, as small island developing states, are extremely vulnerable to climate change and face "fundamental threats" to their sustainable development (CARICOM 2015). CARICOM's position at the COP21 called for "the recently capitalized Green Climate Fund (GCF) to play a critical role in facilitating the Caribbean countries' access to financing to promote the paradigm shift towards low-carbon and climate-resilient development pathways and limiting temperature rise to 1.5°C" (CARICOM 2015).

With respect to agriculture, the global financial crisis of 2007 and the subsequent global food crisis, which triggered scarcity and high prices, reinforced the need for CARICOM countries to address as an urgent priority the issue of food security within the context of poverty reduction and inclusive, sustainable development (CARDI 2011, 9). Globally, food prices have continued to trend upward, with marked increases in staples such as wheat, maize, sugar and edible oils (CARDI 2011, 11) which have precipitated increases in the price of feedstock and final products in this region. Meanwhile, there has been no commensurate increase in extra-regional agricultural exports of mainly sugar and bananas for the region, as small size, outdated production methods, high production costs, frequent occurrence of tropical storms and hurricanes[1] and more rigorous health standards and regulations exacerbate the region's lack of export competitiveness in this sector.

Most CARICOM countries, with the exception of Belize and Guyana, have experienced worsening agricultural deficits, which have facilitated a shift in production for the local markets, where standards are not as rigorous (Agritrade 2012). Agriculture's contribution to employment and GDP in the region has fallen during the last decade and had become negligible by 2014 (table 7.1). Its contribution to GDP declined by more than 50 per cent, from 6.3 per cent in 1997 to 3.2 per cent in 2006 (FAOSTAT), due in part to the transformation of the Organisation of Eastern Caribbean States from agriculture- to service-based economies.[2]

In the case of energy-producing Trinidad and Tobago, Dutch disease has negatively impacted the agriculture sector's growth. Its inability to attract labour because of the high-wage competition from energy, as well as several social work programmes, have accelerated this decline. A recent survey found that the average wage for workers in the petroleum sector in 2009 was "almost 5 times higher than the average wage of persons in the other sectors" and that workers in domestic agriculture earned the lowest wages in 2000 (Mahabir et al. 2013, 8–9). Unfortunately, the position in 2015 is not much different, as government-funded "make work" programmes have effectively outcompeted this sector for affordable labour.

Despite substantial support given to the agricultural sector, there has been a steady decline, with the sector accounting for only 0.6 per cent of GDP and under 4 per cent of employment in 2010 (WTO 2012). This is reflected in the country's food import bill, which amounted to 10.06 per cent of total imports in 2010 (MFPLMA 2011, 4), or an estimated TT$4 billion annually (Rakhal-Fraser 2015). The government embarked on a National Food Production Action Plan for the period 2011–15 as a means of diversifying the economy and transforming agriculture into a dynamic sector capable of generating sustainable employment and careers, reducing the food import bill and contributing significantly to the country's food and nutrition security.

Table 7.1. Agriculture Contribution to GDP and Labour Force Composition in Caribbean Community Economies, 1960–2014

	Agriculture (Per Cent of GDP)			Agriculture Employment (Per Cent of Labour Force)		
Country	**1960[a]**	**2009[b]**	**2014**	**1981[c]**	**2007[d]**	**2014**
Antigua and Barbuda	11	4	2.4	3	3	n.a.
Dominica	38	20	15.9	28	21	n.a.
Grenada	27	6	7.1	20	14	n.a.
St Kitts and Nevis	19	3	1.5	51	n.a.	n.a.
St Lucia	15	5	2.8	23	15	n.a.
St Vincent and the Grenadines	18	7	7.8	25	15	n.a.
Bahamas	2	1	1.8	5	2	n.a.
Barbados	21	4	n.a.	9	3	n.a.
Belize	31	12	n.a.	24	20	n.a.
Guyana	26	28	18.3	28	21	n.a.
Jamaica	8	6	7.0	27	18	n.a.
Suriname	11	5	n.a.	17	8	n.a.
Trinidad and Tobago	3	1	n.a.	10	4	n.a.

Source: Author's compilation from World Bank Development Indicators, 2016. http://data.worldbank.org/data-catalog/world-development-indicators.

Notes: n.a. = not available.

[a]For some countries contribution to GDP data start in 1977, Antigua and Barbuda, Dominica, Grenada, St Kitts and Nevis, St Lucia, and St Vincent and the Grenadines; 1984, Trinidad and Tobago; 1989, Bahamas; and 1993, Jamaica.

[b]For some countries contribution to GDP data end in 2005, Barbados; and 2006, Bahamas.

[c]For some countries employment data start in 1986, Bahamas; 1988, Dominica and Grenada; 1991, Jamaica, St Lucia, and St Vincent and the Grenadines; 1993, Belize; and 2001, Antigua and Barbuda.

[d]For some countries employment data end in 2001, Antigua and Barbuda; 2004, Barbados, St Kitts and Nevis, and Suriname; and 2005, Belize, Haiti, Jamaica, and Trinidad and Tobago.

Most CARICOM countries are now attempting to increase local food production as a means of improving their food security positions and reducing their food import bills. For this reason, a more balanced approach to growth and sustainable development is required, one that can generate revenue and long-term employment and also contribute to poverty reduction while ensuring the protection and longevity of natural inputs upon which such economic growth is predicated. Despite differing levels of development and resource endowments, both tourism and agriculture continue to be important contributors to GDP, foreign exchange earnings and employment for CARICOM countries. If they are to contribute meaningfully to growing these economies and placing them on a more secure development footing, both sectors will need to increase output, introduce differentiated and high-quality goods and services that can build competitiveness, secure market share and earn revenue.

The challenge for CARICOM countries will be to avoid a "race for resources" as each tries to compete in the same market with the same products. This chapter advances the need for a more harmonized approach to industry expansion and diversification as specified in the Revised Treaty of Chaguaramas, in which standards, best practice and protection of natural assets became key drivers. Utilizing a green growth framework to guide the process of "dynamizing" critical sectors provides a realistic option for smaller economies like those of CARICOM to better address growth and development challenges within the framework of very limited resources in areas such as financial capital, skilled human capacity, natural endowments and investment in innovation and research.

Green Growth for Sustainable Development of the Tourism and Agriculture Sectors in CARICOM Countries

While many CARICOM countries have attempted to diversify their economies to reduce dependence on one or two resource-intensive or resource-related activities, most remain anchored to these traditional exportables, primarily because they provide a consistent source of revenue. For this reason, applying green principles and practices to the sectors will be critical for maintaining their viability over time.

Green Growth and Sustainable Development

Green growth is defined as the "pursuit of economic growth and development while preventing costly environmental degradation, climate change, biodiversity loss and unsustainable natural resource use" (OECD 2010). Green growth utilizes mutually supportive economic and environmental policies to ensure economic progress and sustainability over time.

A key component of green growth strategy is the creation of competitive conditions to address environmental risks that may impede economic and social progress. This provides the space for investing in the environment, which can trigger new sources of economic growth. Since the ultimate goal of green growth is to enhance well-being, it not only is concerned with the economic viability of countries but approaches development from a holistic standpoint that focuses on issues such as poverty reduction, sustainable livelihoods and equitable and balanced development in line with the UN Millennium Development Goals.[3] It emphasizes economic growth for sustainable, inclusive development based on a more prudent approach to resource and environmental usage. Green growth thus provides a framework for linking the economy, the environment and social objectives to achieve concrete measurable progress. As such, green growth should be viewed as a key component of the concept of sustainable development rather than distinct from it.

It should be noted that the concept of a green economy in the context of achieving sustainable growth outcomes for developing countries is a somewhat contentious one. While the UN Environment Programme (UNEP), the Organisation for Economic Co-operation and Development and various environmental and non-governmental groups support greening as a more viable means for poorer countries to achieve inclusive growth in line with the UN Millennium Development Goals, many argue that this is impractical on two fronts.

First, the transformation to a green economy requires a quantum of investment, research, innovation and expertise for the creation of new industries which are beyond the capacity of poor or small developing countries. Since these countries depend on a few areas of economic activity for revenue and employment generation, there is little room for sector replacement. This is simply not an option. Second, McAfee (2012) contends that assigning prices to ecosystem services, biodiversity banking and carbon-offset sales, rather than benefiting the poor, can result in "upward redistribution of wealth from poorer to wealthier classes and from rural regions to distant centres of capital accumulation, mainly in the global North" because these are based upon the logic of neoclassical economics, in which the market model for profit maximization is the main objective.

Cognizant of these arguments, what is advocated is not the *replacement* of major revenue earners, such as tourism and agriculture, but rather the *transformation* of these into more sustainable sectors capable of increasing contributions to employment and foreign exchange without unduly diminishing natural resources or negatively impacting the environment.

Greening the Tourism and Agriculture Sectors in CARICOM Tourism

Efforts at diversification or the search for alternative development options have tended to focus on growth initiatives which would significantly transform current models which either have failed or have remained stagnant. While green growth may sound like a major transformation involving policy changes, technological input and tax restructuring, in reality, incremental measures involving improvements along the value chain could significantly alter the product in question to allow it to earn the green growth label.

Various "tools" can be adopted by countries depending on their resource endowments and technical capacities and the subsectors in which they operate. These include investment in solar panels and wind-generated devices (renewable energy), energy efficiency practices, waste management and recycling, water conservation, eco-tourism, eco-labelling and green certification.

Currently there are attempts to apply some elements of green practices and principles to the tourism sector of most CARICOM countries, with Barbados emerging as a clear leader in this area. Recognizing that despite the country's flagging economy, tourism remains the principal driver of the economy, accounting for 15 per cent of GDP (Henry 2011) and fourteen thousand direct jobs, in 2014 (WTTC) major inhibitors to this sector's growth were identified as high energy and water demands, intensive land use and high energy costs, while waste was a significant output generated by this sector. To address these concerns and spiralling energy costs, Barbados has developed a Tourism Policy Framework which emphasizes a sustainable tourism development approach in keeping with its National Strategic Plan 2006–25 to make Barbados a developed country by 2025, along with the broader vision of making the country the most environmentally advanced green economy in Latin America and the Caribbean (Henry 2011).

In December 2010, the Government of Barbados and UNEP entered a formal partnership to develop a resource-efficient green economy in Barbados.

As part of this project, a Green Economy Scoping Study was launched in March 2011 to analyse linkages between key growth sectors such as tourism, transportation and agriculture and the implications for cross-cutting issues such as energy, waste and water.

The National Strategic Plan recognized the importance of energy security for attaining sustainable development and has set specific targets of increasing the renewable energy supply on the country's electricity grid and increasing the number of households with solar water heaters by 50 per cent by 2025 (Henry 2011). However, energy efficiency and renewable energy have been directed particularly at the tourism industry since it is such a heavy consumer of energy. The hotel industry and wider tourism sector have been encouraged to conserve energy and to adopt other green practices, including the use of solar water heaters, green building design in accordance with industry standards and certification such as that for Leadership in Environmental Engineering and Design; eco-labelling;[4] recycling; using solar vehicles for tourist transport as well as other eco-friendly modes of transport – trams, seaways and bicycles; and eco-branding as means of differentiating the product and attracting a different market segment. Many of these measures are driven by the private sector.

The hotel industry in countries such as St Lucia, Jamaica, Dominica and Guyana have also begun to introduce measures designed primarily for energy and water conservation. Some destinations and attractions have focused on branding their products as eco-intensive and have been successful in acquiring international green certifications and standards, such as Earth Check, Green Key and Green Globe.[5] Hotels such as Fond Doux Plantation (St Lucia), Spice Island Beach Resort (Grenada), Galley Bay Resort (Antigua) and Accra Beach Resort (Barbados) have been able to gain Green Globe certification by adopting one or more of the following green strategies:

- Use of solar photovoltaic systems for electricity and heating water
- Use of water from desalinization plants
- Use of rainwater harvesting systems
- Incorporation of salt-based pool purification systems instead of chlorine-based ones
- Use of energy-efficient or smart systems in buildings and energy-efficient appliances

- Development of waste management systems
- Conversion of food waste to compost

While there is a concerted attempt to reduce costly fossil fuel and water consumption and adopt practices that reduce harmful impacts on natural environments in these countries, including energy-producing Trinidad and Tobago, there is no discernible attempt to strengthen and sustain backward linkages with the agriculture sector to reduce the food import bill, reduce the carbon footprint and grow the local food sector.[6] Although several countries have articulated sustainable development plans,[7] the Barbados "model" is supported by an actionable policy and an institutional and legislative framework which has identified clear targets and time frames and provided appropriate concessions to drive green growth. Notwithstanding differences in resources across the region, development of similar frameworks to provide the enabling environment will be necessary for successful replication in other CARICOM countries, since the problems of all tend to be similar.

Agriculture

Like tourism, agriculture continues to be a key contributor to employment in the region. Global food scarcity and price fluctuations have reignited concerns for CARIOM's food security and its balance-of-payments position. The Community Agricultural Policy, provided under Article 56 of the Revised Treaty of Chaguaramas, and the Regional Strategic Plan, which emerged from the Jagdeo Initiative,[8] were introduced to address these critical issues and assist member countries in developing national agricultural policies under a harmonized regional agriculture policy that could effect "transformation of the agricultural sector towards market-oriented, internationally competitive and environmentally sound production of agricultural products; (56 (1) (a))", through "efficient management and sustainable exploitation of the Region's natural resources, including its forests and living resources of the exclusive economic zone (56: (1) (f))".

The Caribbean Agricultural Research Institute, the regional centre for applied research in agriculture, has identified three strategic axes – (1) development of sustainable industries, (2) establishment of strategic linkages and (3) capacity building – which will drive its *Medium-Term Plan 2011–13* (CARDI

2011). Heavy emphasis will be placed on the application of technology, research and innovation to develop new, more commercially viable crops and livestock varieties and to assist national agricultural departments in introducing these. This is particularly important as countries attempt to move up the agriculture value chain in livestock and foodcrop production by (1) expanding agro-based industrial activities; (2) increasing the variety of local fruits, vegetables and flowers for the domestic and international markets; and (3) increasing the scope for agricultural exports by extending their life cycle to include niches in organically produced crops and related products.

Key to the development of viable, competitive agricultural sectors will be the application of research and innovations that are internally generated or adapted from external sources via strategic partnerships. Adhering to relevant food regulations and standards, as well as increasing the food-testing laboratories across the region, will also be major factors in determining the export viability of agricultural and related products. Application of eco-labels can also be used as a green growth measure to identify products that were produced sustainably with few to no lasting effects on the environment. These can range from crops to processed foods to fertilizers and pesticides used in plant products and the feeds and living conditions of animal products. Additionally, harmonization of agricultural policies and standards, increased budgetary allocations for agricultural research and capacity building must be seen as urgent priorities to address intensive land use, unsustainable farming practices and types of pesticides and fertilizers since these impact natural resources, habitats and the environment and thus the sustainability of this sector.

While the perception that such initiatives are technology- and investment-intensive may be valid, many of the success stories are due to initiatives undertaken by entrepreneurs with little tangible support from government. The Tobago Cocoa Estate WI produces gourmet chocolates from organically grown cocoa for the international market and copped a Gold Star at the UK Great Taste Awards of 2011. It is now certified organic and has moved up the value chain by introducing sustainable agri-tourism as part of its line. The Belmont Estate in Grenada has also followed this sustainable agri-tourism model and is producing award-winning chocolates from certified organic cocoa. Hotel Chocolat in St Lucia plans to build a fully solar-powered chocolate factory that will utilize harvested rainwater and locally sourced milk and sugar.

These green success stories can also be found in vegetable production. By applying hydroponic techniques one entrepreneur in Trinidad created Mama's Green Garden which supplies organic vegetables to local supermarkets and restaurants (*Trinidad Guardian* 2012). A key strategy in building demand for these products and services has been the formation of alliances with international partners, both from a marketing and a technical standpoint. Growing sustainable industries requires more active collaboration on the part of local entrepreneurs and government, in addition to accessing strategic international partnerships to assist in areas such as quality, branding and marketing. It also requires a modification of strategies by trade facilitation and promotion agencies, such as Export-TT, Invest-TT and Trinidad and Tobago Manufactures Association, as well as financial institutions, toward promoting and financing these types of goods and services.

Green Growth Frameworks for the Tourism and Agriculture Sectors

UNEP's *Green Economy and Trade* report for 2013 identifies sustainable tourism and agriculture as emerging opportunities that can be used by developing countries to engage in sustainable trade (UNEP 2013, 19). It should be noted that because these sectors are so interconnected, enabling frameworks will have basic elements with certain aspects tailored to the specific demands of each sector.

In the case of tourism, sustainable tourism represents a potentially lucrative growth subsector for the region, since eco-tourism is now the fastest-growing segment of this subsector (UNEP 2013, 22). A Travel Insights report issued in November 2011 noted that environmental awareness and sustainability issues were growing among UK consumers and that future travel trends revolved around issues of sustainability, exploring unseen places, increased eco-tourism and social responsibility (Henry 2011).[9]

CARICOM countries have a comparative advantage in eco-tourism because each has a distinctive natural environment and a rich culture which can be developed as sustainable, certified tourism products[10] and attract a growing market on the export side while potentially reducing negative environmental and social impacts such as air and water pollution, biodiversity loss and pressures on utilities and waste management systems. UNEP (2013, 22) notes that protected areas in Costa Rica attract over a million visitors annually and generate entrance-fee revenues of US$5 million, while in Mexico these attract 14 million visitors and generate over twenty-five thousand jobs.

Sustainable agriculture, too, represents a viable export segment as consumers globally become more conscious of organically certified foods. According to the Organic Trade Association (2013), Canada's organic market grew to Cdn$3.7 billion in 2012, of which certified organic foods amounted to Cdn$3 billion. It noted that the value of the Canadian organic food market has tripled since 2006, outpacing other agri-food sectors, and attributes this to public-private partnerships, citing government's role in implementing, at industry's urging, "strict national standards and label requirements in 2009 to uphold consumer confidence in organic claims" and funding by major private-sector companies including supermarket and food giant Loblaws. Public awareness of agriculture and certification in it is very limited in CARICOM countries. A few sustainable farms have received international certification, such as Rainforest Alliance, but adaptation of these techniques across the region remains limited.

Community-based cooperative initiatives modelled on the Integrated Watershed and Coastal Area Management Cuban demonstration project, which used innovative technologies such as Vermiculture along with soil conservation measures to increase agricultural yield (Clauzel 2011), can be an ideal way of linking the agricultural and tourism sectors in pursuit of green growth initiatives in CARICOM.

While sustainable tourism and agriculture present new trade and employment opportunities for this region, certain limitations can act as inhibitors and so must be considered in developing green growth frameworks. These include limited financing for green activities, low investment in research and development or in technology adaptation, lack of public "buy-in" to greening and low-incentive structures for shifting to greener activities. Government support should focus on introducing policies and development initiatives that are geared towards educating and informing small farmers about the viability of these initiatives, providing technical assistance to facilitate adaptation of these new initiatives, offering low-interest financing and marketing merchandise and access to markets. Such initiatives will be critical for the development, growth and commercialization of these sectors.

An Integrated Approach to Sustainable Development Planning

A key component of the green growth framework will be the situation of sustainable tourism and agriculture strategies and targets within the broader national development objectives so that there is a clear link between sector strategies, inputs, outputs and national development outcomes. Moreover, the success of green growth requires more than endorsing policy. It requires effective coordination of decision-making, monitoring and accountability systems to ensure that green growth policies are implemented to produce the intended outcomes within specified time frames. These procedures will facilitate more effective allocation of limited financial and technical resources and avoid costly duplication while building confidence in the green growth process.[11]

Targeted Government Investment and Strategic Partnerships: Capacity Building and Research and Development

The development of sustainable sectors like tourism and agriculture requires greater emphasis on land, water, energy and waste efficiency while introducing new products and services with market appeal. Targeted incentives for infrastructure, such as compressed natural gas to reduce fossil fuel consumption in Trinidad and Tobago and solar energy initiatives in Barbados and Trinidad and Tobago, are necessary to encourage private-sector interest. Development of strategic partnerships with industry leaders locally, regionally and globally is also important for building capacity, standards and benchmarks and securing investments and technology. Investment in public awareness building and education and skills-training programmes are key inputs to support the development and commercialization of green activities along the tourism and agriculture value chains. A major inhibitor is low levels of expenditure on research and development across CARICOM.

CARICOM spends less than 0.13 per cent of its GDP on and receives less than 1 per cent of its GDP as returns from science, technology and innovation (*Jamaica Gleaner* 2012). Expenditure on research and development in Trinidad and Tobago (table 7.2), which has the highest research and development expenditure among CARICOM countries, is still very low.

Table 7.2. Trinidad and Tobago: Expenditure on Research and Development as a Percentage of GDP, 2005–2011

Year	2005	2006	2007	2008	2009	2010	2011
Percentage	0.09	0.06	0.05	0.03	0.05	0.05	0.04

Source: NIHERST (2013), expenditure on research and development as a percentage of GDP, 2005–10 and 2006–11.

This is in stark contrast to the richest countries (table 7.3), which allocate approximately 30 per cent of their budgets for research and development and derive over 50 per cent of their GDP from science, technology and innovation.[12]

Table 7.3. Research and Development Expenditure of OECD Countries, 2012

	Budgetary Expenditure on R&D, Private and Public Sector (Per Cent)	Returns from R&D to GDP (Per Cent)
Organisation for Economic Co-operation and Development Countries	30	> 50
Caribbean Community Countries	0.13	< 1

Source: *Jamaica Gleaner* (2012).

This is compounded by a general lack of investment in research and development within CARICOM countries, due in part to their small size, segmented markets and high operating costs arising from high levels of energy and other imported inputs. Given the pressing constraints on revenue generation in this region and the challenges for financing even basic government operations, there is an urgent need to increase strategic alliances and partnerships at the bilateral and multilateral levels, including at research and teaching institutions, to better access technology and skills sharing, adaptation and upgrading to facilitate greening and commercialization opportunities.

Further, intensifying regional collaborations with research centres such as the Inter America Institute for Cooperation in Agriculture, the Caribbean Agricultural Research Institute, the Caribbean Industrial Research Institute, the Caribbean Regional Organisation for Standards and Quality, the University of the West Indies and the University of Trinidad and Tobago for targeted projects can augment the capacity and technological adaptation required to drive more sustainable industries. The Caribbean Development Bank's Climate Resilience Strategy 2012–17 "seeks to finance investments and strengthen capacity to utilise financing, design and implement policies and strategies to address resilience and deliver on sustainable development objectives" (CDB Annual Reports 2012, 18, and 2014, 16–19).

There is also a dire need for more efficient utilization of resources, particularly highly trained human capital. This approach requires not only targeted investment for training and certification in specific industry-related programmes but ensuring that these skilled resources can get employment in their chosen specializations. Misallocation of human capital continues to be a major impediment to real growth in this region.

Harmonization of Policies, Standards and Regulations

Several CARICOM countries have developed or are in the process of developing variants of a sustainable development action plan.[13] For agriculture or tourism, meeting international certification, standards and regulations and producing green goods and services appear to beyond the capacity of governments and many firms in the region. It is for this reason that the Revised Treaty of Chaguaramas calls for the harmonization of sector policies and enabling legislation across CARICOM. Additionally, it safeguards against possible environmental impacts as countries compete to attract investment to the tourism sector and intensify agricultural activity. To date, however, CARICOM has made little progress beyond recommending the establishment of guidelines and standards. To be effective and meaningful, CARICOM must set enforceable monitoring and accountability standards to ensure that standards set are being met and sustained.

This may help the region in developing its own Caribbean green standards linked to leading global standards for agricultural practices and outputs and for hotel and destination experiences. Such regional certification bodies can distribute costs and help brand the region as "environmentally progressive". Further, guidelines should be established for different industries to enable firms to find the simplest ways to "green" their production processes. Regional tertiary education bodies such as the University of the West Indies can partner with industry to determine green growth measures suited to the region. These bodies would also train the human resources needed to carry out the certification process and ensure compliance.

Incentives and Private-Sector Initiatives

Although commercialization of tourism and agricultural activities is primarily private sector– driven, entrepreneurship building in these areas will require an incentives framework, including subsidies and tax relief, that can attract both large firms and smaller entrepreneurs. For instance, Barbados offers incentives to both households and firms to encourage the installation of solar water heaters, which has led to the growth of a few importers and manufacturers of solar panels, while this has been slow to take off in Trinidad. However, a Green Fund levy of 0.1 per cent on gross income is applicable to all companies operating in Trinidad and Tobago to balance the impacts of growth on the environment. In the case of agriculture, incentives for the production of organic products and sustainable farming can be tied to industry certification to stimulate the growth of such products.

For the private sector, understanding the growth potential of the sustainable goods and services market and how these goods and services can be replicated in or developed for the domestic market will be key to the commercialization of new products. The Cariloha brand of apparel is a good example of innovation and commercialization.[14] Products are made from 100 per cent recycled bamboo, and the line has been expanded to include bedding, accessories and fitness wear. Cariloha (cariloha.com) is the only multistore retailer in the world to provide an entire store experience completely merchandized with products made from bamboo. It has successfully branded itself not only as a green brand but as a leisure brand to appeal to an even wider market.

Good Governance

The successful operation of green growth frameworks is predicated on good governance since the introduction of new industries and activities will require significant investments that should be carefully managed. Linked to this is the need for transparency in decision-making to build confidence in the system and ensure that potential gains are shared by all, while the risks associated with such investments are not only minimized but do not negatively impact certain groups, particularly the poor and vulnerable. Additionally, the private sector and non-governmental organizations must be active participants. The former provides initiative and leadership to drive green growth, particularly in the area of corporate social responsibility, whether voluntary or based on industry standards, and sets the tone for government to adopt similar attitudes towards sustainable growth and decision-making. The latter monitor both the private and the public sectors, ensuring performance, adherence to standards and accountability.

Conclusion

Sustainability is a concept that will require new ideas and fresh thinking. As CARICOM countries devise strategies to grow their economies and position themselves more firmly along a sustainable development path, this will also require commitment and buy-in by all stakeholders. It will require, too, more efficient utilization of limited resources, particularly human capital, and reinforces the case for greater regional cooperation for accessing technology, training and financing, as well as for developing or adopting internationally recognized industry standards and certifications. Additionally, this approach requires a concerted shift in attitudes to recognize the potential financial and environmentally sustainable benefits of greening industries and sectors. This is even more urgent now with Trinidad and Tobago's energy-driven economy experiencing a recession since 2015. While governments will remain the principal drivers of the economy for the foreseeable future; greening sectors such as tourism and agriculture present new, dynamic opportunities for entrepreneurs and the possibility of greater diversification and resilience building. Targeted support from government must be accompanied by clear private-sector strategies to turn green activities into commercially viable industries and translate them into more sustainable livelihoods.

Notes

1. Eastern Caribbean countries have been shown to be the most disaster-prone in the world on account of the large number of hurricanes experienced.
2. The Organisation of Eastern Caribbean States is comprised of nine members – Antigua and Barbuda, Dominica, Grenada, Montserrat, St Kitts and Nevis, and St Lucia, as well as Anguilla, St Vincent and the Grenadines, and the British Virgin Islands (associate members).

3. These eight goals are eradication of extreme poverty and hunger, universal primary education, gender equality, reducing child mortality rates, improving maternal health, combating diseases, environmental sustainability, and developing a global partnership for development.
4. An "eco-labelling" refers to a voluntary method of environmental performance certification and labelling. This allows environmentally conscious consumers to patronize producers that practice sound and environmentally safe methods of production.
5. Green Globe certification has been awarded to hotels in Antigua and Barbuda, Belize, Grenada, Barbados, and Jamaica.
6. For instance, St Lucia's food import bill was EC$350 million (2012), and Barbados's food imports totalled Bd$700 million (2012).
7. For example, Antigua and Barbuda has its National Environmental Strategy, Barbados a Sustainable Development Policy, Guyana a National Development Strategy, and Trinidad and Tobago a plan called Working for Sustainable Development in Trinidad and Tobago.
8. The Jagdeo Initiative recognized nine binding constraints to agricultural development on the region – limited financing, deficient risk management measures, a fragmented agricultural private sector, inadequate research and development, outdated agricultural health and safety systems, inefficient land and water management systems, lack of skilled human resources, inadequate transportation systems, and weak information and intelligence systems and markets.
9. Travel Insights is a leading online UK provider of information on all aspects of travel.
10. These include the world-famous Asa Wright Nature Centre and Pointe-à-Pierre Wildfowl Trust in Trinidad; Tobago's Main Ridge rainforest, the oldest of its kind in the Western Hemisphere; Soufrière Hills volcano in Montserrat; and the World Heritage site Pitons in St Lucia.
11. The Sustainable Development Report produced by the Trinidad and Tobago Ministry of Planning, Housing and the Environment (2012) and the Barbados National Strategic Plan (2006–25) are good examples of this integrated planning approach.
12. This represents the private sector and government combined.
13. These include Antigua and Barbuda, which is developing a sustainable tourism plan and a sustainable energy action plan; Bahamas, which is designing a national environmental management action plan, and Belize, which is preparing a national sustainable development report.
14. Developed by American entrepreneurs in 2007, these green products were marketed to reflect the ease and comfort of Hawaiian and Caribbean lifestyles.

References

Agritrade. 2012. *Agritrade: Executive Brief Update 2012: Caribbean: Agricultural Trade Policy Debates and Developments*. Wageningen, Netherlands: Technical Centre for Agricultural and Rural Cooperation.

BCG (Boston Consulting Group). 2009. *Capturing the Green Advantage.* www.bcgperspectives.com/content/commentary/consumer_products_sustainability_capturing_the_green_advantage_mit/.

Bourse Securities Limited. 2013. *Regional Review: Barbados Time to Diversify!* www.bourseinvestment.com.

CDB (Caribbean Development Bank). 2012. *Annual Report 2012.* Bridgetown, Barbados: CDB.

———. 2014. *Annual Report 2014.* Bridgetown, Barbados: CDB.

CARDI (Caribbean Agricultural Research and Development Institute). 2011. *Medium Term Plan, 2011–2013.* www.cardi.org/wp-content/uploads/2011/01/Medium-Term-Plan-2011-2013.pdf.

CARICOM. 2015. *CARICOM Heads in France to Push for Climate Action.* CARICOM press release, 30 November. http://caricom.org/media-center/communications/press-releases/caricom-heads-in-france-to-push-for-climate-action.

Cariloha. 2016. *About Cariloha.* Cozumel, Mexico: PW Companies. www.cariloha.com/about/about-us.

Clauzel, S. 2011. *A Model for Integrated Watershed and Coastal Area Management: The Case of Cienfuegos Bay, Cuba.* Castries, St Lucia: Global Environment Facility-Funded Integrated Watershed and Coastal Areas Management Project. http://iwlearn.net/iw-projects/1254.

Deloitte Financial Advisory Services Limited. 2009. Deloitte Report: Risk and Rewards for Building Sustainable Hotels, Tourism, Hospitality and Leisure. New York: Carter Ledyard and Milbur. www.clm.com/docs/Deloittearticle.pdf.

Fritz-Krockow, B., and Y. Sun. 2009. Six CARICOM Countries Seek IMF Support. *Abeng News,* 6 May. www.abengnews.com/2009/05/06/five-caricom-countries-seek-imf-support/.

Henry, G. 2011. Tourism and Energy in Barbados: Opportunities and Challenges. Paper presented at the Coco Reef Hotel for Greening Tobago Why and How? Conference, Tobago, 10 November.

Jamaica Gleaner. 2012. Invest More in Research and Development: Scientists. 27 July. http://jamaica-gleaner.com/gleaner/20120727/news/news6.html.

Mahabir, R., V. Jagessar, C. Neptune and D. Cox. 2013. Understanding Wages in a Small Open Economy: The Case of Trinidad and Tobago. Working Paper No. 11. Central Bank of Trinidad and Tobago, Port of Spain, February. https://www.central-bank.org.tt/sites/default/files/Understanding%20Wages%20in%20a%20Small%20Open%20Economy%20The%20Case%20of%20Trinidad%20and%20Tobago%20Mahabir%20Jagessar%20Neptune%20Cox%20-%20Feb%202013.pdf.

Massachusetts Institute of Technology. 2011. The Future of Natural Gas: An Interdisciplinary MIT Study. Cambridge, Mass: MIT.

McAfee, K. 2012. The Contradictory Logic of Global Ecosystem-Services Markets. *Development and Change* 43 (1): 105–34.

McCarthy, M. 2010. Rising Sea Level Threatens "Hundreds" of Caribbean Resorts, Says UN Report. *Independent,* 1 December. www.independent.co.uk/environment/climate-change/rising-sea-level-threatens-hundreds-of-caribbean-resorts-says-un-report-2148034.html.

MFPLMA (Ministry of Food Production, Land and Marine Affairs, Government of the Republic Trinidad and Tobago). 2011. The National Food Production Action Plan, 2012–2015. Port of Spain, Trinidad. http://www.agriculture.gov.tt/pdf/National%20Food%20Production%20Action%20Plan%202012-2015.pdf.

Mintel Group. 2014. *Mintel Identifies Four Key UK Consumer Trends for 2015*. London. www.mintel.com/press-centre/social-and-lifestyle/mintel-identifies-four-key-uk-consumer-trends-for-2015.

NIHERST (National Institute for Higher Education, Research, Science and Technology). 2013. *Science, Technology and Innovation (STI) Indicators: Research and Development*. Port of Spain, Trinidad and Tobago. www.niherst.gov.tt/research/research-sti.html.

OECD (Organization for Economic Co-operation and Development). 2010. *The Green Growth Strategy: How Can We Get to a Greener Economy?* Paris, November. www.oecd.org/greengrowth/46141709.pdf.

Organic Trade Association. 2013. *Canada's Organic Market Now Worth $3.7 Billion Growth Driven by Broad-Scale Support of Organic Food*. Newswire (Canada). www.newswire.ca/news-releases/canadas-organic-market-now-worth-37-billion--growth-driven-by-broad-scale-support-of-organic-foods-512246601.html.

Rakhal-Fraser, T. 2015. Grow More of Our Own Food. *Trinidad Guardian*, December 7. www.guardian.co.tt/columnist/2015-12-07/grow-more-our-own-food.

Ramsaran, R. 2016. Public Policy and Economic Growth: Some Insights into the Caribbean Experience. In *The Modern Caribbean Economy*, vol. 2, *Economic Development and Public Policy Challenges*, edited by N. Karagiannis and D. A. Mohammed, 1–54. New York: Business Expert Press.

Trinidad Guardian. 2012. Hydroponics: Mama's Green Garden. 20 August. www.guardian.co.tt/lifestyle/2012-08-20/changing-agriculture-throughhydroponics.

UNEP (United Nations Environment Programme). 2013. *Green Economy and Trade Report 2013*. Nairobi: UNEP.

US Department of Commerce. 2010. *Measuring the Green Economy*. Washington, DC: Economic and Statistics Administration. www.esa.doc.gov/sites/default/files/greeneconomyreport_0.pdf.

World Bank. 2016. *World Development Indicators*. Washington, DC. http://data.worldbank.org/data-catalog/world-development-indicators.

WTO (World Trade Organization). 2012. *Trade Policy Review: Trinidad and Tobago*. Report by the Secretariat No. 260, March. Geneva. www.wto.org/english/tratop_e/tpr_e/tp360_e.htm.

WTTC (World Travel and Tourism Council). 2013a. *Data Gateway*. www.wttc.org/datagateway/.

———. 2013b. *Travel and Tourism Economic Impact 2013: Caribbean*. www.wttc.org/research/other-research/big-data-the-impact-on-travel tourism/.

———. 2014. *Travel and Tourism Economic Impact 2014: Caribbean*. http://www20.iadb.org/intal/catalogo/PE/CM%202014/14031.pdf.

CHAPTER 8

Marshalling Transnational Partners for Caribbean Development: The Role of the Diaspora

Indianna D. Minto-Coy

The Commonwealth Caribbean is at a pivotal point in its development. Many gains have been secured since independence, with many states noted for their levels of democracy and rule of law. Gains have also been secured in education and health while some economies have fared relatively well. As the experiences of colonialism fade further, the region finds itself trying to survive among a number of local, regional and international challenges which highlight the need for new and inventive methods for securing past gains and providing a future for its citizens. Among these challenges is the pressing need to identify new strategies and partners for growth and development.

Migration is a definitive aspect of the Caribbean's past and present, and it has defined society in the region (see Lapointe 2004; Nurse 2004; Reis 2007). According to Foner (1998, 47), the region has been "more deeply and continuously affected by migration than any other region in the world". Linguistics, culture, institutions, practices and economies have been shaped by migration in different ways. Included here are experiences of colonialism, slavery and the sugar trade. More recently the focus has been on migration out of the region. By all indications, migration might continue to be a major area of focus due to challenges in providing for the region's citizens.

The resulting members of the global Caribbean diaspora community are increasingly being viewed as credible development partners for their home countries or countries of origin (Newland and Tanaka 2010). Since the acknowledgement of diasporas as a largely untapped source of development and growth (for example, by Lowell and Gerova 2004; Minto-Coy 2009a), many efforts have been made globally to engage this group, particularly in developing countries. This is largely an acknowledgment of the historical role that the group has played, the increasing significance of their engagement and their desire to contribute to their countries of origin. Diasporas have therefore moved from being overlooked concerning policy to being more formally acknowledged by governments (Minto-Coy 2011, 2016a).

This notion of diasporas as development actors is reflected in discussions on the "diaspora option" (Meyer 2003), which refers to the marshalling of the diasporas' skills and resources to aid in the development of the countries of origin. This notion is also embodied in policy and praxis as mainstreaming the diaspora in national development (see, for example, Minto-Coy 2013). For developing countries, therefore, diasporas are now viewed as vital transnational actors (Bauböck and Faist 2010; Cohen 2008; Quayson and Daswani 2013; Rafael and Sternberg 2009; Sahoo and Pattanaik 2013) with the ability to utilize their multiple perspectives to the benefit of the country of origin (see, for example, Brinkerhoff 2008; Plaza and Ratha 2011).

Therefore, this chapter suggests giving attention to Caribbean nationals and their offspring living outside the region – the Caribbean diaspora – as critical transnational actors, offering immense possibilities concerning the search for new sources to reignite and fund growth and development in the twenty-first century. Indeed, countries within the region have been awakening slowly to the prospect of the diaspora option, taking steps towards mainstreaming this group in national development (for instance, Minto-Coy 2013). Such a move is significant for the Caribbean small island states, as brain drain (that is, the loss of the skilled and educated to migration) has been said to have affected small states more directly than other countries and regions (Thouez 2005).

The chapter reviews the role of diasporas in development more generally, reviewing a select body of literature and global experiences. It then reviews the Caribbean experience enroute to making a case for the relevance of the diaspora option in a Caribbean context. Next it draws broad conclusions on strategies and guides for Caribbean governments in their effort to mainstream diasporas into national and regional development and ends with a summary and conclusion. The growing interest in this area globally (Agunias and Newland 2012; Chikanda, Crush and Walton-Roberts 2016; Minto-Coy 2009a; Mercer, Page and Evans 2008; Plaza and Ratha 2011; Tai Yong and Rahman 2013) suggests that the presentation and discussion will have resonance beyond the Caribbean.[1]

The information for this chapter has been collated via desk research and interviews (between 2011 and 2016 in the United Kingdom and Jamaica) and is informed by my role in putting together the first draft of the Jamaica Diaspora Policy in 2013 for the Government of Jamaica (Minto-Coy 2013) and a 2009 working paper published by the Centre for International Governance Innovation in Canada (Minto-Coy 2009a).

The Diaspora Option in Context

Diaspora remains a contested term (see, for example, Baser 2016). From its original application to Jews dispersed from their homeland with an implication of force, disaster or tragedy, a number of other definitions and perspectives have emerged (Cohen 1998; Chander 2001). Definitions diverge based on, for instance, reason for or length of departure. The International Organization for Migration defines the *diaspora* as "the collective of long-term emigrants and the descendants of long-term emigrants, who are currently living abroad" (2012, 33). A number of terms have also been used to refer to the diaspora, or specific groups within the diaspora, including "absent migrants", "nationals abroad", "expatriates" and "transnational citizens" (see, for example, Cohen 2008; Vertovec 2009; Agunias and Newland 2012). A suitable definition befitting the notion of transnationalism and diaspora engagement in the Caribbean context is that of Agunias and Newland, which sees diasporas as emigrants and their descendants living outside their home country (that is, their country of birth, ancestry or origin) on a temporary or permanent basis but maintaining sentimental or material ties to the country of origin (2012, 5–6). Nonetheless, it is noted here that the issue of sentimentality or material ties (that is, the conscious exercise of affiliation with the country of origin) is not a delimiting factor for membership in a diaspora.

The development of the home country is a core diaspora theme (Plaza and Ratha 2011). From an initial "silent" or informal partnership in which the diasporas' role was largely unrecognized in policy and official government discourse, diaspora's are increasingly being given a voice and greater visibility nationally and beyond (Minto-Coy 2011, 2016a), particularly in unofficially helping to deliver public goods and services (for example, see Sheffer 2003, 174). In so doing, the diaspora has performed a social and economic role, meeting unmet demand for government services and poverty reduction. Within the last three decades, there has been a noticeable shift in this relationship towards acknowledgement in policy and the discourse on development. Therefore, formal emphasis on diasporic engagement, diaspora and development or the "diaspora option" is a growing tradition, covering the many ways in which countries now engage their diasporas.

Among these issues is remittancing, which has tended to preoccupy thinking and investigations on the role of the diaspora (Ratha 2005; Minto-Coy 2009a, 2010). Less attention has been focused on non-private transfers, including investment, trade and the transfer of skills and rights protection (Ionescu 2006, 11). More recent are attempts to consolidate and highlight the activities of diaspora business and diasporas in business (Minto-Coy 2016c), while Orozco's depiction of the diasporic economy helps to map the contribution made by the diaspora to economies in Latin America and the Caribbean (2003; see also Minto-Coy 2011, 2016a). Orozco's focus is on the *five Ts:* trade, telecommunications, tourism, transport and transfers (including remittances). Orozco's classification is somewhat limited in its ability to capture the full extent of the diaspora's contribution.[2] Nonetheless, the typology is a useful one for the closer investigation of the diaspora's role in regional economies.

It is important to note that the diaspora country of origin relationship is not unidirectional but is far more dynamic, involving government efforts to assist the diaspora in their country of residence and in the country of origin as well. This is important, since the notion of the diaspora as a transnational community suggests flow and exchange between the country of origin and adopted countries. The extended view is particularly relevant. It accounts for the informal movement and networks, as well as the circulatory nature of movement between the Caribbean and the rest of the world. Importantly, too, diasporic engagement denotes the stake of the home country in the progress and overall development of its diaspora. Therefore, diaspora and development and diasporic engagement suggest a number of issues regarding the diaspora, the country of origin, the relationship between the two, that between the diaspora and the country of residence and the interaction between governments in the home and host countries, other actors and institutions in each setting and how these conditions affect the diaspora. The ideal is at the core or intersection, where the interests and resources of the diaspora meet the supportive environment and policies of the host and home countries.

A Review of Select International Experiences

The perception of the diaspora as a potentially positive force for the benefit of the home country is not unique to the Caribbean. Indeed, countries such as Israel, Ireland and China have helped to make a case for governments engaging their diasporas more integrally in national growth and development (Saxenian 1999, 2002, 2003; Coogan 2000).

Countries have initiated different diaspora engagement strategies. Global strategies include opportunities for portfolio investment, direct investment, technology and skills transfer and trade links. Latin American countries have, for instance, encouraged their diasporas to create small businesses and manufacturing enterprises in the country of origin. Governments have also introduced favourable terms for the diaspora to invest and modernized rules and regulations governing investments, while countries such as India and Israel have been noted for the introduction of financial instruments such as diaspora investment bonds.

Countries such as the Philippines focus largely on remittancing, one of the most obvious forms of engagement. China and India are among the countries with the largest diaspora populations and also the recipients of the highest remittances in absolute terms (Haitao 2015, 203). The focus in these countries is also on investments and identifying ways in which contributions can be improved. Of note is the fact that while India and China are widely noted for their share of foreign direct investments (for instance, Buckley et al. 2010, 251), less attention has been paid to the fact that the bulk of investments originate from locations with the largest diaspora populations, including Mauritius and Singapore (*Economist* 2011). The suggestion is that the diaspora not only provides investments but also assists country of origin–based firms to navigate their entry into international markets and international businesses to enter the home market (Minto-Coy 2013, 2016c).

The diaspora has also received some credit for the success seen in other countries, such as the Celtic Tiger in 1990s Ireland (Burnham 2003; Minto-Coy

2009a). This has been mainly through their involvement in key industries such as intelligent technology, banking and pharmaceuticals. In this case, the government's investment body strategically approached members of its diaspora in countries such as the United States with incentives for repatriation. The diaspora's role here, as in other countries, has been that of investors, networkers, employers, employees, and bearers of expertise and knowledge.

The value of information and communications technologies in offering more seamless communication and transfers between the diaspora and home has also been recognized. For instance, an online platform now allows the Ethiopian diaspora to access information on investments, taxes, and so on. Australia also uses the Internet as a means for organizing professional networks with information on local jobs and repatriation being made available to the diaspora.

It is worth noting that not all the efforts to attract the diaspora have been along the lines of economic linkages, as China's initial efforts were based on cultural engagement with its diaspora and Armenian diasporas have been more focused on humanitarian issues (Freinkman 2001). Ireland offered financial assistance to its diaspora from Europe to Latin America up to the second and third generations. Assistance was also given towards becoming more organized in their countries of residence. Thus, more complex and symbiotic linkages were created, with governments offering direct support to their diasporas to build a sense of nationhood and assist in meeting social and welfare needs. The Latin American region has also seen engagement around health and education (Lapointe 2004; Lowell and Gerova 2004).

Finally, significant attention has been placed on the formation of diaspora knowledge networks (see, for example, Meyer and Brown 1999; Kutznetsov and Sabel 2006; Saxenian 2002; Séguin, Singer and Daar 2006). These groups are differentiated by size, the extent of their independence from the state (both country of origin and country of residence), membership and activities. Such networks offer opportunities for linking skills, expertise, ideas and contacts within and across national diasporas for the benefit of the home country. As with remittancing, much of what has unfolded here has been independent of government, having been instigated mainly by the members of the diaspora themselves.

The experiences of these frontrunners have helped to galvanize international aid and development. The work of international development and multilateral agencies such as the International Organization for Migration, World Bank and USAID have been critical here (Minto-Coy 2009a, 1, 16; Luginaah and Kerr

2016). The advice and support of these groups have combined with the practical experiences of the frontrunners to encourage more and more countries to consider measures for engaging their diasporas. Therefore, countries have begun engaging their diasporas more formally through the establishment of special sections within ministries and the formulation of diaspora policies and events, as well as by assisting them in becoming more organized in the countries in which they reside. An example is Home Town Associations, representing the pooling of remittances for scaled-up impact (Orozco and Welle 2005).

Governments have supported such initiatives through match funding. The Philippines has provided measures to assist its workers in the diaspora, including helping to protect their labour rights in the countries of residence. Kenya has also announced plans to grant dual citizenship status using the model of India's Non-Resident Indians and Persons of Indian Descent programmes (see Newland and Patrick 2004; Agunias and Newland 2012, 96).

One form of engagement is through return of the diaspora to the country of origin, bringing with them skills, capital and contacts acquired in the country of residence. For example, Ireland, with returning diasporans helping to turn around the country's long migration history in the 1990s with more immigrants than emigrants. India and China have not left contribution and return up to the goodwill of the diaspora but have introduced policies to encourage engagement, such as returning students' venture parks in China. In India, professionals are enticed to return to teach in Indian universities (Saxenian 2002; Séguin, Singer and Daar 2006).

The experiences just described are some of the more common engagement initiatives. Of note is the value of an enabling environment for investments and "knowing" the diaspora in order to design suitable policies and strategies for engagement, along with the importance of having clear lines for diasporic engagement and communication and a clear point (for instance, an agency or organization) for such engagement, clear governance structures and also a range of options to facilitate involvement. The preceding accounts also suggest that the relationship is not unidirectional or lopsided (that is, diaspora to home) or unidimensional (that is, related to remittances or economics). Engagement also has to do with governments securing the rights and welfare of citizens overseas and offering them protections and rights at home and abroad. Engagement can also be social and psychological and ultimately about mutual gain.

Overview of the Caribbean Diaspora

It is not a coincidence that many Caribbean countries are now viewing diasporic engagement as a means of addressing many developmental challenges. While many of these experiences have developed organically, they have also been influenced by developments in some of those countries. As the situational analysis that follows demonstrates, too, the actions of some of the Caribbean's governments are not without basis, particularly given indications of the diaspora's sustained goodwill and desire to contribute to the region.

The Caribbean has had a long history with migration. The physical institutions and culture have been shaped by this force (Richardson 1983; Minto-Coy 2016b). The diaspora's emergence and growth can be attributed largely to economic factors (Greenidge 2007), with Caribbean people leaving home in search of employment opportunities from the early twentieth century to Latin America and the United Kingdom (see Palmer 2007; Reis 2007; Moss-Solomon 2012), for example. In 1948, some 492 Jamaicans migrated to the United Kingdom, and these and successive emigrants contributed to rebuilding that country following World War II. Independence across the Commonwealth, largely in the 1960s and 1970s, and the opportunities for travel to North America saw many Caribbean nationals turning their attention to the United States and Canada. The Immigration and Nationality Act of 1965 was instrumental in the United States' allowing Caribbean nationals to enter that country and work in it legitimately (Palmer 2007, 2–3).

Still others, who had moved to the United Kingdom, later settled along with their families in Canada, given their view of Canada as a more welcoming environment. Further motivations included politics, as in the case of the emigration of many middle-class Jamaicans during the country's tryst with democratic socialism in the 1970s (see McNeil and Adams 1978; Palmer 1990).[3] Crime has also played a role, as people left their countries out of fear for their lives and livelihoods. The region's proximity to the United States and Canada and the reality that the region is mainly a grouping of middle-income countries have also facilitated emigration (Adams and Page 2003).

Consecutively, the United States, the United Kingdom and Canada have been the main destinations, though South-South migration has also been featured. For instance, in 2009 six million persons in the United States identified themselves as being among the Caribbean diaspora.[4] Of these a majority reside in areas such as New York–Northern New Jersey–Long Island (34.2 per cent) and Miami–Fort Lauderdale–Pompano Beach in Florida (30.2 per cent) (McCabe 2011). This figure does not include the unauthorized or hidden diaspora and those who chose other destinations. As for those claiming citizenship up to the third generation as well as dual citizenship, it can be assumed that this figure is significant. While a precise figure remains elusive, it has been suggested that there is a 1:1 ratio between the home and diaspora populations (World Bank 2013). With an estimated home population of almost 43.5 million in 2016, the Caribbean diaspora represents a sizeable group, particularly when considered as a proportion of population size.

Diasporas and Development: Evidence from the Caribbean

The diaspora's desire to contribute has driven the evolution of an independent and largely unacknowledged role for the diaspora in promoting the Caribbean and engaging with the region in ways which have helped to ease the practical losses (emotional and numerical, as well as in terms of skills) sustained through migration in the Caribbean. Perhaps the dominance of an economic motivation for departure has caused this group to sustain their engagement with the region upon departure. In such a context, things Caribbean (such as food, music and culture) have taken on profound resonance in a search for ways of maintaining their links with home.

Remittancing

It is interesting to note that many of the first generation of migrants, especially to the United Kingdom, left the region with the intention of working, saving, and returning to the region with enough funds to build their lives at home. Therefore, their "diaspora" status was never meant to be permanent, with their orientation towards home as opposed to the country of residence. Money was sent to the region as savings to sustain families left behind and to build homes. While a majority never returned, such practices hailed the beginning of remittancing. Much attention has been placed on remittances, now a major contributor to national economies (see table 8.1 and figure 8.1). Remittances contribute to reducing balances of payments (Cassells 2007), constituting a major source of income for communities and households (Dade and Unheim 2007).

Table 8.1. Migrant Remittance Inflows to the Caribbean Community Region, Including Haiti and the Dominican Republic, 2000–2013 (US$ Millions)

	2000	2001	2002	2003	2004	2005	2006	2007	2008	2009	2010	2011	2012	2013	Remittances as a Share of GDP (%)
Antigua and Barbuda	21	27	18	20	21	18	19	21	22	21	20	20	21	21	1.7
Barbados	115	131	125	131	131	94	87	139	101	114	82	82	82	85	n.a.
Belize	26	31	28	34	35	45	64	73	76	79	78	75	76	81	n.a.
Dominica	16	17	17	18	23	22	22	22	23	22	23	23	23	23	4.8
Dominican Republic	1,839	1,982	2,194	2,325	2,501	2,719	3,054	3,397	3,606	3,415	3,430	3,651	3,615	3,655	6.1
Grenada	46	47	48	49	72	27	28	29	29	28	28	29	29	30	3.7
Guyana	27	22	51	99	153	201	218	283	274	262	368	412	469	493	16.5
Haiti	578	624	676	811	932	986	1,063	1,222	1,370	1,376	1,474	1,551	1,612	1,696	20.6
Jamaica	892	1,058	1,260	1,398	1,623	1,762	1,924	2,122	2,157	1,889	2,026	2,106	2,145	2,277	14.5
St Kitts and Nevis	27	28	29	30	31	30	33	36	40	39	47	45	45	45	6.0
St Lucia	26	27	27	27	29	27	28	29	29	28	29	29	30	30	2.5
St Vincent and the Grenadines	22	23	23	24	26	22	26	29	27	29	29	29	30	31	4.2
Suriname	n.a.	0	15	24	9	4	2	3	2	5	4	4	8	8	0.2
Trinidad and Tobago	38	41	79	87	87	92	91	109	95	109	91	126	126	132	0.5
Caricom (including Dominican Republic)	3,675	4,057	4,590	5,076	5,672	6,050	6,659	7,513	7,849	7,415	7,730	8,182	8,312	8,609	6.8

Source: World Bank (2014); in Minto-Coy (2016a).

Note: No data available for the Bahamas and Montserrat. n.a., not available.

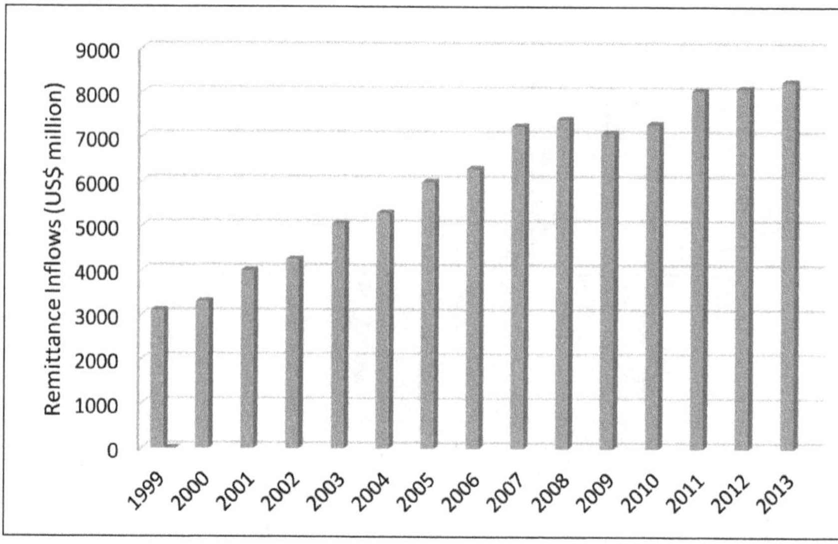

Figure 8.1. Migrant remittance inflows to the Caribbean Community Region, including Haiti and the Dominican Republic, 1999–2013
Source: World Bank (2013).
Note: No data available for the Bahamas and Montserrat.

The value of this funding becomes even clearer when placed alongside other economic indicators. Table 8.2 demonstrates that remittances consistently surpass Jamaica's exports and rivals the main income earner, tourism, even surpassing tourism receipts in 2011. The latter was also the case at the onset of the Global Financial Crisis in 2007 (Minto-Coy 2010). When compared

Table 8.2. Remittances as a Percentage of Select Indicators for Jamaica, 2009–2014

Selected Indicators (US$ Millions)	2009	2010	2011	2012	2013	2014
GDP	14.9	14.4	14.0	13.9	14.5	15.5
Tourist Expenditures	93.0	95.3	100.8	98.7	99.6	95.6
Exports	129.0	143.2	124.3	118.2	130.7	144.3
FDI Inflows	331.0	837.0	924.9	494.2	348.8	362.5
Imports	34.8	36.2	31.0	31.9	33.3	36.5

Source: Adapted from Bank of Jamaica (2016, 12).

to the main sources of income (tourism, exports and foreign direct investment inflows), remittancing emerges as a more consistent source of income, a point which underscores its relevance as a source of development funding.

The Diasporic Economy

Interestingly, while the direct economic contribution can clearly be seen from the level of remittancing, what tends to be more hidden are contributions through Orozco's five Ts of the diasporic economy (see Orozco 2003; Minto-Coy 2016a, 2016c). Remittances fits the category of transfers reviewed previously. The remaining elements of this economy will be reviewed now, namely tourism, trade (to which investment has been added), transport and telecommunication (expanded to information and communications technology).

Tourism constitutes the main source of income for most of the region's economies. Yet practitioners, planners and marketers have in the past focused scarce attention on the role of the diaspora in the success of this product. For example, Ying and Manderson (2013) noted that diaspora tourism accounts for roughly 11–15 per cent of Jamaica's tourism industry, while Nurse (2004) noted that members of the diaspora constitute around 70 per cent of actual visitors to the region. Return has largely been for special events and leisure activities, including vacation travel, and for ethnic and cultural tourism. Marketing campaigns and the structuring of the tourism services have tended to ignore this group. Additionally, the multiplier effect of the diaspora's spending may be seen in the fact that they stay not only in large hotels but also in other establishments, spending in their communities and buying local products for travel.

Previously highlighted by Orozco was the contribution to trade and investments which is evident in the Caribbean experience. As noted by Rampersad (2007, 10), the diaspora is "deeply sympathetic to nation building". This sympathy contributes to their desire to "invest their resources [given that] their drive is more zealous and passionate than [that of] potential non West Indian investors". Trade and investment here includes their establishment of businesses in their country of residence and country of origin and their facilitatory and networking role in linking businesses in the country of origin and country of residence, providing market and brand recognition for country of origin–based businesses. In so doing, they are helping to overcome challenges to growth and entering new international markets (*Economist* 2011).[5] Their role here is visible not only in traditional ethnic business areas such as restaurants, hair salons and shipping services but also in banking and finance (Minto-Coy 2011).

This suggests that diasporic trade is not limited to nostalgic services but also to traditional services such as banking and finance, which later provide opportunities for growth and internalization for related services. Businesses established by the diaspora also create multipliers and opportunities for related services and products to grow and internationalize. The Jamaican diaspora–owned Port Royal Patties, based in the United Kingdom, imports curry powder from Jamaica, creating an additional market for imports from that country. Golden Krust has also partnered with the local soft drink maker, offering its products in its restaurants.

Strategic business support from country of origin governments also extends to the diaspora in establishing businesses in the country of residence, as in the case of Jamaica's national investment promotions body (Jampro), which supported the start-up of Port Royal Patties in 2001. The company is now the largest producer of Jamaican patties in the United Kingdom. Opportunities have also emerged for artists and musicians to work in foreign markets given the spread of Caribbean music and culture via the diaspora. Caribbean businesses such as Laparkan have emerged, grown and internationalized, having identified economic opportunities for services geared towards the diaspora.[6] Ultimately, the diaspora also serves gate-opening function for Caribbean enterprises much beyond their limited physical boundary (see Minto-Coy 2016a, 2016c).

The Laparkan case also resonates in terms of diasporic engagement and development in the transportation sector. Whereas the diaspora's contribution in the area of transportation can already be seen via their direct travel to the region for tourism and other purposes, this case underscores the indirect ways in which they also contribute via travel. That is, Laparkan has grown from a small company to a multinational employing over a thousand by shipping the diaspora's goods to relatives and friends in the region. The remittance of actual cash and the sending of barrels of goods arguably represent the two most important emblems of care for and sustained ties with Caribbean families separated by distance. Not to be ignored are concerns around the contribution to the region's high import bill, its proclivity for foreign goods and the income generated from regional businesses that have been able to grow and diversify into other sectors thanks to the diaspora market.

Information and communications technologies underscore another area in which the diaspora has contributed to the region.[7] Its involvement is complex and multifaceted, with the term "telecoms-mediated diasporic engagement" (Minto-Coy 2011) coined to represent this role. It includes the introduction of the latest technologies into local communities. In so doing, the diaspora has helped to reduce the digital divides on many islands, with the first introduction to information and communications technologies in some communities (such as radios and mobile phones) facilitated by the diaspora (Minto-Coy 2011). The members of the diaspora have contributed to the success of telecom firms in the region mainly via income received for telephone calls terminating in the region that originate with the diaspora. From the reform of international settlement regimes at the end of the 1990s and into the first decade of the twenty-first century, rates earned from such calls contributed vital foreign exchange to the region. Domestic telephone rates were also subsidized through income earned from international calls. The desire to protect this lucrative income constituted the basis for cable and wireless's protection of its monopoly in countries such as Jamaica up to the end of the 1990s. Information and communications technologies have also diversified the modes of engagement between the diaspora and the region, helping to reduce physical and emotional distance and providing a tool for organizing within the diaspora. Thanks to the Internet, activities such as organizing, networking and fundraising among the members of the diaspora are possible regardless of location. Governments have also developed websites to provide information for their diasporas, though the maintenance and interactivity of such platforms remain wanting. Nonetheless, technology has meant that return is not only physical or permanent but also virtual (including via e-commerce).

The Diaspora, Politics and Governance in the Caribbean

The diaspora's impact has also been felt in the development of regional politics through the return of Caribbean nationals who studied mainly in the United Kingdom and have brought home with them ideas honed in their transnational locations. These people were to shape the independence debate, and later some occupied political office under self-rule and later independence, for example, Trinidad and Tobago's Eric Williams, Guyana's Forbes Burnham, Barbados's Errol Barrow and Jamaica's Michael Manley.

More recent efforts at political organization have seen more engagement via online platforms and radio talk shows, allowing for participation in local debates. Such engagement has allowed the diaspora to monitor regional governments and governance. Greater organization within the group has also seen some successful lobbying in the countries of residence to the benefit of the countries of origin. One prime example is the successful lobbying against the imposition of the UK travel tax (UK Air Passenger Duty) between 2009 and 2014 in the United Kingdom (see, for example, JIS 2009; *Jamaica Observer* 2014; Ransome 2014). While other interests (including UK-based travel groups) played a role here, the diaspora was instrumental in strengthening the Caribbean's voice in the United Kingdom. However, the members of the region's diaspora have not mobilized as effectively as other national diasporas, including the Irish and Israeli.[8]

The diaspora's role in resettlement and the consequences thereof are not to be discounted. Islands such as Grenada and St Kitts have seen annual labour migration rates of around 12 per cent of their total populations (Nurse 2004, 3). Related governance challenges here relate to the diminished capacity for effective human resource management, with fields such as teaching and nursing experiencing skills gap. Nevertheless, migration has helped to reduce unemployment (Palmer 1990, 9). This has been done tacitly and directly through initiatives such as the Canadian and US farm work programmes and the hotel work programme, which offer opportunities for overseas employment and higher wages. Migration here has helped to reduce social dislocation and tension, helping citizens towards levels of self-actualization not readily available to all in the Caribbean.

A sustained form of engagement may be seen in the indirect partnerships with governments in providing social and welfare services. Personal transfers have grown to become an important contributor to national income. They also fill the void in public-sector capacity, providing vital welfare goods and services to citizens. Sector-specific diaspora groups have also helped to strengthen capacity in critical sectors such as health and education via the provision of school and hospital supplies and equipment and the construction of hospitals and health clinics. According to the Jamaica Diaspora Institute, the diaspora may be credited with having established 132 health missions offering free health care in underserved communities in Jamaica.

Contributions towards disaster risk reduction, relief and management in response to natural disasters are also well known (Minto-Coy 2009a, 2011).

The diaspora has been able to tap into its networks and resources in their countries of origin to raise funds and other forms of contributions for assisting the region. Through such initiatives they have introduced efficiencies and helped modernize the region's practices and machinery. Indeed, for many who do not remit cash or who do not have families and communities with which they can readily associate (including those beyond the second and third generations), corporate and individual philanthropy offers a direct route to the maintenance of connections with the country of origin.

Challenges to Diasporas and Development in the Caribbean

Notwithstanding the positives highlighted, the Caribbean region has experienced some pernicious effects of migration. For the most part, the negative connotations of diaspora and migration have tended to be bound up in the notion of brain drain. Indeed, such acknowledgement is critical in any review of the diaspora option. For instance, the issue of brain drain remains, particularly given that nearly 80 per cent of the most educated and highly skilled have been lost from the region since independence (see Carrington and Detragiache 1999; Minto-Coy 2009a). The tendency towards preferential treatment of such groups in migration practices in countries such as Canada (via skilled migration programmes) has also contributed to this depletion. Further, and notwithstanding the value of remittances, it has also been suggested by Funkhouser (1992) that remittance recipients in countries such as Nicaragua tend to have lower rates of participation in the labour market than do non-recipients. While Funkhouser's study did not focus on the English-speaking Caribbean, the findings are nonetheless relevant given the implications for realizing the full impact of remittances directed towards more sustainable Caribbean economies.

Other challenges, such as trans-border crime and cross-border criminal networks (Minto-Coy 2009a, 15; Bagley 2014, 34) that benefit from increased ease in communication and organization, have also emerged. The existence of undocumented segments of the diaspora also means that some members of the diaspora are absent from formal regimes. This has negative implications for their ability to improve their prospects in their countries of residence, as well as for country of origin–based governments to design policies around the group and to offer assistance and protections. Even with increased opportunities for exporting to and by the diaspora, existing challenges to businesses within the region as well as the absence of supportive policies from host-country governments (Morrison 2006) complicate the ability of the diaspora and country of origin–based businesses to access these markets, e-commerce notwithstanding.[9]

A low level of trust in governments in the region also inhibits the extent to which the diaspora is willing to engage with governments and increase their activities beyond their families and communities. Other challenges relate to the investment climate and specifically to the insufficient advice and support for diaspora investors in some countries. Critical too has been the absence of institutional support and mechanisms to facilitate the diaspora's engagement at home with issues such as voting rights.

Furthering the Diaspora Option in the Caribbean

Many of the initiatives just discussed have evolved organically (without much government intervention), with the private sector and the non-governmental organization community featured prominently in facilitating diasporic engagement in the Caribbean. The diaspora has also made direct overtures to regional governments, demonstrating their desire to engage even in the absence of formal routes to engagement.

Formal government involvement has come largely in response to the developments covered earlier. The continuing search for much-needed support for regional development has been a catalyst for the increased interest at the policy level in the support and funding of bodies such as the International Organization for Migration. Mainly since the late 1990s, Caribbean governments have become more interested in engaging their diasporas for development, addressing their absence from this space.

Developments from the point of view of regional governments include the introduction of a number of institutions, ranging from government bodies and diaspora conferences to special diaspora events and attempts to organize the diverse groups within the diaspora into an overall governance framework which links back to the country of origin governments (see Minto-Coy 2016a for a description of many such measures). This has had varying effects, including some frustration that what was a private grassroots movement is now being captured by government. The challenge remains in achieving a balance between government (country of origin and country of residence) involvement and the diaspora's private ownership of their activities and desires with the concern of organizing and engaging with government on a sustained basis. Nonetheless, clearer lines of communication are opening up to the diaspora. Important, too, are the opportunities afforded by way of the dual citizenship which has been extended to members of the diaspora, including, tax exemptions and opportunities to invest locally. However, many of the rights of citizenship and how to access these are still not known by many in the diaspora.

Among the most significant opportunities, however, is the development of specific policies aiming to mainstream diasporas into national development. Action at this level is important in formalizing engagement as well as making the diaspora a permanent focus beyond a change in the political administration of a country. For example, the governments of Guyana and Trinidad and Tobago are moving towards the formulation of diaspora policies, while Dominica's were passed in 2010. Jamaica is the first in the region to draft both a national migration and a diaspora policy, the latter specifically noting the intent to mainstream the diaspora in national affairs. Such policies aim to provide the institutional and policy framework for engagement, forming a synergy between the developmental goals of the country and the diaspora's involvement. Haiti is one of the regional pioneers in that it first introduced a special government arm for the diaspora in 1994. Policies and governments have an important role to play as enablers, facilitating inclusion and the building of partnerships and acting as catalysts in stimulating engagement at all levels and among all stakeholders.

There has also been a focus on mapping the diaspora. Such efforts involve the gathering of information to facilitate greater knowledge and information on national or regional diasporas, with attention given to areas such as their interests, skills, sizes and locations. The undercurrent to such efforts is the desire to secure greater information to assist the country of origin in designing more specific policies and strategies for involving the diaspora in development. Guyana and Jamaica have attempted to map their diasporas, but the success of such efforts remains largely unknown. Indeed, the suggestion is that these efforts have not borne much fruit, with many of the fears among the diaspora (for example, those related to privacy and security and lack of trust of government) limiting responsiveness among the members of the diaspora.

Despite the efforts of governments, there are concerns that insufficient levels of support are still being offered to the diasporas where they are, including labour protections and means of securing their rights in the country of residence. Even acknowledging the limits to small island governments' exercising power or offering similar support as the Irish, for example, deepening engagement may mean that Caribbean governments will have to make more of an effort toward lobbying for its diaspora. This will include measures for reaching youths, those beyond the second and third generations and those who migrate to study in order to engender emotional and psychological attachment to sustain their engagement.

Efforts by private-sector firms in the diasporic economy, including the Jamaica National Building Society and GraceKennedy Limited, provide examples of what can be achieved and how. For example, GraceKennedy's Birthright Programme provides internships for persons of Jamaican heritage living in Canada, the United Kingdom and the United States.[10] These also suggest the need for more diverse forms of engagement seeking to utilize the diverse resources of the group.

Conclusion

The chapter has focused on the diaspora option in the Caribbean context, underscoring the value of this transnational actor to the region's future development, as well as some challenges to this end. An attempt has also been made to discuss the concept of the diaspora option and international experiences as a means of situating the region's experiences within a wider context. In so doing, the relevance of the Caribbean experience globally and the implications beyond the region are also clear, certainly insofar as there is some similarity in the issues and arguments for engaging diasporas with more countries looking to this group for development resources. As noted, the experiences of Caribbean countries such as Jamaica are already under review by others, even as the region has benefited from the experiences of others. As a small space, the Caribbean also offers a microcosm of global experiences demonstrating the possibilities, even though there may be some peculiarities in its experiences.

Certainly the coverage has also been selective, given the breadth of issues that could be considered in such a discussion. For instance, voting rights and the potential conflict between the home-based population and the diaspora have barely been reviewed. The presentation given here is not meant to minimize the importance of these and other issues. Additionally, while growing attention is being placed on diasporas and their role in development, a challenge remains in definitively tying any country's development solely to its diaspora.

There is a need for more investigations and research that verify the precise contribution of this group to states globally. This includes the need for more sophisticated statistical analyses in the emerging field of diaspora studies, which seeks to quantify much of the diaspora's contribution. This may be a very complex task, given the hidden and informal nature of a significant portion of the diaspora's engagement. The very nature of the engagement (largely private, bottom-up and multilayered) has a role to play here. The tangible evidence of the diaspora's contribution, as seen in the ratio of remittances to gross domestic product and other economic indicators, suggests the significance of its contribution, whether in terms of direct funds to government or not. The concept of diaspora economy offers a means of mapping the contribution, but this concept or tool also has its limitations.

Overall, the presentation here suggests that the Caribbean region has benefited tremendously from its diaspora and in diverse ways. Considering the noted challenges, much of the developments across the region over the past decades have helped to move the focus to the "brain chain" and possible ways the region could benefit from brain gain. Much support and direction are still needed towards actually scaling up the positive aspects of engagement detailed here while minimizing the negatives. This speaks not only to supportive policies at the level of governments, a safe investment climate and more strategic engagement towards regional growth and development but also strategies towards assisting the members of the diaspora to become more active and successful in their countries of residence. The latter may be taken as counterintuitive, but a strong and successful Caribbean diaspora is a strong a successful Caribbean.

Notes

1. For instance, in 2015 the Government of Jamaica hosted a study tour for top officials from the Government of Moldova who wanted to learn from the Jamaican experience in diaspora policy development and engagement more generally.
2. Thanks to participants in the Diaspora Business: The Diaspora and Business Project First Global Meeting held 15–16 July 2015 in the United Kingdom.
3. The extent to which this was political versus economic motivation may still be debated, given the fears over possible appropriation of wealth as opposed to political persecution.

4. This figure includes Cuba, the Dominican Republic and Haiti as well as the English-speaking region.
5. The diaspora's role in overcoming challenges addressed in traditional business and marketing literature, including the liabilities of foreignness and brand cross over have already been noted (e.g., Minto-Coy 2016b).
6. See Laparkan's company profile (n.d.).
7. Much of the material in this section is informed by Minto-Coy (2011).
8. An exception outside of the Commonwealth Caribbean may be Cuba. More recently, the increasing size of the Haitian diaspora in the southern United States has also accompanied that diaspora's increased visibility in political representation in that country and increased lobbying for Haiti.
9. Of course one could question the extent to which a host government has a responsibility for securing opportunities for its migrant entrepreneurship and business in this way. However, as the diaspora option resonates for countries of origin, there also exist opportunities for accessing the talents and skills of diasporas by country of residence governments in much the same way as members of the Chinese diaspora have helped to broker businesses opportunities for US-based firms in China and elsewhere (e.g., see *Economist* 2011).
10. See the GraceKennedy Birthright Programme, available at: https://www.thecaribbeancurrent.com/gracekennedy-jamaican-birthright-programme-2017/.

References

Adams, R., and J. Page. 2003. International Migration, Remittances and the Brain Drain: A Study of 24 Labour-Exporting Countries. *Policy Research Working Paper 3179*. Washington, DC: World Bank.

Agunias, D.R., and K. Newland. 2012. *Developing a Road Map for Engaging Diasporas in Development: A Handbook for Policymakers and Practitioners in Home and Host Countries*. Geneva and Washington: International Organization for Migration and Migration Policy Institute.

Bagley, Bruce. 2014. Globalisation and Latin American and Caribbean Organised Crime. In *Global Crime Today: The Changing Face of Organised Crime*, edited by Mark Galeotti, 32–53. New York: Routledge.

Bank of Jamaica. 2016. *The Balance of Payments: Remittance Report December 2015*. Kingston, Jamaica: Bank of Jamaica. http://boj.org.jm/uploads/pdf/rem_updates/rem_updates_dec2015.pdf.

Baser, Bahar. 2016. *Diasporas and Homeland Conflicts: A Comparative Perspective*. New York: Routledge.

Bauböck, R., and T. Faist. 2010. *Diaspora and Transnationalism: Concepts, Theories and Methods*. Amsterdam: Amsterdam University Press/IMISCOE.

Brinkerhoff, J.M. 2008. Diasporas and Development: What Role for Foreign Aid? In *Foreign Aid and Foreign Policy*, edited by Louis A. Picard et al., 375–93. New York: M.E. Sharpe.

Buckley, P.J., J. Clegg, A.R. Cross, X. Liu, H. Voss, and P. Zheng. 2010. The Determinants of Chinese Outward Foreign Direct Investment. In *Foreign Direct Investment, China and the World Economy*, edited by P.J. Buckley, 81–118. Basingstoke: Palgrave Macmillan.

Burnham, J. 2003. Why Ireland Boomed. *Independent Review: A Journal of Political Economy* 7 (4): 537–56.

Carrington, W.J., and D.E. Detragiache. 1999. How Extensive Is the Brain Drain? *Finance and Development* 36 (2). http://www.imf.org/external/pubs/ft/fandd/1999/06/carringt.htm.

Cassells, E.D. 2007. Matching Desire with Capacity. Paper presented at the Caribbean Diaspora and Regional Development Conference, Conference on the Caribbean: A 20/20 Vision. Washington, DC, 19–21 June.

Chander, A. 2001. Diaspora Bonds. *New York University Law Review* 76:1005–99.

Chikanda, A., J. Crush and M. Walton-Roberts, eds. 2016. *Diasporas, Development and Governance*. New York: Springer.

Cohen, R. 1998. Cultural Diaspora: The Caribbean Case. In *Caribbean Migration: Globalised Identities*, edited by Mary Chamberlain, 21–35. London: Routledge.

———. 2008. *Global Diasporas: An Introduction*. London: Routledge.

Coogan, Tim Pat. 2000. *Wherever Green Is Worn: The Story of the Irish Diaspora*. 1st edition. London: Hutchinson.

Dade, C., and P. Unheim. 2007. Diasporas and Private Sector Development: Impacts and Opportunities. FOCAL. http://www.focal.ca/pdf/diaspora_DadeUnheim_diasporas%20private%20sector%20development%20impacts%20opportunities_April%202007.pdfV.

Economist. 2011. The Magic of Diasporas: Immigrant Networks Are a Rare Bright Spark in the World Economy. 19 November 2011. http://www.economist.com/node/21538742

Foner, N. 1998. Towards a Comparative Perspective on Caribbean Migration. In *Caribbean Migration: Globalised Identities*, edited by Mary Chamberlain, 47–60. New York: Routledge.

Freinkman, L. 2001. Role of the Diaspora in Transition Economies: Lessons from Armenia. Paper presented at the 11th Annual Meeting of the Association for the Study of the Cuban Economy. Coral Gables, FL, 2–4 August. Available at: http://lanic.utexas.edu/project/asce/pdfs/ volume11/freinkman.pdf.

Funhouser, Edward. 1992. Migration from Nicaragua: Some Recent Evidence. *World Development* 20 (8): 1209–18.

Greenidge, C. 2007. ICTs, Caribbean Diaspora and Knowledge Mobility Management: Networking the Caribbean Economy. Paper presented at the Conference on the Caribbean, Washington, DC, 19–21 June.

Haitao, J. 2015. New Indian Migrants in Guangzhou and Its Vicinity. In *Indian and Chinese Immigrant Communities: Comparative Perspectives*, edited by J. Bhttacharya and C. Kripalani, 197–218. London: Institute of Southeast Asian Studies/Anthem Press.

IOM (International Organization for Migration). 2012. *Migration in Jamaica: A Country Profile 2010*. Geneva: IOM http://mfaft.gov.jm/jm/images/IOM-MigrationinJamaica2010_FINAL_311012.pdf.

Ionescu, D. 2006. *Engaging Diasporas as Development Partners for Home and Destination Countries: Challenges for Policymakers.* Geneva: International Organization for Migration.

JIS (Jamaica Information Service). 2009. UK Jamaicans Urged to Lobby Against Proposed Travel Tax. Jamaica Information Service. 18 March. Available at: jis.gov.jm/uk-jamaicans-urged-to-lobby-against-proposed-travel-tax/.

Jamaica Observer. 2014. Jamaica, Caribbean Welcome UK Air Passenger Duty Reforms. 19 March. www.jamaicaobserver.com/news/Jamaica-Caribbean-welcome-UK-Air-Passenger-Duty-reforms.

Kutznetsov, Y., and C. Sabel. 2006. International Migration of Talent, Diaspora Networks, and Development: Overview of Main Issues. *Diaspora Networks and the International Migration of Skills: How Countries Can Draw on Their Talent Abroad.* Washington: IBRD/WB, 3–21.

Laparkan. N.d. Company Profile. www.laparkan.com/index.php?option=com_content&view=article&id=89&Itemid=149. Accessed 19 April 2016.

Lapointe, Michelle. 2004. *Diasporas in Caribbean Development.* Report delivered at the Inter-American Dialogue and World Bank for The Caribbean Diaspora as a Development Agent Workshop, Washington, DC, 14 April.

Lowell, L., and S. Gerova. 2004. *Diasporas and Economic Development: State of Knowledge.* Washington, DC: World Bank and Georgetown University, Institute for the Study of International Migration. http://siteresources.worldbank.org/INTPROSPECTS/Resources/334934-1322593305595/8287139-1327608098427/LowellDiaspora.pdf.

Luginaah, I. and R.B. Kerr. 2016. *Geographies of Health and Development.* Surrey, England: Ashgate.

McCabe, K. 2011. *Caribbean Immigrants in the United States.* Washington, DC: Migration Policy Institute. www.migrationpolicy.org/article/caribbean-immigrants-united-states/.

McNeill, W., and R. Adams. 1978. *Human Migration: Patterns and Policies.* Bloomington: Indiana University Press.

Mercer, C., B. Page and M. Evans. 2008. *Development and the African Diaspora: Place and the Politics of Home.* London: Zed.

Meyer, Jean-Baptiste. 2003. Policy Implications of the Brain Drain's Changing Face. *Science and Development Network Policy Briefs* (London), May 2003.

Meyer, Jean-Baptiste, and M. Brown. 1999. Scientific Diasporas: A New Approach to the Brain Drain. Discussion Paper presented at UNESCO-ICSU at the World Conference on Science, Budapest, 26 June–1 July.

Minto-Coy, Indianna D. 2009a. Diasporas and Development: The Case of Ireland and the Caribbean. Caribbean Paper No. 7. Centre for International Governance Innovation, Waterloo, Canada, April.

———. 2010. The Impact of the Global Financial Crisis on Remittancing. In *What Others Manifest? The World Economy in the Theoretical Turbulence of the Global Financial Crisis,* edited by I. Günaydın and E. Yayla, 2–18. Gümüşhane, Turkey: Gümüşhane University Press.

———. 2011. Beyond Remittancing: An Investigation of the Role of Telecoms in

Facilitating and Extending the Diaspora's Contribution to the Caribbean. *Canadian Foreign Policy Journal* 17 (2): 129–41.

———. 2013. Draft Jamaica Diaspora Policy Paper. Prepared for the Government of Jamaica to guide the production of the national diaspora policy.

———. 2016a. Diaspora Engagement for Development in the Caribbean. In *Diasporas, Development and Governance in the Global South*, edited by A. Abel Chikanda, J. Crush and M. Walton-Roberts, 121–39. New York: Springer.

———. 2016b. The History of Public Administration in the Commonwealth Caribbean. In *Public Administration and Policy in the Caribbean*, edited by I. Minto-Coy and E. Berman, 33–60. Boca Raton, FL: CRC.

———. 2016c. The Role of Diasporas in the Growth and Internationalisation of Businesses in Countries of Origin. In *Diaspora Business*, edited by E. Maria and L. Riddle. Oxford, UK: Inter-disciplinary.Net.

Morrison, Dennis. 2006. Growing Economic Dependence on Diaspora. 25 June, http://www.Diaspora.org.jm/content/home/StaticPages/Conf2006/growingeconomicdependence.asp.

Moss-Solomon, J. 2012. *Jamaica and GraceKennedy: Dreams Converging, Roads Diverging.* GraceKennedy Foundation Lecture. Kingston: GraceKennedy and Company Limited.

Newland, K., and R. Patrick. 2004. *Beyond Remittances: The Role of Diaspora in Poverty Reduction in Their Countries of Origin.* Washington, DC: Migration Policy Institute.

Newland, K., and H. Tanaka. 2010. *Mobilizing Diaspora Entrepreneurship for Development.* Washington, DC: Migration Policy Institute.

Nurse, K. 2004. Diaspora, Migration and Development in the Caribbean. FOCAL Policy Paper FPP-04-6. Canadian Foundation for the Americas, Ottawa.

Orozco, M. 2003. The Impact of Migration in the Caribbean and Central American Region. Focal Policy Paper FPP-03-03. Canadian Foundation for the America, Ottawa.

Orozco, M., and K. Welle. 2005. Hometown Associations and Development: A Look at Ownership, Sustainability, Correspondence, and Replicability. Inter-American Development Bank, New York. http://idbdocs.iadb.org/wsdocs/getdocument.aspx?docnum=561678.

Palmer, R. 1990. Caribbean Development and the Migration Imperative. In *Search of a Better Life: Perspectives on Migration from the Caribbean*, edited by R. Palmer, 121–39. New York: Praeger.

———. 2007. Contemporary Caribbean Migration to the United States. *Conference on the Caribbean: A 20/20 Vision*, Washington, DC, 19–21 June.

Plaza, S., and D. Ratha. 2011. *Diasporas for Development in Africa.* Washington, DC: World Bank.

Quayson, A., and G. Daswani. 2013. *A Companion to Diaspora and Transnationalism.* Hoboken, NJ: Wiley-Blackwell.

Rafael, B., and Y. Sternberg. 2009. *Transnationalism: Diasporas and the Advent of a New (Dis)order.* Boston: Brill, 2009.

Ransome, D. 2014. APD: A Lobby Victory for the Caribbean. *Caribbean Intelligence*. www.caribbeanintelligence.com/content/apd-lobby-victory-caribbean.

Rampersad, I. 2007. Crime as an Obstacle to Diaspora Investment. Conference on the Caribbean: A 20/20 Vision. Washington, DC, 19–21 June.

Ratha, D. 2005. Workers' Remittances: An Important and Stable Source of External Development Finance. Paper No. 9, Global Development Finance Economics Seminar Series. World Bank, New York. http://siteresources.worldbank.org/INTRGDF/Resources/GDF2003-Chapter7.pdf.

Reis, M. 2007. Vision 2020: The Role of Migration in Trinidad and Tobago's Plan for Overall Development. Paper presented at the Sir Arthur Lewis Institute of Social and Economic Studies at the 8th Annual Conference, Crisis, Chaos and Change: Caribbean Development Challenges in the 21st Century, St Augustine, Trinidad and Tobago, 26–28 March. https://sta.uwi.edu/conferences/salises/documents/Reis%20%20M.pdf.

Richardson, Bonham C. 1983. *Caribbean Migrants: Environment and Human Survival on Saint Kitts and Nevis*. Knoxville: University of Tennessee Press.

Sahoo, S., and B.K. Pattanaik. 2013. *Global Diasporas and Development: Socio-Economic, Cultural and Policy Perspectives*. New Delhi: Springer.

Saxenian, A. 1999. The Bangalore Boom: From Brain Drain to Brain Circulation? In *Bridging the Digital Divide: Lessons from India*, edited by K. Kenniston and D. Kumar, 169–81. Bangalore: National Institute of Advanced Study.

———. 2002. Transnational Communities and the Evolution of Global Production Networks: The Cases of Taiwan, India and China. *Industry and Innovation* 9(3): 183–202.

———. 2003. Brain Circulation and Capitalist Dynamics: The Silicon Valley-Hsinchu-Shanghai Triangle. CSES Working Paper No. 8, Centre for Economy and Society, Cornell University.

Séguin, B., P.A. Singer and A.S. Daar. 2006. Scientific Diasporas. *Science* 312 (5780): 1602–3.

Sheffer, G. 2003. *Diaspora Politics: At Home Abroad*. Cambridge: Cambridge University Press.

Tan, Tai Yong, and Md Mizanur Rahman. 2013. *Diaspora Engagement and Development in South Asia*. Basingstoke, Hampshire: Palgrave Macmillan.

Thouez, C. 2005. The Impact of Remittances on Development: International Migration and the Millennium Development Goals. Selected Papers of the UNFPA Expert Group Meeting, Marrakesh, Morocco, 11–12 May.

Vertovec, Stephen. 2009. *Transnationalism*. London: Routledge.

World Bank. 2013. *Unlocking the Economic Potential of the Caribbean Diaspora*. Washington, DC: World Bank.

Ying, Neville, and Melesha Manderson. 2013. *Quantifying Diaspora Healthcare and Education Contributions to Jamaica: Research Project Preliminary Report*. Kingston: Jamaica Diaspora Institute.

Part 3

Globalization and Special Challenges

CHAPTER 9

New Dimensions of Regionalism in the Caribbean: An Analysis of the Shanique Myrie Case

Wendy C. Grenade

This chapter explores new dimensions of regionalism in the Global South using the case of CARICOM.[1] It concentrates on the 2013 judgement of the Caribbean Court of Justice (CCJ) in the case of *Shanique Myrie and the Government of Jamaica versus the Government of Barbados* [2013] CCJ 3 (OJ). The case exposes the contradictions of regionalism, the paradoxes of sovereignty and the unequal gender relations which characterize Caribbean societies. The central question is, how can the *Shanique Myrie* case advance a more nuanced understanding of regionalism in the Caribbean? This chapter consists of four parts. Following the introduction, the first section provides theoretical insights to frame the discussion. The next section presents a brief overview of CARICOM. The third analyses the *Myrie* case and the implications for the study of Caribbean regionalism. The final section offers conclusions.

Theoretical Insights

Regionalism is a pervasive force in global affairs that challenges the traditional centrality of states in the study of international relations.[2] There is no universal definition of regionalism. During the 1950s, functionalist and neofunctionalist scholars explained the early stages of European integration citing the importance of supranational institutions (Haas 1958). As European integration experienced turbulence in the 1960s and 1970s, regional integration studies was influenced by realism, which focused on the centrality of the sovereign state and its national interests (Hoffman 1966; Schmitter 1970). Haas reflected on his earlier works and argued that the effort to cope with turbulence was unlikely to lead to any final set of regional institutions (Haas 1976). For such scholars, no one grand theory could explain the messiness of regionalism.

Early studies also focused on economic integration, which is central to the study of regionalism. Drawing on the work of Viner (1950), trade economists concentrated on preferential trading agreements, which were categorized as free trade agreements, customs unions, common markets, and economic and monetary unions. The debate focused, in part, on whether regional trade blocs were trade-creating or trade-diverting and whether they were stepping stones or stumbling blocks to global trade (Bhagwati and Panagariya 1996; Krueger 1999). However, by narrowly focusing on markets, economic theories often overlook the institutional arrangements, common rules, policies and cultural norms that govern regional economic spaces. For developmental scholars, regionalism was and still is viewed as a means to achieve development (Brewster and Thomas 1967; Demas 1976; Axline 1977; Girvan 2008).

The end of the Cold War coincided with the intensification of globalization and trade liberalization and a new wave of regionalization. For post-colonial societies, traditional issues and actors converged with new ones to shape a complex world. Within this maze, transnational forces, cross-border movements and intermestic issues are intertwined. Increasingly, sovereign states are finding it difficult to cope, on their own, with prevailing and new insecurities, whether climate change, the global illicit drug trade, communicable diseases, financial contagion or terrorism. Global governance institutions such as the International Monetary Fund, the World Bank and the World Trade Organization are becoming more intrusive and are further eroding the autonomy of sovereign states, particularly small, relatively weak, dependent states. Therefore, regionalization often provides a collective platform from which small developing states can navigate globalization.

Beyond traditional discourses, open regionalism (Bergsten 1997), alternative regionalism (Keet 2007), comparative regionalisms (Laursen 2010; Fanta, Shaw and Tang 2013; Knight, Castro-Ra and Ghany 2014) and "New Regionalism" (Hettne and Söderbaum 2000; Hettne 2005) are central to debates on regionalism. New Regionalism refers to a situation in which "state, market, civil society and external actors often come together in a variety of mixed-actor collectivities, networks and modes of regional governance" (Söderbaum and

Shaw 2003, cited in Hettne 2005, 555). Development and security regionalism are core concepts of New Regionalism. These are pertinent to regionalisms in the global south.

It is necessary to note that the European Union is the most advanced regional integration scheme in the world. McCormick (2014) provides a concise introduction to the workings of the European Union. However, since the recent eurozone crisis, many scholars have critiqued European integration and have questioned its viability (see, for example, Bootle 2014 and Majone 2014). Importantly, on 23 June 2016, some 52 per cent of British citizens voted in a referendum to leave the European Union, while 48 per cent voted to remain. This is a watershed moment in world politics and has far-reaching implications for the United Kingdom, the European Union and the rest of the world. The United Kingdom's proposed exit from the European Union brings to the fore contradictions of regionalism, paradoxes of democracy and the contentious issue of sovereignty.

In the study of international relations, "the concept of 'sovereignty' is usually taken to mean that a nation state has power and control over its own future. A loss of sovereignty implies a loss of legal and actual control over the determination of the direction of national policy" (Held 1990, 407, cited in Rudolph 2005, 3). However, as globalization intensified, the concept of sovereignty became fiercely debated (Barrow-Giles 2003; Harvey 2005; Agnew 2009; Krasner 2009; Bishop and Payne 2010; Joseph 2011). As Premdas observes, "New actors have proliferated in the international arena of the contemporary international system, some affirming the jurisdiction of state sovereignty, others undermining it" (2002, 50). Rudolph (2005) contends that "patterns of trade and capital flows provide a strong argument that the global economy readily transcends national boundaries. In contrast, other scholars observe that the globalization of migration flows has served to increase the importance of territoriality as a central component of sovereignty and as an ordering principle in world politics (Albert, Jacobson and Lapid 2001, cited in Rudolph 2005, 2). Krasner (2009) argues that Westminster is compromised given "sovereignty bargains and trade-offs". However, Watson (2013) maintains that it is necessary to rethink the sovereignty paradigm away from the state-centric framework.

Given global uncertainty, shrinking state resources and security dilemmas, governments are forced to engage in deeper multilateralism and regionalism. This is reinforced by legal treaties that are ratified by sovereign states and adjudicated by regional or international courts that are established by states.

However, as states become more embedded in systems of global and regional governance, territoriality and autonomy are compromised, bringing to the fore the perennial tension between regionalism and nationalism.

The tension between regionalism and nationalism is not new. However, it is compounded in the context of a gendered capitalist world economy. The duality of capitalism and patriarchy perpetuate the subjugation of many working-class women and men. In a related way, neoliberal state policies, which aim to create fiscal balances, sustain macroeconomic stability and spur growth, can erode social safety nets, generate citizen insecurities, undermine environmental and social sustainability and compound unequal gender relations. Additionally, the multiple jeopardies of gender, class and race often give rise to the feminization of poverty and the ensuing outward migratory flows, which have implications for development.

The Caribbean's political economy is gendered (Barriteau 2002), as manifested in the gendered division of labour (Reddock 1994). Gender norms are also at the core of multiple forms of violence against women (DeShong 2015; DeShong and Haynes 2016). Kempadoo, for example, has written extensively on tourism and sex work (1999); on gender, race and sexual labour (2004); and, with Sanghera and Pattanaik, on trafficking and prostitution (2012). Gender stereotypes often lead to injustices at ports of entry as women, in particular, search for economic security in their daily lives.

Given the issues just mentioned, the following section examines CARICOM to throw light on the complexity of regionalism in the twenty-first century.

The Caribbean Community: Assessing the Record

The Caribbean has had a long history of regional integration (O'Brien 2011). CARICOM was established by the signing of the Treaty of Chaguaramas in 1973. It is, for the most part, an intergovernmental community of independent sovereign states. CARICOM's main pillars are functional cooperation, foreign policy coordination, economic integration and security.

A critical assessment of CARICOM presents a mixed scorecard. CARICOM has achieved relative successes in the realm of functional cooperation, particularly in the areas of health, education, disaster management and security (Thomas 2008). Several CARICOM institutions and associate institutions have created a regional institutional framework to address some of the developmental challenges that confront the region. In fact, functional cooperation has evolved as the catalyst of Caribbean integration. It is both a means to deepen regional integration and a tangible outcome of the regional integration process. Based on research, it can be observed that functional cooperation has advanced social development in the region. Yet, despite the collective gains in the social realm, "functional cooperation has been awarded little prominence given the (over)emphasis on economic integration as the basis for regional development" (Grenade and Skeete 2012, 50).

In the realm of foreign policy coordination, CARICOM countries have "punched above their weight". In several instances, they have used their numeric advantage and collective exercise of sovereignty to advance their individual and collective interests in the international community (see Ramphal 2012). They have forged strategic partnerships and alliances to increase their bargaining power, enhance their voice and reach in the international system, build solidarity, facilitate access to markets and promote a sense of collective identity for the Caribbean in the world. Caribbean countries have championed issues that are critical to small states, particularly in the United Nations and in the Commonwealth (Ramphal 2008). Yet, despite the collective gains that can be realized, foreign policy coordination does not negate national interests and the bilateral relations that ensue. In several instances, CARICOM states have failed to coordinate their foreign policies. A glaring instance is in their relations with China and Taiwan (Grenade 2013). In fact, a major development within the Caribbean is the emergence of overlapping memberships in regional groupings such as UNASUR, the Union of South American States, and in the Bolivarian Alternative for the Americas (Girvan 2011). In essence, CARICOM has had mixed outcomes in the area of foreign policy coordination (see Braveboy-Wagner 2008).

In response to an interwoven maze of insecurities, in 2008 the Conference of Heads of Government of CARICOM agreed that security should be recognized as the fourth pillar of the community, given its ever-increasing importance to the community and its crosscutting and fundamental nature. Thus, a CARICOM Crime and Security architecture has been established, and security cooperation is high on CARICOM's agenda (see works on Caribbean security by Griffith [2004] and Grenade [2012]).

One of the defining features of CARICOM in the twenty-first century is the Revised Treaty of Chaguaramas (2001). The Revised Treaty of Chaguaramas is the instrument that governs the CARICOM Single Market and Economy (CSME), which was established in 2006. The CSME was envisioned to provide full employment; completely utilize all factors of production, inclusive of natural resources; and improve the standards of work and living across the region. The main goal of the CSME is to integrate the economies of CARICOM into a unified market in which people, goods, services and capital move freely and into a single economy that functions under the same harmonized economic policies (CARICOM 2001). Importantly, there is a growing body of literature on the CSME (Brewster 2003; Hosein and Thomas 2007; Girvan 2008; Gilbert 2013; Kaczorowska-Ireland 2015; Mohammed 2008; Nelson 2007). As the literature shows, economic integration is as necessary as it is problematic. Some of the negative ramifications include the simultaneous formation of poles of growth and poles of stagnation; perceived "winners" and "losers"; and tensions between state-market imperatives and citizenship rights. Consequently, effective regional governance is critical.

Regional Governance

Regional governance is the overarching collectivity of institutions, rules and norms, underpinned by a body of law, that legitimizes countries' voluntary participation as regional actors in a particular historical, political-legal, socio-economic and cultural context. Regional governance is one dimension of multilevel governance. It is distinct from, yet intricately linked to, global and national systems of governance.

One of the weaknesses in CARICOM's approach to integration is its attempt to use an intergovernmental framework while seeking to deepen economic integration through the CSME. This "half-way house" approach creates an implementation deficit that slows down the pace of integration. A report of the West Indian Commission stressed that CARICOM suffered from "an implementation paralysis" which was viewed as "a chronic CARICOM deficiency" (West Indian Commission 1992, 54).

In 2003, through the Rose Hall Declaration, the CARICOM Heads agreed to establish a CARICOM Commission or other executive mechanism to address deficiencies in regional governance. Subsequently, a Prime Ministerial Expert Group on Governance was set up to formulate recommendations for the operationalization of the commission. However, to date, member states have found it difficult to arrive at a consensus on a suitable structure for regional governance. In his analysis of the Rose Hall Declaration, Brewster argued, "It is rare, perhaps unknown, for states forming a Community to begin by affirming their national sovereignty, and that regional integration will proceed in that political and juridical context" (Brewster 2007, 48). Brewster (2007, 47) further observed that "the CARICOM nation-states thus find themselves in the ambivalent situation of being, at one and the same time, the guardians of national sovereignty and the (unwilling) promoters of supranationalism". This dilemma has stymied the process of Caribbean integration.

The Caribbean Court of Justice

The idea of a final indigenous court for the anglophone Caribbean had its genesis as long ago as 1947, at the meeting of colonial governors in Barbados which reflected on the need for a West Indian Court and urged its establishment (Rawlins 2000, 5). As Caribbean integration evolved, in 1998 the Heads of Government adopted, in principle, the Agreement Establishing the Caribbean Supreme Court under the new appellation of the Caribbean Court of Justice (CCJ) with two jurisdictions: an appellate jurisdiction and an original jurisdiction. In the exercise of its appellate jurisdiction, the CCJ considers and determines appeals in both civil and criminal matters from common law courts within the jurisdictions of member states of the community, which are parties to the Agreement Establishing the CCJ. Given the adversarial political culture within member states, a major challenge that faces the CCJ in its appellate jurisdiction is the need to gain parliamentary approval in member states. To date only Barbados, Belize, Dominica and Guyana are members of the CCJ in its appellate jurisdiction.

In the exercise of its original jurisdiction, the CCJ discharges the functions of an international tribunal applying rules of international law with respect to the interpretation and application of the Revised Treaty of Chaguaramas. In this regard, the CCJ performs functions like those of the European Court of Justice, the European Court of First Instance, the Andean Court of Justice and the International Court of Justice. In its original jurisdiction, the CCJ can hear disputes between member states, disputes between member states and the community, referrals from national courts or tribunals of member states and applications by individuals with the special leave of the court. Pollard (2007a,

193) outlines three significant functions of the CCJ in its original jurisdiction: ensuring uniformity in the interpretation and application of the Treaty; determining *Locus standi* for both public and private entities in matters of which the Court is seized; and developing community law pursuant to decisions taken within the CARICOM process (*stare decisis*). The role of the CCJ is critical for the effective functioning of the CSME. Pollard continues:

> In the absence of this institution to pronounce authoritatively and definitely on the rights and obligations of Member States of the Community and their nationals, rights may tend to become illusory and obligations vacuous. An integration regime compromising an association of sovereign States, requires an institution like the Caribbean Court of Justice to assist the justice sector in the delivery of services expected of the sector in any progressive, stable, national environment. (Pollard 2007b, 217)

The European experience suggests the significance of the European Court of Justice. For example, in 1963 in the case *Van Gen Loose* the court established the doctrine of direct effect in that EU nationals had the right to expect their governments to adhere to EU obligations. In the 1964 *Costa versus ENEL* case the court established the supremacy of community law. That is, if a domestic law contradicts an EU obligation, EU law prevails. The *Cassis de Dijon* case of 1979 greatly simplified completion of the single market by establishing the principle of mutual recognition. That is, a product made and sold legally in one member state cannot be barred from another. Such cases strengthened European jurisprudence and helped to consolidate the European Union. The following section discusses one of the significant rulings of the CCJ in its original jurisdiction.

Shanique Myrie and the Government of Jamaica vs the Government of Barbados [2013] CCJ 3 (OJ)

On 14 March 2011, a twenty-two-year-old female Jamaican citizen and CARICOM national, Shanique Myrie, entered Barbados and alleged that she was discriminated against because of her nationality, subjected to a body-cavity search, detained overnight in a cell, deported to Jamaica the following day and subjected to derogatory remarks by a Barbadian immigration officer. Myrie asked the CCJ to determine the minimum standard of treatment applicable to CARICOM nationals moving around the region (*Jamaica Gleaner* 2013).

As part of the process to deepen Caribbean integration, freedom of movement of CARICOM nationals is expressed as a goal in article 45 of the Revised Treaty of Chaguaramas. Salient to this case is the fact that, in 2007, the CARICOM Heads of Government agreed that all CARICOM nationals should be entitled to an automatic stay of six months upon arrival in order to enhance their sense that they belong to, and can move in, the Caribbean Community, subject to the rights of member states to refuse undesirable persons entry and to prevent persons from becoming charges on public funds. The conference noted the reservation entered by Antigua and Barbuda in this regard. The Government of Barbados argued that, first, the conference decision of 2007 was ineffective because it used the word "agreed" and not "decided". Second, the fact that Antigua and Barbuda entered a "reservation" rendered the decision ineffective since a decision is binding only if it is unanimous; and, third, section 240 of the Revised Treaty of Chaguaramas requires a conference decision to be domestically enacted before it becomes binding (CCJ 2013).

The CCJ declared that the decision of the Conference of the Heads of Government of CARICOM on the right of entry of CARICOM nationals to CARICOM member states for six months was legally binding on member states without the requirement that it be enacted into their domestic law. The court further held that a community national would be refused entry only if such national were "undesirable" or would become "a charge on public funds". In this context, undesirability refers to protection of public morals, maintenance of public order and safety and protection of life and health (CCJ 2013). The CCJ ruled that refusal on the basis of "undesirability" may be based on national law and on community law, with the proviso that where national law does not conform to the parameters laid down by community law, it will be the latter that ultimately must prevail (CCJ 2013). Myrie was awarded approximately J$3.6 million in pecuniary and non-pecuniary damages by the CCJ on 4 October 2013. The Government of Barbados has since complied with the CCJ's ruling, and Ms. Myrie has been paid (Singh 2014).

Without any claim to the notion of Barbadian exceptionalism, it is important to emphasize that traditionally, Barbados has been one of the most stable Caribbean economies (Downes 2001; Grenade and Lewis-Bynoe 2011). It is not surprising, therefore, that Barbados, along with Antigua and Barbuda and Trinidad and Tobago, is among the countries receiving the largest numbers of regional migrants (Wiltshire 2010). However, given the negative impact of the global financial and economic crisis which began in 2008, Barbados experienced a severe economic downturn (IMF 2014).

Responding to the *Myrie* case, Barbados's attorney general, the Honourable Adriel D. Brathwaite, was reported to have said that there were not enough structures in place to ensure that free movement works. He expressed concerns about the capacity to provide adequate housing and education for Barbadians and other CARICOM nationals. According to the *Jamaica Gleaner*, Brathwaite insisted that there was nothing "earth shattering" about the *Myrie* judgement and that Bridgetown had already made moves to retrain its border personnel in keeping with the CCJ ruling. He stressed that all member states must follow suit to make free movement a reality (*Jamaica Gleaner* 2013).

Implications of the Myrie Case

The *Myrie* case has several implications for regionalism. First, it contributes to Caribbean jurisprudence. Although Caribbean integration is treaty-based, the outcomes of integration were predominately influenced by political and economic imperatives. Joseph (2005) argues that one of the main reasons for the slow record of implementation of CARICOM decisions in the past has been too-heavy reliance on executive action as the main strategy of integration. For Joseph, under the new dispensation a greater role must be accorded the use of law as a medium of integration (Joseph 2005, 14). This case has laid the foundation for community law as a catalyst to boost integration.

Also significant regarding the CCJ's ruling is that the case has scope to address the deficiencies in regional governance and the implementation deficit within CARICOM. For Prime Minister Ralph Gonsalves, "The decision of the CCJ in the Myrie case effectively gave teeth to the RTC [Revised Treaty of Chaguaramas] and implemented, through the judicial channel, a significant plug to the implementation gap in CARICOM" (Gonsalves 2014, 25–26). For the late Norman Girvan (2013, 8),

> the recent ruling of the Caribbean Court of Justice in the Shanique Myrie case is a major development in rescuing the Caricom regional

> project. Not only does it give justice to an aggrieved Caricom citizen in her treatment by functionaries of another Caricom state, it also establishes minimum standards for unobstructed hassle-free travel with which all states are bound to comply; and it gives much greater legal force to decisions of the Caricom Conference of Heads of Government than hitherto been thought to obtain.

This is a new dimension of regional governance in the Caribbean.

The case also elucidates the nuances of gender and regionalism. I have argued elsewhere that in the context of the CSME, the free movement of skills of both men and women is critical to advance human resource capacity and promote economic security in the region. Yet the search for economic security can undermine other dimensions of security (Grenade 2012, 200). This is particularly important for Caribbean women, given the power differentials between women and men and the gendered nature of intraregional migration (see Thomas-Hope 2007). As Hinds-Harrison (2012) points out in relation to CARICOM trade relations, these issues are not gender-neutral. The case demonstrates that regional integration transcends disciplinary boundaries.

Additionally, discourses on regionalism have focused on states, institutions and markets and have missed the centrality of people. Despite successes in functional cooperation, mixed outcomes in foreign policy coordination and the promise of security cooperation, for the most part CARICOM is prime ministerial, paper-based, piecemeal and peopleless. Many observers have pointed to the disconnect between the community of Caribbean states and the community of Caribbean people. The West Indian Commission reported that the needs of Caribbean people are real and immediate: "Unemployment, poverty, deteriorating health services, severe shortcomings in education systems, a huge rise in crime, the new menace of the evil trade in narcotics, a serious lowering of standards of behaviour and discipline, the continued desperately disadvantaged state of most women bringing up children alone, were all scourges deeply disturbing West Indians through the Region" (West Indian Commission 1992, 23).

Two decades following the report of the West Indian Commission, the needs of Caribbean people are perhaps even more "real and immediate". Yet, at the time of the *Myrie* case, many observers lamented that CARICOM was on pause. According to Singh (2011), "Sick CARICOM" needed a dose of "people power". However, the court's action in *Myrie* seems to support the claim that the Caribbean was in the midst of one of its greatest experiments in citizenship in the post-independence era with the creation of the CCJ (Kamugisha and Trotz 2007). Importantly, the case has the potential to advance citizenship rights and enhance democracy within CARICOM. I maintain that integration is meaningless if it does not positively impact the lives of ordinary people as they live and move throughout the Caribbean community.

Finally, the case also illustrates the complex relationship between sovereignty and regional integration. As Pollard (2007b) reminds us, despite its misleading nomenclature of "Caribbean Community", the regional integration movement, from its very inception and up to the present time, remains an association of sovereign states. However, several scholars have questioned CARICOM's narrow conceptualization of sovereignty (Brewster 2003; Bishop and Payne 2010; Wiltshire 2010; Girvan 2011). The CCJ's ruling in the *Myrie* case seems to introduce a supranational dimension to Caribbean integration. The action taken by Myrie and the subsequent ruling by the CCJ creates space for rethinking about the role of the state in this new dispensation. However, a key question arises: If the CCJ is the construct of states, where does power lie? I am of the view that the CCJ's ruling in the *Myrie* case presents an opportunity for deep reflection on the relationship between regionalism and nationalism in the twenty-first century.

How will CARICOM member states respond going forward? While this case can inject new blood into CARICOM, there is cause for caution. Gonsalves contends that the case has captured the community's imagination and has bolstered the faith of the regional public in the possibilities of CARICOM (Gonsalves 2014, 6). However, he questions whether the "empire of Heads of Government and State" will strike back. According to Gonsalves, "CARICOM Heads will be more careful in crafting its decisions in the future". He argues that "only time will tell [b]ut . . . a new ball game is certainly on!" (Gonsalves 2014, 46).

Ironically, in 2004 during one of the parliamentary debates on whether Jamaica should accede to the CCJ, then-leader of the opposition Jamaica Labour Party, Edward Seaga, had warned that the CCJ was a disguise to bring political union through the back door (see Jones 2004). For Seaga, Jamaica's political destiny was not intertwined with the rest of the Caribbean. Reminiscent of the referendum on the West Indies Federation in 1961, the Jamaica Labour Party fiercely opposed Jamaica's membership in the CCJ. It is noteworthy that the

Government of Jamaica has recently established a CARICOM Review Commission to properly research and evaluate the situation before deciding Jamaica's future as part of the community. Importantly, the Brexit debates in the Caribbean bring into question the future of CARICOM.[3] I am of the view that while Britain may be able to recover from its ill-fated decision to leave the European Union, it is ill-advised for any CARICOM country to seek to individually navigate the global system.

Conclusion

The *Myrie* case draws attention to possibilities and contradictions. On the one hand, regionalism is an indispensable necessity to foster the overall well-being of Caribbean people and to enhance the region's bargaining power as it asserts its role in a complex world. The case has the potential to (re)engineer regional governance in the Caribbean through new dimensions of Caribbean jurisprudence. Yet the case also brings to the fore issues of sovereignty and national interests. The reality is, for small developing states, autonomy and viability are threatened in the context of neoliberal globalization. Regionalism thus acts as a buffer against global forces. However, with time, regional institutions take on a life of their own. This, in turn, can undermine state power as states seek to exercise authority over their territory, given an interplay of insecurities. Nevertheless, this case transcends stale discourses on state sovereignty and national security. It draws attention to the concerns of ordinary people who continue to search for freedom, dignity, security and gender justice in their daily lives.

Going forward, a broad-based approach is necessary that involves interdisciplinary research, public education and citizen engagement, and a reengineering of CARICOM to more directly meet the needs of the people of the region.

Notes

1. CARICOM is a regional arrangement which comprises fifteen states in the Caribbean Basin, which include the anglophone, French and Dutch Caribbean. They are Antigua and Barbuda, Barbados, Belize, the Commonwealth of the Bahamas, the Commonwealth of Dominica, the Federation of St Christopher and Nevis, Grenada, Guyana, Jamaica, Haiti, Montserrat, St Lucia, St Vincent and the Grenadines, Suriname and the Republic of Trinidad and Tobago. In this chapter I use "the Caribbean" and "CARICOM" interchangeably.

2. There is a distinct difference between regionalism as ideology and regionalization as a process. "Regional integration" is used interchangeably here with "regionalization".
3. Brexit has triggered a debate in the Caribbean. See "Why Not Have a Referendum on CARICOM Too", *Barbados Today*, 24 June 2016, available at www.barbadostoday.bb/2016/06/24/why-not-have-a-referendum-on-caricom-too/. See also "Could Brexit Lead to Jamexit from Caricom", *Jamaica Observer*, 25 June 2016; "Caricom Urged to Explore the Options to Counter Brexit's Effects", *Jamaica Observer*, 26 June 2016.

References

Agnew, J. 2009. *Globalization and Sovereignty*. Lanham, MD: Rowman and Littlefield.

Axline, W.A. 1977. Underdevelopment, Dependence and Integration: The Politics of Regionalism in the Third World. *International Organization* 31 (1): 83–105.

Barriteau, V.E. 2002. Women Entrepreneurs and Economic Marginality: Rethinking Caribbean Women's Economic Relations. In *Gendered Realities: Essays in Caribbean Feminist Thought*, edited by Patricia Mohammed 221–48. Kingston: University of the West Indies Press and Centre for Gender and Development Studies.

Barrow-Giles, C. 2003. Dangerous Waters: Sovereignty, Self-determinism and Resistance. In *Living at the Borderlines: Issues in Caribbean Sovereignty and Development*, edited by C. Barrow-Giles and D. Marshall, 51–62. Kingston: Ian Randle.

Bergsten, C.F. 1997. Open Regionalism. *World Economy* 20 (5): 545–65.

Bhagwati, J., and A. Panagariya. 1996. Preferential Trading Areas and Multilateralism – Strangers, Friends or Foes? In *The Economics of Preferential Trade Agreements*, edited by J. Bhagwati and A. Panagariya, 1–78. Washington, DC: AEI.

Bishop, M., and A. Payne. 2010. Caribbean Regional Governance and the Sovereignty/Statehood Problem. Caribbean Paper No. 8. Centre for International Governance Innovation, Waterloo, Ontario.

Bootle, R. 2014. *The Trouble with Europe: Why the EU Isn't Working – How Can It Be Reformed – What Could Take Its Place?* Boston: Nicholas Breadley Publishing.

Braveboy-Wagner, J. 2008. *Small States in Global Affairs: The Foreign Policies of the Caribbean Community (CARICOM)*. New York: Palgrave Macmillan.

Brewster, H.E. 2003. *The Caribbean Single Market and Economy: Is It Realistic without Commitment to Political Unity?* Georgetown, Guyana: CARICOM Secretariat.

———. 2007. Review of the Rose Hall Declaration: Provisions on Regional Declaration. In *CARICOM Single Market and Economy Genesis and Prognosis*, edited by K. Hall and M. Chuck-A-Sang, 46–60. Kingston: Ian Randle.

Brewster, H., and C.Y. Thomas. 1967. *The Dynamics of West Indian Economic Integration*. Kingston: Institute of Social and Economic Research.

CCJ (Caribbean Court of Justice). 2013. *Shanique Myrie and Government of Jamaica versus Government of Barbados*, CCJ 03 (OJ).

CARICOM (Caribbean Community) Secretariat. 2001. *Revised Treaty of Chaguaramas*. Georgetown, Guyana.

Demas, W. 1976. *Essays on Caribbean Integration and Development*. Mona, Jamaica: University of the West Indies Institute of Social and Economic Research.

DeShong, Halimah A.F. 2015. Policing Femininity, Affirming Masculinity: Relationship Violence, Control and Spatial Limitations. *Journal of Gender Studies* 24 (1): 85–103.

DeShong, H.A.F., and T. Haynes. 2016. Intimate Partner Violence in the Caribbean: State, Activist and Media Responses. *Global Public Health* 11 (1–2): 82–94.

Downes, A.S. 2001. Economic Growth and Development in Barbados during the Twentieth Century. *Integration and Trade* 15 (5): 145–76.

Fanta, E., T.M. Shaw and V.T. Tang. 2013. *Comparative Regionalisms for Development in the 21st Century: Insights from the Global South*. Farnham, Surrey: Ashgate.

Gilbert, T. 2013. *The Politics of Integration: Caribbean Sovereignty Revisited*. Kingston: Ian Randle.

Girvan, N. 2008. A Single Development Vision. In *Caribbean Community in Transition: Functional Cooperation as a Catalyst for Change*, edited by K. Hall and M. Chuck-A-Sang, 27–44. Kingston: Ian Randle.

———. 2011. CARICOM's Original Sin. Paper prepared for delivery at the CARICOM Regional Civil Society Consultation, Port of Spain, Trinidad and Tobago.

———. 2013. Constructing the Greater Caribbean. Keynote address delivered at SALISES Regional Integration Conference, 2013 Rethinking Regionalism: Beyond the CARICOM Integration Project, Kingston, Jamaica, 7 October 2013.

Gonsalves, R. 2014. *Bridge over Troubled Waters: The Caribbean Community, the Caribbean Court of Justice, Shanique Myrie and Community Law*. Speech delivered at the Norman Manley Law School, Kingston, Jamaica, 17 April.

Grenade, K., and D. Lewis-Bynoe. 2011. Reflecting on Development Outcomes: A Comparative Analysis of Barbados and Guyana. *Journal of Eastern Caribbean Studies* 36 (1): 21–42.

Grenade, W.C. 2012. Engendering Security: HIV/AIDS and Human (In)Security in the Caribbean. In *Love and Power: Caribbean Discourses on Gender*, edited by E. Barriteau, 183–206. Kingston: University of the West Indies Press.

———. 2013. Small States and Risky Global Intercourse: The Grenada-Taiwan Dispute. *Social and Economic Studies* 62 (3): 181–202.

Grenade, W.C., and K. Skeete. 2012. *Report on Regional Integration in Small States: The Case of the Caribbean*. Prepared for the Commonwealth Secretariat.

Griffith, I., ed. 2004. *Caribbean Security in the Age of Terror: Challenge and Change*. Kingston and Miami: Ian Randle.

Haas, E.B. 1958. *The Uniting of Europe: Political, Social and Economic Forces, 1950–1957*. Stanford, CA: Stanford University Press.

———. 1976. Turbulent Fields and the Theory of Regional Integration. *International Organization* 30 (2): 173–212.

Harvey, D. 2005. *A Brief History of Neoliberalism*. New York: Oxford University Press.

Hettne, B. 2005. Beyond '"New"' Regionalism. *New Political Economy* 10 (4): 543–71.

Hettne, B., and F. Söderbaum. 2000. Theorising the Rise of Regionnes. *New Political Economy* 5 (3): 457–73.

Hinds-Harrison, K. 2012. These Issues Are Gender-Neutral Caribbean Gender-Free Trade Relations. In *Love and Power: Caribbean Discourses on Gender*, edited by E. Barriteau, 207–33. Kingston: University of the West Indies Press.

Hoffman, S. 1966. Obstinate or Obsolete? The Fate of the Nation-State and the Case of Western Europe. *Daedalus, Journal of the American Academy of Arts and Sciences,* 95 (3): 862–915.

Hosein, R., and C. Thomas. 2007. Caribbean Single Market and Economy (CSME) and the Intra-Migration of Nurses: Some Proposed Opportunities. *Global Social Policy* 7 (3): 316–38.

IMF (International Monetary Fund). 2014. *Barbados 2013 Article IV Consultation.* Country Report No. 14/52. Washington, DC.

Jamaica Gleaner. 2013. Myrie Case a Turning Point for Regional Integration – Experts. 3 November. http://jamaica-gleaner.com/latest/article.php?id=49042.

Jones, P. 2004. Caribbean Court of Justice: Caribbean Integration or Disintegration. *Economic Working Paper*, vol. 5. Economic Development Institute Information Booklet Series 1.

Joseph, C. 2005. Conceptualizing the Caribbean Community: Reconciling Individual and Collective Exercise of Sovereignty – A Legal Perspective. In *Caribbean Perspectives: Regional Governance and Integrated Development,* edited by K. Hall and D. Benn, 10–21. Kingston: Ian Randle.

Joseph, T.S.D. 2011. *Decolonization in St. Lucia Politics and Global Neoliberalism, 1945–2010*. Jackson: University Press of Mississippi.

Kaczorowska-Ireland, A. 2015. *Competition Law in the Caribbean Single Market and Economy*. New York: Routledge.

Kamugisha, A., and A. Trotz. 2007. Editorial. *Race and Class* 49 (2): i–iv. Institute of Race Relations, London, Sage Journals.

Keet, D. 2007. Alternative Regionalisms: Why and How. *Global Social Policy* 7: 255–58.

Kempadoo, K. 1999. *Sun, Sex and Gold: Tourism and Sex Work in the Caribbean*. Oxford: Rowman and Littlefield.

———. 2004. *Sexing the Caribbean: Gender, Race and Sexual Labour*. New York: Routledge.

Kempadoo, K., J. Sanghera and B. Pattanaik. 2012. *Trafficking and Prostitution Re-Considered: New Perspectives on Migration, Sex Work, and Human Rights*. New York: Routledge.

Knight, W.A., J. Castro-Ra and H. Ghany, eds. 2014. *Remapping the Americas: Trends in Region-Making*. Farnham, Surrey: Ashgate.

Krasner, S.D. 2009. *Power, the State and Sovereignty*. London: Routledge.

Krueger, A.O. 1999. Are Preferential Trading Arrangements Trade Liberalizing or Protectionist? *Journal of Economic Perspectives* 13 (4): 105–24.

Laursen, F. 2010. *Comparative Regional Integratio:n Europe and Beyond*. Aldershot, Hampshire: Ashgate.

Majone, G. 2014. *Rethinking the Union of Europe Post-Crisis: Has Integration Gone Too Far?* New York: Cambridge University Press.

McCormick, J. 2014. *Understanding the European Union: A Concise Introduction*, 6th ed. New York: Palgrave Macmillan.

Mohammed, D. 2008. Size and Competitiveness: An Examination of the Caribbean Single Market and Economy (CSME). *Round Table* 97 (395): 287–303.

Nelson, R. 2007. The Caribbean Court of Justice and the CARICOM Single Market and Economy. In *CARICOM Single Market and Economy: Genesis and Prognosis*, edited by K. Hall and M. Chuck-A-Sang, 164–85. Kingston: Ian Randle.

O'Brien, D. 2011. CARICOM: Regional Integration in a Post-Colonial World. *European Law Journal* 17 (5): 630–48.

Pollard, D. 2007a. The Caribbean Court of Justice: Challenges and Response. In *CARICOM Single Market and Economy: Genesis and Prognosis*, edited by K. Hall and M. Chuck-A-Sang, 186–204. Kingston: Ian Randle.

———. 2007b. The Caribbean Court of Justice in Regional Economic Development. In *CARICOM Single Market and Economy: Genesis and Prognosis*, edited by K. Hall and M. Chuck-A-Sang, 205–18. Kingston: Ian Randle.

Premdas, R.R. 2002. Self-Determination and Sovereignty in the Caribbean: Migration, Transnational Identities, and Deterritorialisation of the State. In *Caribbean Survival and the Global Challenge*, edited by R. Ramsaran, 49–64, Kingston: Ian Randle.

Ramphal, S. 2008. *Sir Shridath Ramphal: The Commonwealth and the World Essays in Honour of His 80th Birthday*. Hertfordshire, UK: Hansib.

———. 2012. *Caribbean Challenges Sir Shridath Ramphal's Collected Counsel*. Hertford: Hansib.

Rawlins, H. 2000. *The Caribbean Court of Justice: The History and Analysis of the Debate*. Georgetown, Guyana: Caribbean Community Secretariat.

Reddock, R. 1994. *Women, Labour and Politics in Trinidad and Tobago: A History*. London: Zed.

Rudolph, C. 2005. Sovereignty and Territorial Borders in a Global Age. *International Studies Review* 7 (1): 1–20.

Schmitter, P. 1970. A Revised Theory of Regional Integration. *International Organization* 24 (4): 836–68.

Singh, R. 2011. Sick Caricom Needs a Dose of "People Power". *Jamaica Observer*, 6 February.

Thomas, C.Y. 2008. The Urgency of Functional Cooperation: Priority Interventions in Selected Areas (Disaster Preparedness, Health, Education and Security). In *The Caribbean Community in Transition Functional Cooperation as a Catalyst for Change*, edited by K. Hall and M. Chuck-A-Sang, 359–82. Kingston: Ian Randle.

Thomas-Hope, E. 2007. Shifting Location and Negotiating Place: Women in Caribbean Intra-Regional Migration. In *CARICOM Single Market and Economy: Genesis and Prognosis*, edited by K. Hall and M. Chuck-A-Sang, 324–45. Kingston: Ian Randle.

Viner, J. 1950. *The Customs Union Issue*. New York: Carnegie Endowment for International Peace.

Watson, H.A. 2013. Transnational Capitalist Globalization and the Limits of Sovereignty: State, Security, Order, Violence, and the Caribbean. In *Caribbean Sovereignty, Development and Democracy in an Age of Globalization*, edited by L. Lewis, 35–67. New York: Routledge.

West Indian Commission. 1992. *Time for Action: The Report of the West Indian Commission*. Black Rock, Barbados.
Wiltshire, R. 2010. Public Policy Lecture Caribbean Migration: Challenges to Leadership. *Journal of Eastern Caribbean Studies* 35 (2): 61–79.

CHAPTER 10

Governance and Security in the Caribbean Region: What Does It Take?

Georgina Chami

Good governance is perhaps the single most important factor in eradicating poverty and promoting development.

—Kofi Annan, former secretary-general of the United Nations

The year 2015 marked a significant watershed for the global development agenda. It was evident that some progress was made on the UN Millennium Development Goals, but it was uneven. The evidence suggests that the uneven progress was related to major differences in the quality of governance across nations. The term *governance* is actually a very old one, but it was revived within recent times due to globalization. Evolving from its original focus on economic processes and administrative efficiency, it now shares deeper ties with democracy, rule of law, participation, transparency and accountability, and responsiveness (to the needs of the people). While there is universal acceptance of its significance, differences exist with respect to the theoretical formulations and conceptualization of the subject itself.

Unlike the 1970s and 1980s, when the focus was on implementing economic reform programmes, today's governance agenda has taken on a broader interpretation in order to accomplish the goals of the Millennium Declaration. Consequently, we saw the convergence of global development and security agendas at the beginning of the new millennium. Therefore, the challenge for many countries was not only improving standards of living but also making enhancements in the areas of education, health and nutrition, environment and security of people, and ensuring a richer cultural life. With the globalization process and the subsequent highly uneven distribution of gains, inequality may deepen further, with all its associated implications. Consequently, governance has become multidimensional in nature.

Included with this widening global development agenda are non-traditional matters such as health, the environment and poverty to ensure greater stability and security within states. In this regard, the post-bipolar world has shown the loss of preeminence of the military dimension and of the state in security affairs (Sheehan 2005). Consistent with this change, different sources of non-military threats led to the inclusion of economic, political, societal and economic factors. Consequently, this broadening of security has led to the emergence of a human security paradigm and a change in focus from the state-centric military sector towards the individual. This concept covers a wide range of problems such as refugees, light arms, human rights violations, international terrorism and transnational organized crime.

In this post-bipolar global landscape, security has assumed a broader meaning and is more challenging. Undoubtedly, there is a growing certainty that many of these security challenges are a reflection of weak governance. Analyses across countries and regions allude to weak governance as the basis for continuing insecurities and development deficiencies in many developing countries. Therefore, it has become essential to devise proper governance mechanisms in order to support security and development. Likewise, sound social and economic policies, democratic institutions and improved infrastructure are necessary for sustained economic growth and poverty reduction. Incorporating these elements as measures of governance success creates an indivisible link between governance and human development outcomes.

As a group, Caribbean countries face numerous security challenges that hold deep implications for governance. These include increased crime and violence, transnational organized crime and socioeconomic insecurities associated with global financial crises, environmental hazards and diminishing market opportunities. Consequently, there must be greater efforts at regional governance in order to strengthen and enhance security within the region. Given the present global climate, which can impact these economies, the region is presented with a good opportunity to be introspective and reactive on regional governance and to forecast future options. Similarly, it is important to understand the factors (internal and external) that shape and influence the concept of regional security.

If, as a region, we want to examine regional security, it remains important to understand the nature of security thinking in the Caribbean. Traditionally, security thinking in the Caribbean was shaped and influenced by the bipolar rivalry between the two former superpowers: the United States and the former Soviet Union. According to Ferguson (2002), the historical dominating presence of the United States in the Caribbean region was characteristic of the Cold War climate. Therefore, security during this period was conceived as the ideological rivalry, militarization and primacy of the nation state. In some studies and analyses it was also defined as "high politics" and described as power-based and state-centric. Thus, the goal of states was to pursue their own national interests and even to resort to force as effective tools to deal with threats.

For many years, Caribbean Basin countries had relatively great geostrategic importance for the major powers. In this regard, three areas were considered vital: strategic materials, vital sea lanes of communication and security networks of powerful states in the area (Griffith 2004). First, in the region there was a wealth of resources which were significant for military and civilian purposes at that time. Second, sea lanes of communication provided important links between the Caribbean and other destinations in the United States and Europe. Third, in the area of security networks, the region gained prominence because of the US–Soviet power struggle for dominance over areas in the global political economy. The United States considered the region as its "southern side" and implemented containment programmes to curb the spread of communism within the region.

As the Cold War intensified in the 1950s, the security landscape in the region was dominated by anticommunist sentiments and the containment of its spread. The United States intervened in countries like Guatemala (1954), Colombia (1957) and Venezuela (1958) in order to suppress communist-directed revolutions which could have enhanced Soviet influence in the region. Guatemala, for example, had been pursuing an anti-US policy for several years and supported the North Korean and Soviet position in the United Nations (Smith 1994). Nonetheless, this security environment lasted for only a few more years. The end of bipolarity in the early 1990s heralded new dialogues and discussions for security analysts and scholars in the region.

The post-bipolar world heralded major changes for the concept and analysis of security. First, security was no longer simply state-centric. Second, the individual gained prominence in security discussions. Third, the evolving demands of the conflict and the growing importance of human security led to its redefinition. As the issue of human security emerged, it became the cornerstone of the United Nations Development Programme's 1994 *Human Development Report*. The report emphasized that security was not simply state-centric but included the protection of the individual and freedom from direct and indirect threats of violence. What became clear was that human security and governance had become intertwined, and for security in the Caribbean region to exist, a more multidimensional approach was required.

In the Caribbean, the issue of governance appears to be problematic. Regionally, there is a waning of domestic security arising from innate deficits in governance, which has led to the proliferation of private security firms to deal with the problem. Criminal activity in the Caribbean is complex due to the region's weaknesses and deepening global interconnectedness. In 2013 the UN Office on Drugs and Crime stated that the Caribbean had experienced an increase in its homicide rate, the fluctuations of which were also related to changes in drug trafficking patterns and gang violence (UNODC 2013). Added to this was the growing problem of transnational organized crime in the region. In this context, the region must now reexamine its interpretation of governance to include these new challenges.

Definitions of Governance

Governance is a very general concept that is often defined more narrowly. The concept of good governance emerged in the late 1980s and early 1990s, mainly in the World Bank. The bank defined good governance as the ways public officials and public institutions acquire and exercise authority to provide goods and services (World Bank 2007). Its focus on governance was demonstrative of the universal drive toward political and economic liberalization. This approach emphasized the issues of greater state responsiveness and accountability and the impact of these factors on political stability and economic development. Similarly, regional banks, such as the Asian Development Bank and the African Development Bank, adopted similar language.

Conversely, the bank's interpretation of promoting governance can be contested for its perceived misperceptions. Generally, projects or programmes of the World Bank and other multilateral development institutions on governance examine and manage the operations of economic institutions and public sectors to guarantee transparency and accountability, regulatory reform and enhancement of public sectors and leadership skills. However, the bank has adopted a limited approach, restricting itself to focusing on the economic dimension of governance. It is less likely to emphasize democratic governance and human rights, which remain critical to political governance. As such, the bank, in order to improve governance in developing countries, must adopt a more holistic approach, including issues of power, politics and democracy.

What has been observed is that governance has become distorted and misconstrued by elites. What we have seen is the misuse of resources by these elites in public institutions and international organizations to promote their own interests. Globalization has also created the conditions for this abuse to flourish by creating avenues for illicit activities. In this context, developing countries are pressured by aid agencies and foreign investors to implement policies in line with a neoliberal agenda which has proven detrimental to their development. Likewise, the Washington-based institutions only exacerbate this situation by pressuring developing countries to be more accountable to donor institutions. Yet it must be highlighted that promoting governance is ensuring development based on achieving people's rights.

Generally, there is no clear and specific definition of governance in use by donor countries and donor agencies. However, it is now evident that the concept comprises an economic and a political dimension. Basically three general definitions have emerged. According to Landman and Larizza (2010), *governance* in its simplest form focuses on the economic dimension and refers to sound public financial management. Second, *good governance* refers to a blend of economic and political elements which include appropriate public financial management, accountability, transparency in decision-making and rule of law. Third, *democratic governance* incorporates the economic and political dimensions of good governance and also includes elements of democracy and respect for human rights.

What has become clear is the significant relationship between governance and economic performance. This has in some measure led the donor community to connect aid distribution to governance. The quality of governance in states receiving aid from countries and international organizations such as the World Bank is mixed. All of this implies that no longer is economic performance perceived purely as a matter for economists. Consequently, more attention is now given to the part that governance can play in the realization of social and economic development. The type of governance system in a state will affect its performance in carrying out its core functions and in meeting its main economic and social goals.

The principle of governance covers different ideals for a better society. If we explore this concept from different angles, we can better understand its multifaceted nature. In the economic sphere, the idea is that there must be transparency and accountability in the management of government accounts and public resources. In addition, there must be a stable regulatory environment to allow for private-sector activities. A second need is the strengthening and promoting of democratic institutions as well as tolerance throughout the society (CSCE 1992). Third, democratic governance refers to the legitimacy of government, the accountability of the political elements of government and respect for human rights and the rule of law. These are the main issues for practising good governance in societies.

Governance typically emphasizes leadership and how political leaders use or misuse power to advance social and economic development. This power can also be misused by these leaders to undermine the achievement of better standards of living for their people. Therefore, another fundamental approach in guaranteeing governance, or rather *democratic* governance, is promoting and practising ethical principles such as the rule of law, accountability and participation, transparency, and human and civil rights. These principles contribute significantly to the overall development process of a country. In this regard, it can be affirmed that good leadership can empower people, enhance the standards of the citizenry, and ensure that people enjoy access to public goods without commotion.

While good leadership allows for improved governance by empowering the people, the reverse is also applicable. A good leader must ensure inclusive participation while never overlooking the fact that he is a leader. Group discussion and input from the team motivates team members. This enhances levels of trust and openness in societies and organizations. In truly democratic societies, people can be empowered to demand and influence better policies, hold leaders and the private sector accountable for their actions and seek justice for abuse. Societies possessing strong, democratic institutions can empower people to sway their governments to ensure sustainable and equitable national development. In a true democracy, people can exercise their rights and deliver sustainable and equitable development.

The Interface between Good Governance and Security

There is no single way to achieve good governance and ensure security. Recent debates have focused on what makes institutions and rules more efficient, transparent and accountable to the rule of law. These variables are critical to development, as often ineffective institutions inflict the most harm upon underprivileged and vulnerable peoples. Against this backdrop, the United Nations Development Programme is advocating democratic governance as its main corporate goal to ensure democratization, facilitate the building of inclusive societies and foster participation in the world's poorest societies, with sound strategies and policies to combat poverty and achieve sustainable development goals. Increasingly, it is recognized that a multidimensional approach must be adopted to promote conditions for development, security and governance.

Although governance and security are distinct concepts, they are interconnected. Given the contemporary challenges of conflicts, governance gives meaning to the present nature of security. What has become quite evident is that once there is governance failure the security framework also deteriorates. In this regard, the sustainability of an efficient security system is reliant on the linkage between elements of good governance such as rule of law, accountability and transparency in the management of resources, political stability, provision of basic needs and services, and an absence of corruption. Undoubtedly, there is a strong relationship between the nature of governance and the state of security in any society. With the interplay between security and governance, there has been some progress in response to the complex mounting insecurities.

In many developing countries, both internal and external factors complicate efforts at attaining good governance. In regard to the former, profound poverty and structural weakness, along with susceptibility to external shocks and disasters, challenge governance. On the other hand, external factors such as global financial crises and unjust trade regimes and practices obstruct the realization of development in these countries. Moreover, there have not been adequate policies and programmes to modify the structures of inequality and insecurity caused by these changes. These structures remain exclusionary and are especially ill-suited for promoting a democratic system of governance.

Therefore, developing countries must review their experiences in areas of governance in order to enhance the implementation of policies and programmes to support it.

CARICOM's Governance Experience

Presently, as Girvan (2010) has stated, Caribbean countries are facing many threats that pose serious "challenges to the viability of our states as functioning socio-economic-ecological-political systems". Their vulnerability to natural disasters, climate change and global economic crises, coupled with other ongoing social challenges, has created a serious development problem for these states. In this regard, regional integration has been presented as a viable alternative for addressing threats of marginalization in an increasingly interdependent global system. With the persistence of these threats, there is much to suggest that the sustainability of CARICOM is threatened. It is troubling that there is neither an effective regional governance mechanism in place nor an effective response to the development crisis.

Unfortunately, the lack of an appropriate regional governance framework has hindered efforts towards the achievement of shared development outcomes, including the creation of a single economy. Some factors hindering this process include the failure to include and consult with non-political stakeholders in this decision-making process. Over the years, a number of factors, both internal and external, have influenced governance – or the lack thereof – in the Caribbean. It has been stated that Caribbean leaders seem to have been unsuccessful in correcting an internal governance crisis. This is associated with the establishment and upholding of institutions and processes that are unprepared to address deep-rooted political tradition and to overcome interconnected development challenges.

The Global Dimension

To date, CARICOM states' efforts at establishing a regional governance framework have been hindered by structural limitations, failed attempts at regional integration, and other shared social and economic vulnerabilities. These vulnerabilities include their small size, market thinness, unfavourable terms of trade, large import volume, poverty, susceptibility to natural disasters, limited human and technical capacities, and crime. These structural features have accelerated the pursuit of regional integration as a principal tool not only for increasing development capacity but also for maintaining security. Generally, throughout the region it is accepted that economic integration provides an avenue for overcoming the limitations mentioned by building shared capacity which is critical to the survival of the region socially, economically and politically.

Even though most Caribbean countries are autonomous states, external forces continue to greatly manipulate the decision-making process. These small and dependent economies of the Caribbean region face serious challenges to economic growth and development. Furthermore, external shocks only exacerbate this situation in these economies by creating serious balance-of-payments problems and enormous trade deficits. Owing to the global financial and economic crises, the region's development progress has been retarded. Most of the Caribbean states are highly dependent on tourism for foreign direct investment, foreign exchange earnings and employment. Consequently, multilateral economic institutions have come to the assistance of the region.

The multilateral economic institutions, such as the International Monetary Fund and the World Bank, assist states with managing and resolving the effects of current global financial and economic crises on their economies, especially for small island developing states. While these institutions provide fiscal support and policy advice, their measures are often too strict and thus undermine the economic well-being and stability of these states. These institutions negate the vital role that governance plays in the economic development of countries. Moreover, the Caribbean states continue to be economically dependent and less influential as decision-makers or power players in influencing decisions at these global levels and within these forums.

Political Culture

A strong, healthy political culture is both a condition for and an outcome of effective governance (Grenade 2012). However, the existent political culture in the Caribbean has weakened efforts at effective governance. Undoubtedly, the Caribbean has a strong and long-standing practice of formal democracy, as citizens are seen to benefit from constitutional rights, civil liberties and freedoms. Yet there are ongoing debates on the nature of democracy and governance in the region. Caribbean heads of government or prime ministers have excessive powers and often marginalize and alienate opposing parties, civil society groups and even citizens. This is rooted in the Caribbean's history (Grenade 2010). Caribbean leaders have contributed to the governance crisis by holding steadfast to old political traditions.

Generally, the political culture of any nation is shaped by historical events, and the Caribbean as a region is no exception. Its experiences with colonization, slavery and indentureship have conditioned how these societies have developed politically, socially and economically. Knight (1990, 307) has referred to the Caribbean as consisting of "artificial societies, that is, ones where people, territory, government and economy are not integrated but were contrived to serve foreign powers that denied the people the right to a collective consciousness, civil and political rights to develop as a people, to manage their own governments, to practice their own culture, and to construct their own identity". Thus, Caribbean peoples have always struggled to develop and create a sense of autonomy and nationalism.

Within the Caribbean, domestic politics is highly influenced by the decision-making process, with the dominant role played by the prime ministers in their capacity as heads of governments. As part of their role, the heads ensure that sovereignty and national autonomy are safeguarded. This has only allowed for each member state to advocate for non-regional interference in their affairs. Therefore, at the regional level it is challenging to secure a proper governance system. To date, the regional governance process has not improved the lives of Caribbean people. Thus far, Caribbean politics continues to represent this historical structure. In this milieu, the task ahead for governments is to manage the societies so that their social relations conform to post-independence nation building.

According to Girvan (2001), the Caribbean has developed or evolved from a legacy of slavery and the plantation system. As a region, it comprises many islands with peoples of different ethnicities, religions and shared events which make the Caribbean unique and have influenced its political culture. Having moved into a new phase of globalization, the Caribbean region confronts new issues and concerns in its political, economic, social and cultural spheres. Therefore, it has become vital for the region to consider seriously the idea of regional integration for continued sustainability. The idea of regional integration has been a theme in the English-speaking Caribbean since colonial times.

The Security Landscape

The end of the Cold War heralded a new era in security analyses and studies for the Caribbean Basin. During the Cold War, security was conceptualized in relation to ideological rivalry, militarization, external intervention and nation-state primacy. Moreover, the United States played a pivotal role in the region in curbing the reach of communism and safeguarding continual access to resources in the region. With the end of the Cold War, a new international order emerged and there was a reconfiguration of the global security order. The United States remained the main hegemonic power, but security broadened to include traditional and non-traditional concerns. In the Caribbean, security became more multidimensional in nature, encompassing military, political and economic dimensions.

Drug Trafficking

In the 1970s, the Caribbean was a main hub for cocaine trafficking from Colombia. Given its proximity to the United States and largely unprotected coastlines, cocaine traffickers exploited this area to expand their markets in the 1980s. Approximately 10 per cent of US-bound cocaine was estimated to be trafficked through the region, mostly on speedboats and in cargo containers or privately owned fishing craft and small aircraft. In the mid-1980s, over 75 per cent of the cocaine seized between South America and the United States was taken in the Caribbean, and very little was seized in Central America (UNODC 2012). With vigorous law enforcement by the United States, the Colombian connection declined in the 1990s, and the Mexican connection gradually assumed control of the drug-trafficking chain.

Large amounts of cocaine also entered the United States over the south-western land border. Initially, direct shipments to Mexico were favoured, with stopovers in Central America largely limited to refuelling. With the enacting of laws to curb these transactions in the early 2000s, it became quite risky to ship directly to Mexico. As a result, Central America became a transit and storage area, and parts of the Caribbean region were once again enmeshed in this illicit activity. In 2007 and 2008, cocaine was used by some 16 to 17 million people globally. North America accounted for more than 40 per cent of global cocaine consumption, with the second-largest flow of cocaine directed to Europe (UNODC 2010).

Arms trafficking, corruption, and money laundering are often major spin-off activities that support the drug trade and gravely threaten Caribbean security. The growing flow of drugs to this region is an example of the "balloon effect". In such a situation, increased pressure on one drug route produces a bulge elsewhere.[1] More importantly, intraregional drug trafficking has led to higher levels of crime and violence. This has allowed for institutionalized criminal behaviour and increased property-related crime by drug users and the availability of firearms. According to the *Economist,* the route for this illicit activity is from the Andean region (the main source of cocaine) to the drugs' main consumer markets – the United States and Europe. Conversely, the guns flow south, mainly from the United States to South America.

Crime

When the word *Caribbean* is mentioned, one thinks of scenic beaches and sunny tourist resorts. However, within the last decade this positive image has been slowly fading. The reason is that some countries, particularly in the English-speaking Caribbean, are earning reputations for rising levels of crime and violence. The Caribbean now has one of the highest murder rates globally. On average, it is estimated that there are 30 homicides per 100,000 inhabitants per year in the English-speaking Caribbean (*Economist* 2008). Aside from the societal impact, a country runs the risk of adverse effects on foreign trade, investment and tourism. In the Caribbean this is a major factor challenging efforts at promoting governance and development. Rule of law is an essential prerequisite of governance.

Across the Caribbean, deaths and injuries associated with gun violence have also increased due to the availability and misuse of firearms. Nations such as Guyana, Haiti, Jamaica, and Trinidad and Tobago are experiencing a steady rise in this area. Regionally, firearms are being used more often in the commission of crimes. Gun violence is related to the ease of access to US markets for firearms and to drug trafficking, and it is exacerbated by governments' inability to secure their borders, which makes the Caribbean region viable for organized criminal activities. The relatively easy access to small arms and light weapons, and their accessibility in the Caribbean region, impedes security, democratic processes and economic development. This makes it even more challenging to achieve good governance at state and regional levels.

Adding to the challenge is the fact that Caribbean countries have open coastlines but lack the resources and adequate law enforcement to patrol and monitor these areas. The result is huge flows of drugs into the region. Drug proceeds are often used to buy illegal arms which end up in the hands of competing gangs. The domino effect is an increase in the murder rates and a subsequent rise in kidnappings and extortion. It is estimated that 139,256 homicides occurred in Latin America and the Caribbean in 2012, representing an annual rate of 23.5 per 100,000. The highest levels of homicide by country are associated with the increased use of firearms. On average, 73 per cent of homicides were committed with firearms (80,387 cases) in 2012, according to calculations with data from the Pan American Health Organization (Fleitas, Lodola and Flom 2014).

The economic importance of the drug trade cannot be underestimated. The drug trade is equivalent to roughly 3.5 per cent of formal-sector gross domestic product in the region overall. On the other hand, crime brings with it substantial economic costs. Crime in the English-speaking Caribbean has led to a decline in investment, both foreign and domestic, which in turn slows growth. Due to the employment of additional security measures, crime increases the costs of doing business because it redirects investment away from business expansion and productivity improvement. Therefore, employee morale and productivity diminish as a result of the ensuing economic downturn. Consequently, the society is faced with spin-off effects which include losses through theft, looting, arson, fraud and extortion.

Terrorism

The Caribbean region is not immune to terrorism. Examples of terrorist activities include the *Cubana* airline bombing in 1976 and the 1990 attempted coup in Trinidad and Tobago. The region was adversely affected by the 9/11 attacks in the United States; tourism, the single largest earner of foreign exchange for the Caribbean region, experienced declining revenue and employment. It was estimated that international arrivals to the Caribbean declined by 2.5 per cent between 2001 and 2002. Moreover, the region experienced declining foreign direct investment, increased transportation costs for agricultural and manufactured exports, and reduced market opportunities for its goods and services. This proved very harrowing for the region, especially since there were no viable alternatives to cushion the impact.

The region must explore ways of addressing the decline in monetary assistance from the United States to Latin America and the Caribbean (in areas other than defence and counter-narcotic programmes). The United States is now reinvesting these monies to implement new security systems and security-related operations in their homeland in order to counter terrorism. The Caribbean region remains largely dependent on trade and tourism with the United States and the European Union. Through the Economic Partnership Agreement, CARICOM states have gained significantly both financially and economically. However, Brexit will adversely affect many of these states, from trade relations to immigration, tourism to financial relations and cultural engagements to foreign policy (Gangaya 2016).

With an increase in the number of acts of terrorism globally, many countries are positioning themselves to combat "terrorism with a global reach". Caribbean governments are implementing steps to tighten security at airports and other vulnerable areas. After the 9/11 attack, there were other attacks globally, which warranted a transformation in Caribbean thinking about regional security. The region's borders continue to be avenues for terrorist networks. US intelligence is alleging that would-be militants leave from this region to fight with Islamic extremists in Syria. This is a disturbing trend for small Caribbean nations that fear extremists' returning home to conduct terror operations which they are incapable of addressing. Thus, the region must decide on an integrated approach to address this issue.

Environmental Vulnerability

The countries of the Caribbean share similar sustainable development challenges. One such challenge is the environmental or ecological vulnerability of Caribbean states due to their geographical location. In the region, many islands are located in the hurricane belt. Thus, these islands are faced with natural disasters on a yearly basis, which makes them highly susceptible to deep and adverse effects, especially in regard to sustainable development. Moreover, given the small sizes of the populations and economies of these islands, whenever a disaster strikes it affects a large proportion of the economy and people. Consequently, their development is slowed down by several years. The additional challenge of rising sea levels as a consequence of global warming worsens flooding and soil erosion in this region.

The Caribbean islands are particularly susceptible to external shocks due to climate change and natural disasters. As a possible solution to this situation, countries may consider adapting measures within the limits of their available resources. Adaptation involves reducing risk and vulnerability, seeking opportunities and building the capacity of nations, regions, cities, the private sector, communities, individuals and natural systems to cope with climate impacts, as well as mobilizing that capacity by implementing decisions and actions (Tompkins et al. 2010). Since the Caribbean is not a major contributor to greenhouse gas emissions, attention to mitigation is important in terms of building resilience.

There are numerous challenges ahead in adapting to climate change and creating resilient economies. These will include a more responsive and cross-sectoral approach to resource management and the use of legislation to guarantee that sustainable development is at the heart of the decision-making process. It will also necessitate institutional reform which would allow for a regional environmental governance framework. In this regard, there would be regional interagency coordination of all planning and development programmes, sustained supply of resources, use of technology and adequate training in analysing, producing and using climate change data in decision-making. This would allow for better-designed policies and responses to coordination of efforts and planning for environmental hazards.

Future Implications for the Region

From the foregoing analysis it is evident that there is a deficit in the Caribbean governance process. To the credit of the Caribbean, several initiatives have been implemented to enhance national capacity and attain increased regional cooperation. In the area of security, at the national and regional levels, the Regional Demand Reduction Strategy was developed. Simultaneously, national drug commissions and national joint headquarters were established to coordinate the activities of regional law enforcement agencies. These measures were introduced to address drug trafficking and drug use regionally. The fear is that increased consumption of hard drugs or competition for control of the transshipment markets could lead to increased levels of crime and violence which would pose challenges to promoting regional governance.

In the area of crime, programmes, agencies and strategies for preventing and reducing homicide at various levels have been established. Caribbean states have signed many conventions, such as the Inter-American Convention against Corruption and the Inter-American Convention against Illicit Manufacturing of and Trafficking in Firearms, Ammunition, Explosives and other Related Materials. Firearms legislation has been employed in various countries in an effort to reduce homicides committed with such weapons. With the adoption of the Arms Trade Treaty (April 2013), it is notable that Trinidad and Tobago is lobbying for the secretariat to be stationed there. This would be an asset to the region given the challenges faced in this area.

Also established was the multilateral crime and security management architecture – the Caribbean Community Implementation Agency for Crime and Security. Other initiatives include the Joint Regional Communications Centre used during the Cricket World Cup in 2007 to prescreen travellers and the Security Assistance Mechanism to respond to man-made and natural disasters and manage and diffuse conflicts. In order to address climate change threats, CARICOM had established the Caribbean Community Climate Change Centre, the Adaptation to Climate Change in the Caribbean Project (2011–14) and the Special Programme on Adaptation to Climate Change (2007–10).

An added feature is the region's ongoing efforts at establishing the CARICOM Single Market and Economy (CSME). The introduction of this structure reaches to the heart of economic integration and is a strategy to alleviate the adverse effects of economic globalization. It is meant to enhance competitiveness regionally and heighten bargaining power in different forums of international economic negotiations. To date, this initiative is regarded as one of the most advanced forms of regional integration among developing countries. The deepening of the integration process increases the need for formal community institutions and arrangements and for increasing the region's stake in national governance. Despite the setbacks faced thus far in putting the CSME into practice, these states must continue to work on resolving the implementation issues.

Attempts at regionalism are important to Caribbean states' continuing to sustain themselves in an increasingly interdependent world. With diminishing opportunities and markets for goods and services, alliance formation and revamping the economy are key factors towards social and economic governance in the region. A robust economic system will no doubt address the issue of poverty. It is impossible to address security and promote peace and sustainable development with the degree of poverty in some of these countries.

Jeffrey Sachs (2007) argued that poverty leads to desperation in people and an unhealthy struggle for available resources. This creates a fertile ground for insecurity. Therefore, seeking mutually beneficial options for the region is vital to its survival in a rapidly changing global world.

In spite of close consultations with general and legal interest groups on the role of the CCJ, this initiative is yet to be realized. The creation of such a court was the recommendation of the West Indian Commission, which viewed it as essential to the functioning of the CSME. But the region must be commended for its efforts at seeking to establish bodies to adjudicate its own affairs in areas of law (the CCJ), economics (the CSME) and security (the Implementation Agency for Crime and Security). Other initiatives include the development of the Assembly of Caribbean Community Parliamentarians, the Youth Parliament, the CARICOM Task Force on Crime and Security and the Pan Caribbean Partnerships against HIV/AIDS. These measures can all assist in overall regional governance efforts.

But for this region an active and lively civil society has a key role to play. In this regard, an organized civil society serves as a watchdog for the activities of government, thereby ensuring that there are no excesses and that there is accountability. According to Mulgan (2003), accountability is about calling and holding institutions and officials to account in understanding their functions or duties. Therefore, civil society can pressure political entities into safeguarding the democratic interests of its citizenry by advocating for their freedom to exercise political will. On the other hand, it acts as a "promoter" in attracting, encouraging and sensitizing individuals to political participation and the rights of a democratic citizenry. The existent Charter of Civil Society for the Caribbean acknowledges that there is a role for civil society in the integration process.

A critical component of any democratic system is the inclusion and observance of social principles; these include tolerance, moderation, willingness to compromise and respect for opposing viewpoints. Civil society is considered a crucial arena for the development of the latter. As a group entity, it not only allows for the development of more organized participation in civil society but influences the types of societies and values that are adopted or nurtured. These inculcate within a society the relevant attitudinal dispositions and behavioural patterns and other values that promote good governance and democracy. Furthermore, policies and institutions must represent the interests of women and men and promote equal access to resources, rights and voice. This is a central element of good governance.

It is evident that the states in the region are part of a wider system of multi-level governance. In this regard, a multitude of actors are now included and involved in the decision-making arenas. No longer is the state the sole arbiter of affairs within the states. Actually, this role of the states is in decline as we observe the legitimating of political authority by elections and party politics. Citizens have become more involved in the political affairs of states in different ways. Therefore, civil society has a prominent role in shaping politics. In this regard, it enhances the bargaining power of interest groups, provides inclusive mechanisms for them, helps in the recruitment and training of new political leaders and inculcates standards of public responsibility and transparency.

Conclusion

Undoubtedly, the historical experience of the Caribbean has influenced the nature of governance. Added to this, the region has failed to successfully tackle the development needs of its citizens. This has led to problems of insecurity in the region. While there are weaknesses in governance, the Caribbean must work assiduously in addressing them because of global interconnectedness. These weaknesses can be corrected through the adoption of a multifaceted approach to regional governance. What is required is the realization of an active, participative civil society, a revitalized economy, and the inclusion of other social, economic and political elements aimed at enhancing efforts at regional governance. Promoting good governance is essential for security and sustainable development within the region.

But all is not lost; there have been commendable efforts on the part of the region at achieving political and economic integration from the Caribbean Free Trade Association to the CSME. What was perhaps easier for Europe to achieve in the form of the European Union will require a greater level of political will in CARICOM. But part of the problem has to do with the historical and political contexts in which CARICOM has evolved. Traditionally, these states have seldom interfered or got involved in the domestic affairs of member states. However, the end of the Cold War and the consequent changes in global polity have yielded several implications for regional governance. Therefore, the Caribbean has recognized that, in pursuance of good governance, there is a deeper interface in the domestic affairs of states than previously existed.

While there is regional support for the idea of Caribbean unity, there is a need for greater intraregional trade and for addressing the obstacles that hinder the region in achieving political integration and the full implementation of the CSME. Education plays a critical role in this process, as it sensitizes Caribbean people to the importance and usefulness of the CSME for the region. Furthermore, it is important to implement policies and strategies aimed at boosting sustainable economic development, not only at the country level but also within the region. This should be complemented with closer collaboration and deeper integration efforts in the Caribbean and between its people. It is critical that sensitization of the wider Caribbean population to the benefits of integration be undertaken.

Caribbean leaders must also increase their participation at the decision-making tables of international forums such as the International Monetary Fund, G20, United Nations and World Bank. Their decisions directly or indirectly impact our economies. The region must be proactive and provide logical and informed contributions to influence these forums. But it is also important that the region develop an understanding of what it is, what is in its best interest, what makes it unique and how it can become a powerful player in these forums. With diminishing forms of support in terms of remittances, foreign aid and handouts, it is critical that CARICOM revisit this issue. As a region, we must seek to devise solutions to our problems and not import ideas and perceptions that are *a*-historical and *a*-cultural to our context.

Perhaps there should be a shift in focus and effort towards rethinking how to shape our destiny from within while simultaneously finding relevant global partners with which to harness mutually beneficial interests. CARICOM must lobby in its outreach efforts, hosting consultative meetings with civil society and business leaders on issues which would incorporate the interests and opinions of both excluded countries and non-state actors and attracting our people, both abroad and locally, who possess the ingenuity to facilitate its growth. But regional integration can be achieved only with the political backing and will of states and sound understanding of its benefits for the region. In this regard, CARICOM must explore ideas both regionally and internationally to enhance its visibility, increase its resilience and efforts at regionalism and be a global trading partner.

Note

1. Until recently, the favoured northbound route for cocaine from South America was through Honduras. The drug was transported – mainly via Venezuela after Colombia's interdiction efforts in the 1990s – by small aircraft.

References

CSCE (Conference on Security and Cooperation in Europe). 1992. *CSCE Helsinki Document 1992: The Challenges of Change*. Helsinki.

Economist. 2008. A Caribbean Crime Wave: Crime Damages Society and the Economy. 20 March.

Ferguson, T. 2002. Caribbean Basin Security in the Contemporary Period. Paper presented at the conference Governance and Security in the Caribbean Basin, University of the West Indies, St Augustine, Trinidad and Tobago.

Fleitas, Diego Manuel, Germán Lodola and Hernán Flom. 2014. *Delito y violencia en América Latina y el Caribe: Perfil de los países de la región*. Buenos Aires: Asociación para Políticas Públicas.

Gangaya, T. 2016. *EU Referendum: A Brexit Reality, EU and the Caribbean*. First Citizens Research and Analytics. Port of Spain: First Citizens Bank.

Girvan, Norman. 2001. Reinterpreting the Caribbean. In *New Caribbean Thought: A Reader*, edited by Brian Meeks and Folke Lindahl, 3–23. Kingston: University of the West Indies Press.

———. 2010. Are Caribbean Countries Facing Existential Threats? *Caribbean 360*, November 2. www.caribbean360.com/opinion/are_caribbean_countries_facing_existential_threats.

Grenade, Wendy C. 2010. Governance in the Caribbean: Toward Renewal. In *Governance in the Commonwealth: Current Debates*, edited by Seth Lartey and Deepti Sastry, 33–39. London: Commonwealth Foundation.

———. 2012. Governance in the Caribbean: Challenges and Prospects. In *Commonwealth Governance Handbook, 2012–13: Democracy, Development and Public Administration*, commissioned and researched by Andrew Robertson and Rupert Jones-Parry, 54–57. Cambridge: Nexus Strategic Partnerships.

Griffith, Ivelaw Lloyd. 2004. *Caribbean Security in the Age of Terror: Challenge and Change*. Kingston: Ian Randle.

Knight, Franklin W. 1990. *The Caribbean: The Genesis of a Fragmented Nationalism*, 2nd ed. New York: Oxford University Press.

Landman, Todd, and Marco Larizza. 2010. *EU Policy Discourse: Democracy, Governance, and Human Rights*. Stockholm: International Institute for Democracy and Electoral Assistance.

Mulgan, R. 2003. *Holding Power to Account: Accountability in Modern Democracies*. Basingstoke, Hampshire: Palgrave Macmillan.

Sachs, J. 2007. Peace through Economic Development. *Economist's View*, July 25. http://economistsview.typepad.com/economistsview/2007/07/jeffrey-sachs-p.html.

Sheehan, M. 2005. *International Security: An Analytical Survey*. Boulder: Lynne Rienner.

Smith, Robert Freeman. 1994. *The Caribbean World and the United States: Mixing Rum and Coca-Cola*. New York: Twayne.

Tompkins, Emma L., W. Neil Adger, Emily Boyd, Sophie Nicholson-Cole, Keith Weatherhead and Nigel Arnell. 2010. Observed Adaptation to Climate Change: UK Evidence of Transition to a Well-Adapting Society. *Global Environmental Change* 20 (4): 627–35.

UNODC (United Nations Office on Drugs and Crime). 2010. *World Drug Report, 2010*. New York.

———. 2012. *Transnational Organized Crime in Central America and the Caribbean: A Threat Assessment*. Vienna.

———. 2013. *Global Study on Homicide, 2013: Trends, Contexts, Data*, edited by Jonathan Gibbons. Vienna.

World Bank. 2007. *Strengthening World Bank Group Engagement on Governance and Anticorruption: Main Report*. Washington, DC.

CHAPTER 11

Advancing Caribbean Competitiveness: The Potential of Business Analytics

Gour C. Saha and Kamla Mungal

The results of the Global Competitiveness Survey conducted by the World Economic Forum each year have historically demonstrated that most of the Caribbean economies are less competitive than countries with similar socioeconomic conditions. The "Business Sophistication" pillar of the study offers an important area for consideration in the overall plan to improve competitiveness. Business analytics, or BA, is a rapidly growing area in business, society and government, and BA tools can be utilized by organizations to enhance their overall performance and competitiveness. Organizations today have access to enormous data sets, and BA provides the methods and techniques needed to harness the tremendous potential of these data to improve day-to-day decision-making. Applications of business analytics extend to nearly all managerial functions in any organization. Big data analytics, text analytics, content analytics, speech analytics and predictive analytics are commonly used forms of analytics in organizations. Companies see the need to position themselves well in BA to optimize their performance in all areas in which they function.

Similar to the adoption of technology, the use of BA in firms depends on the interplay of the awareness and attitudes of adopters and the level of institutional and organizational support. In order to harness the potential of BA, firms develop BA capabilities at the individual and organizational levels. BA capabilities include skills, data management and leadership that drive a culture of evidence-based decision-making (Kiron, Prentice and Ferguson 2014, 63–68).

The capabilities in firms are built over time as awareness of BA increases, positive attitudes develop and a culture of evidence-based decision-making is promoted. Firms with high levels of BA capabilities generally use or adopt BA routinely and strategically for enhanced competitiveness. A firm's level of adoption of BA is the result of adopters' perceptions and experiences that present barriers or serve as facilitators.

This chapter seeks to provide insights into the adoption of BA in Caribbean firms and examines factors that impact the adoption process in Caribbean countries. It includes a summary of an empirical study of BA in Trinidad and Tobago which sought to address two major objectives: (1) to better understand the levels of awareness, attitudes and adoption of BA in firms across the country as well as the drivers of and barriers to effective adoption of BA solutions and (2) to assess the level of adoption of BA against the performance of firms.

The results of the study are used to develop a framework to guide companies to improve their levels of adoption of BA and enhance their overall competitiveness. Suggestions are proposed to increase the level of adoption in firms in order to realize a greater impact on the firm and, consequently, on country competitiveness.

Caribbean Business Environment

The Caribbean region is challenged to significantly increase its competitiveness. Firms in the region, on average, demonstrate medium and low levels of business and innovation sophistication (Schwab and Sala-i-Martín 2014). The impact of information and communications technology on new services, products and business models is also very low (Beñat, Dutta and Lanvin 2014). In general, there is a lack of a culture of using analytical data and empirical evidence for planning and decision-making. Feedback received at a consultation session on BA held in Trinidad and Tobago in December 2010, with participants from the financial services, telecoms and retail sectors, included a reported general perception of a low level of BA adoption or usage, some level of commitment of local C-level executives to BA,[1] a lack of analytics competency and capacity in the majority of the sectors, and the need for improved analytics-driven decision-making within the business community.

Today's business environment, characterized by rapid technological advances and voluminous, real-time data, requires self-direction and increased ability to respond to market and stakeholder demands. BA presents an opportunity for Caribbean firms to create a robust decision-making support infrastructure that facilitates a bottom-up, emergent and flexible strategy-making process. It is therefore imperative for firms to promote organizational changes that address cultural and analytical capabilities that would facilitate the increasing adoption of BA.

The English-speaking Caribbean comprises a number of small countries with populations of less than four million. These countries share a similar history of colonization and have been challenged with respect to their integration into global markets and positioning in the world economy. The theory of plantation economy proposed by Lloyd Best contends that the institutions, structures and behaviours of the plantation system continue to be deeply entrenched in Caribbean societies and affects the development pathway of these economies (see Best and Levitt 2010). Caribbean economies suffer from a dependency syndrome characterized by passive integration into global markets. This syndrome presents deep barriers to transformation and adoption of the new practices required for local industrial growth and competitiveness (Karagiannis and Polychroniou 2015). The scenario remains unchanged to date with respect to the market, organizational and institutional realities of these countries. The challenge is to break this syndrome and establish technically proficient industrial growth strategies that could lead to domestic and competitive developments, ultimately enhancing export promotion (Karagiannis and Polychroniou 2015). BA provides ready access to data to all market players and can be an empowering force for small Caribbean businesses aiming to address their competitiveness challenge.

Caribbean firms also face challenges related to the size of the market, which include the associated realities of lower economies of scale, the prevalence of small- and medium-sized operations and strong interdependencies in the supply chain. In this environment, there is a demand for breadth of information rather than depth. Firms need to have a more sophisticated understanding of the activities of their suppliers locally and globally, as well as logistics factors and the local market environment. Analytics data must be drawn from various sources and will be of multiple types. BA will therefore be a more complex, shared and clustered activity to generate the broad localized information that will enable the market to be better served.

Although Caribbean countries are heterogeneous in structure and have had varying growth performances (Ramkissoon 2002), there are several commonalities with respect to the conditions of BA adoption. Caribbean countries possess similar low levels of information and communications technology usage and network readiness (Marius 2015) and will benefit from increased BA adoption. Their economies are also impacted by the presence of large companies from Trinidad and Tobago across the region. For example, in the areas of air travel, manufacturing and finance, the dominant firms come from Trinidad and Tobago, and this sets the tone, as the adoption of BA by these firms will eventually impact country competitiveness across the region.

BA and Competitiveness

International research speaks to the link between BA and competitiveness and the impetus towards increasing the adoption of analytics in firms. According to a 2012 survey by Bloomberg, 97 per cent of companies with revenues of more than US$100 million were using some form of BA, up from 90 per cent just two years prior (Kalakota 2012). While businesses have embraced the idea of fact-based decision-making, only one in four organizations believes its use of BA has been "very effective" in helping it to make decisions. The view of BA as continuing to provide a competitive edge is now eroding as firms develop similar capabilities very quickly and lower-level analytics loses its competitive potential (Kiron, Prentice and Ferguson 2014, 63–68). However, the explosion of big data arising from the increased volume, velocity and variety of data provides the next opportunity for business advantage. The declining advantage of unsophisticated BA and the onset of big data suggest that firms must consider upgrading their analytics capabilities to be recognized in the competitive space. The challenge to innovate in analytics is growing stronger.

Studies on BA have attempted to address the question of what makes firms better able to compete on analytics. Studies at both MIT and Harvard identified BA capabilities for competitive advantage as culture, data management and skills. These capabilities require the application of both "hard" and "soft" skills and behaviours in order to successfully utilize BA for competitive advantage. The competitive use of data, for example, requires the "soft" ability to creatively source the right data and the "hard skill" of establishing the information technology infrastructure necessary to integrate the internal and external data. This relationship between "hard" and "soft" skills is dynamic and mutually reinforcing. A company's competitive advantage is enhanced when both hard and soft skills are developed at higher levels. At the highest level, the soft skills tend to prevail over the hard skills as they begin to define the culture of the organization.

While BA capabilities are understood as critical for the competitive advantage of a firm, studies on how these capabilities are developed are limited. Firms differ with respect to the extent to which they have adopted appropriate practices to build BA capabilities. An organization's level of adoption is the extent to which it uses BA and is structured and operates to enhance its BA capabilities. Organizational factors that contribute to building BA capabilities include leadership, talent management, technological tools, decision-making approaches and company culture (McAfee and Brynjolfsson 2012, 66). BA adoption is facilitated by leadership that combines insight with clear goal-setting and definition of success as well as the ability to ask the right questions. With respect to talent, the combination of business savvy with technological skills is perhaps the most valuable and difficult to find as firms progress with the adoption of big data and analytics (Davenport and Patil 2012, 70–76). Decision-making that puts data and related decisions in the same location is deemed the most appropriate to optimize big data and analytics in the organization. Overall, the company culture must move from decision-making that is mainly intuitive to decision-making that is evidence-based, or from "What do we think?" to "What do we know?" (McAfee and Brynjolfsson 2012, 63). Firms with high levels of BA adoption have instituted behaviours, values and decision-making norms that treat data as a core asset and guide to strategy.

The Conceptual Framework: Factors Affecting BA Adoption

The empirical study of BA in Trinidad and Tobago recognizes that adoption of innovations is a staged process and is designed to explore the factors that are important at different stages in the adoption process. This study draws on innovation diffusion theory, which underscores the importance of awareness and attitudes in the adoption of new knowledge and practices. The first stage of the adoption process is knowledge or awareness; the potential adopters seek information about the existence of the innovation and gain understanding of its functionality. Awareness generally depends on the personalities and status of the potential adopters, such as their ages or positions in the organization, and organizational characteristics such as firm size, complexity of managerial structure, complementary investments available in the firm and quality of human resources (Wang, Wang and Yang 2010, 806). Some adopters, based on personal characteristics, are generally more receptive to new ideas and often function as strategically important target groups for marketers and policy-makers to stimulate the diffusion of innovations like BA.

At the second stage, the level of awareness of adopters impacts their attitudes, which may be favourable or unfavourable towards the new technology. Attitudes are mostly dependent on the adopters' beliefs about the usefulness or riskiness of the technology to the firm. The five technological characteristics that appear to influence adoption decisions in the innovation diffusion theory are relative advantage, compatibility, complexity, trialability and observability.

In the third stage the firm develops its BA capability through the interactions of like-minded individuals, as the collective skills of individuals and other factors such as culture and data management impact the overall firm capability. When individuals in a firm possess a positive attitude towards BA and the culture of the firm is conducive to BA, there is a high level of BA capability and, consequently, firm-level adoption.

In the final stage adopters make a choice to adopt or reject an innovation. The level of adoption includes stages of, future plans and future trends of BA adoption. When BA and organizational factors reinforce each other, superior business value results. When BA and organizational factors work against each other, business value may be negatively affected (Cao 2010). Therefore, organizational factors are important to understand for the diffusion and performance of BA in businesses. Figure 11.1 presents the conceptual framework of the study.

Studies of BA adoption and competitive utilization of BA in firms generally seek to understand the contextual nuances of BA adoption and the way in which individual and organizational practices present as barriers or facilitators in particular firms. This study of BA in Caribbean firms seeks to understand the levels of awareness of BA, attitudes towards BA and the general organizational factors that are deemed important for BA adoption. Caribbean firms, challenged by size and historical and cultural norms of passive inclusion in the global economy, are particularly susceptible to marginalization in the global

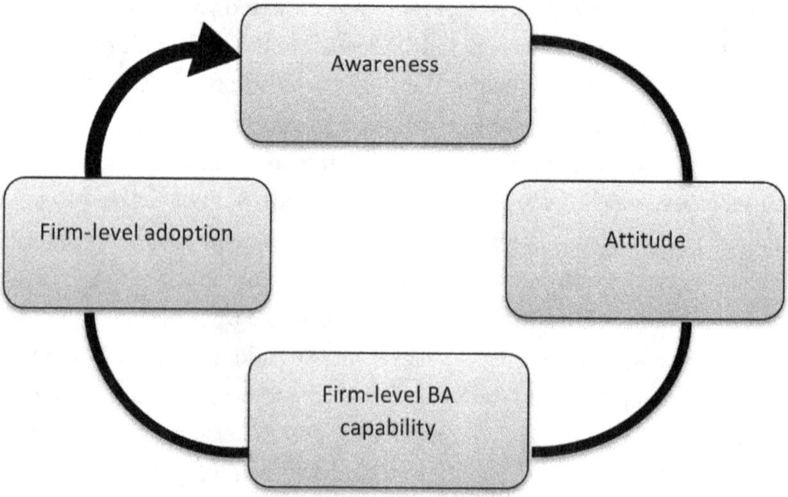

Figure 11.1. Conceptual framework for the study

competitive space. It is therefore important to understand their states of BA adoption and the extent to which their structures and processes will promote or impede actions towards BA competitiveness.

Research Design

The research study was designed to obtain insights into the knowledge and attitudes of C-level executives related to the adoption of BA. More specifically, the researchers sought to better understand the levels of awareness, attitudes and adoption of BA in firms across the country as well as the drivers of and barriers to effective adoption of BA solutions. The findings of the study were used to devise a strategy to increase the levels of adoption and guide executives in a range of sectors to address issues and solve problems using BA.

Some 184 executives from 57 local firms in the category "more than 50 employees" completed a personal interview survey in 2013. According to a Central Statistical Office publication, there are about 927 firms in the category of "more than 50 employees" in Trinidad and Tobago. The sample of 57 firms equaled the number required at a 95 per cent confidence level. The survey was a non-trivial investment of time for C-level executives, the target group of the study. Therefore, respondents were selected from firms based on their receptiveness to answering the survey questions. Multiple respondents from the same firm were included in the sample.

Findings and Discussion

Awareness

The respondents were asked about their levels of awareness of the terms, components and benefits of BA. Their levels of awareness were determined from respondents' knowledge and experience and the actual use of BA by their respective firms. Respondents were sufficiently acquainted with names or terms in BA; however, almost all of them termed BA as "Reporting" (98.9 per cent) and "Management Information Systems" (92.4 per cent). About three quarters of the respondents understood BA as "Business Analytics" or "Business Intelligence". Other common BA terms, such as "Informatics" and "Decision Engineering" were known by fewer than one-third of the respondents.

The percentage of awareness of BA items indicates that respondents were largely unaware of core items in BA (table 11.1). This suggests that firms are operating at the most basic level of SAS classification of BA sophistication. The SAS levels are reporting, basic analytics and advanced analytics. A large majority of the respondents indicated that their firms deal with manageable sets of structured, unstructured or semi-structured data and that spreadsheets are often used to handle these data sets for reporting purposes. Knowledge ("Just Heard of" or "Used in This Company") of basic analytics items, such as interactive data visualization (41.3 per cent), statistical analysis (70.6 per cent) and advanced analytical items, such as big data (53.8 per cent), as well as advanced BA solutions such as Hadoop (31.5 per cent), was very limited.

With respect to BA benefits, respondents' knowledge is mostly around managerial decision-making in the areas of profit, cost and customer experience. About 95 per cent of the respondents understood that BA is used for improved decision-making. Three quarters of the respondents thought that BA is used for maximizing profit, lowering cost or enhancing customer experience.

Despite the high level of general awareness and appreciation of the benefits of BA, adoption of BA is challenged by respondents' confusion about what is needed for BA adoption in organizations. In terms of data source, almost three quarters of them thought that data for BA should be primarily internal and should be obtained from individual data sources across functions within the enterprise. There was some degree of emphasis on external data, structured data and real-time data. However, big data or unstructured data were not seen as important for BA adoption in the organizations. The

Table 11.1. Awareness of Business Analytics Items

	Never Heard of or Never Used		**Just Heard of; Not Used**		**Used in This Company or Elsewhere**	
BA Items	**Count**	**%**	**Count**	**%**	**Count**	**%**
Open-Source Programming Languages	107	58.2	66	35.9	11	6.0
Statistical/analytics software suites	54	29.3	79	42.9	51	27.7
Data Visualization	108	58.7	60	32.6	16	8.7
End User Productivity Tools and Spreadsheets	2	1.1	7	3.8	175	95.1
Business Intelligence Platforms	24	13.0	59	32.1	101	54.9
Structured Data	14	7.6	61	33.2	109	59.2
Unstructured Data	25	13.6	54	29.3	105	57.1
Semistructured Data	36	19.6	53	28.8	95	51.6
Use of Data from Internal Source	9	4.9	20	10.9	155	84.2
Use of Data from External Source	9	4.9	27	14.7	148	80.4
Big data	85	46.2	58	31.5	41	22.3
Data That Are Changing Constantly	21	11.4	36	19.6	127	69.0
Real-Time or Near-Real-Time Data	10	54.0	32	17.4	142	77.2
BA Process	36	19.6	69	37.5	79	42.9
Advanced BA Solution	126	68.5	42	22.8	16	8.7

Source: Inter-American Development Bank (Project ID TT-T1037), 2015.

lack of appreciation of the importance of enterprise-wide big data is a major limitation to BA adoption.

The research explored respondents' knowledge of BA tools to assess the extent to which they were familiar with more sophisticated tools. Tools at varying levels of sophistication based on SAS categorization, including spreadsheets, interactive visualization, statistical software, BA processes and advanced BA solutions were named in the survey, and respondents were asked about their knowledge of these tools. Respondents were categorized by the types of businesses in which they were involved and their positions, reporting authority and length of association with the organization. The research found that knowledge of spreadsheets, which is at the lowest level of sophistication, is the highest for all the respondents in all categories, while advanced BA solutions, the highest level of BA sophistication, is least known by respondents, despite varying levels of experience, reporting relationships, positions and types of firms (table 11.2). Although in the literature interactive visualization is considered low in terms

Table 11.2. Factors Discriminating the Awareness Level (Per Cent)

Factors	Spreadsheet	Interactive Visualization	Statistical Software	BA Processes	Advanced BA Solution
Type of Business: B2B	100.0	45.6	70.2	85.9	33.3
Type of Business: B2C	100.0	26.1	65.2	78.3	34.8
Type of Business: B2B and B2C	98.1	42.3	72.1	77.9	29.8
Position: Analyst	97.8	46.2	67.0	83.5	40.7
Position: Manager	100.0	36.7	74.2	77.4	22.6
Report to: Functional Manager	98.3	41.4	63.8	81.0	36.2
Report to: Board or CEO	99.2	41.3	73.4	80.2	38.9
Length of Association: <3 years	98.8	47.6	69.8	86.0	34.9
Length of Association: <4–9 years	97.9	39.6	77.0	87.5	35.4
Length of Association: >10 years	100.0	32.0	66.0	64.0	22.0
Academic degree: Associate	100.0	16.7	38.9	44.4	16.7
Academic degree: Undergraduate	98.4	45.3	79.7	76.6	32.8
Academic degree: Graduate and PhD	98.6	48.6	78.4	93.2	35.1
Academic degree: Others	100.0	28.6	50.0	78.6	28.6

Source: Inter-American Development Bank (Project ID TT-T1037), 2015.

Notes: B2B, business-to-business firm; B2C, business-to-consumers firm.

of sophistication, the awareness level is very low for this category (about 40 per cent). However, awareness of statistical or analytics software suites such as SAS, SPSS or STATA, and of BA processes such as decision tools, neural networks and so on is sufficiently high for certain characteristics of firms or respondents (about 80 per cent), and therefore does not readily conform to the SAS categorization of the sophistication of analytics use.

An examination of the differences in respondents' awareness of BA tools based on the respondents' characteristics reveals that, with the exception of their levels of education, awareness of BA tools does not differ significantly across respondent categories. Differences are exhibited in interactive visualization in terms of type of business, respondent's job position, length of service in the firm and academic qualifications. It is seen that business-to-consumers firms have a lower level of awareness of data visualization than do business-to-business firms. Similarly, an employee who is a manager or who has many years of service association with the firm, or one who has no academic degree, often tends to know less about interactive visualization. The academic qualifications of an employee also appear to be important discriminators for the use of statistical software, BA processes and advanced BA solutions. An employee with less than a bachelor's degree is often less acquainted with the BA items (figure 11.2).

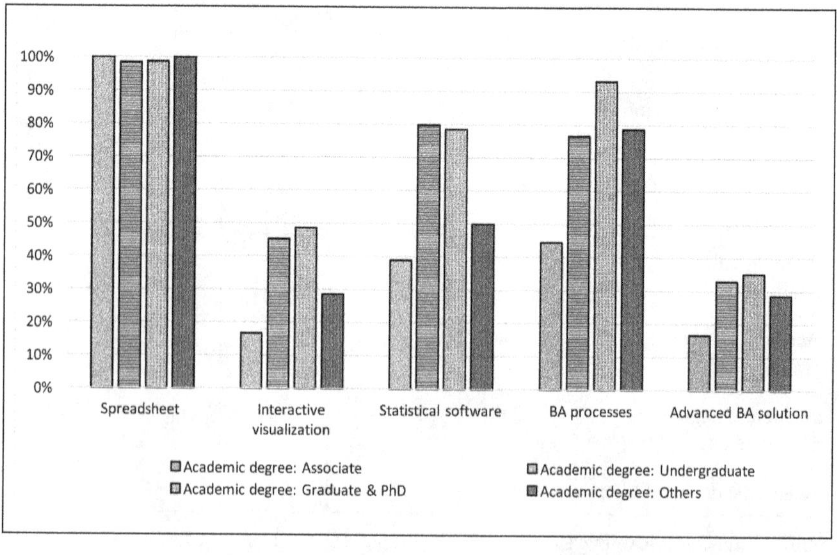

Figure 11.2. Awareness of BA sophistication by respondents' academic qualifications

The sample suggests that generally firms in Trinidad and Tobago have an appreciation of the concept of BA but do not understand what it truly is or its true potential. There is an opportunity to increase BA adoption through BA education, which should serve to enhance awareness of BA and improve the sophistication of firm processes for BA adoption.

Attitude, Drivers and Barriers

The essence of innovation diffusion theory has been used in this study to understand the BA adopters' attitudes. The study sought to assess respondents' attitudes towards BA based on their perceptions of BA's usefulness, barriers to adoption and the extent to which BA is appreciated by critical actors in their organizations. Respondents felt that BA adoption would increase organizational performance (table 11.3). Mean scores for their attitudes towards all seven attributes of BA are in a range higher than the neutral point on the scale of "Strongly Disagree" (1) to "Strongly agree" (5).

Table 11.4 presents perceived BA complexities that designate barriers to or drivers of BA adoption. It is hypothesized that the more complexities associated with BA, the lower the adoption level. Respondents rated their perceived

Table 11.3. Descriptive Statistics for Perceived BA Usefulness

Perceived BA Usefulness	*N*	Mean	Standard Deviation
Analytics would be critical for our company's success in the near future	180	4.48	.672
Companies in my industry are benefiting from analytics in a significant way	174	3.67	.970
Analytics work gives our company a significant competitive advantage	158	3.65	.896
Our internal customers effectively leverage the data and results	165	3.37	1.025
Analytics is central to our company's products and services	181	3.62	.984
The most important decisions are based on data and analysis	177	3.59	.956
Our analysts are used to making key decisions within the company	173	3.80	.919

Source: Inter-American Development Bank (Project ID TT-T1037), 2015.

Table 11.4. Perceived BA Barriers (Per Cent)

BA Barriers	Not a Problem	To Some Extent	To a Great Extent	No Idea
Lack of understanding of how to use analytics to improve the business	13.0	64.7	14.7	7.6
Lack of mindshare due to competing priorities	7.1	59.8	22.3	10.9
Lack of internal skills	11.4	72.8	12.0	3.8
Inability to get the data	13.6	67.4	15.2	3.8
Existing culture does not encourage sharing information	18.5	62.0	15.2	4.3
Ownership of the data is unclear or governance is ineffective	20.7	58.2	12.5	8.7
BA projects are lower priority than other business initiatives for top managerial attention and funding	10.3	65.2	15.8	8.7
Users believe that BA projects take too long	8.7	66.8	10.3	14.1
Stakeholders do not really use BA to drive intelligent business decisions	12.5	61.4	17.4	8.7
Lack of user buy-in	10.9	63.0	15.2	10.9
Does not know where to start	25.0	62.5	6.0	6.5
Poor data quality	20.1	63.0	12.0	4.9
Technical challenges related to extract, transform, and load (ETL) data for analysis	12.0	63.6	10.9	13.6
Merging structured and unstructured data	9.2	59.2	13.6	17.9
Dealing with heterogeneous data (text, numeric data, images, etc.)	12.0	61.4	12.0	14.7
Insufficient budget for adoption	17.9	58.7	12.5	10.9
History of failed efforts in analytics	20.7	53.8	3.8	21.7
Competitors in my industry are not adopting it	14.7	41.3	7.6	36.4
Executives jump the line with their latest emergency	11.4	59.8	17.9	10.9
Overall	14.2	61.3	13.0	11.5

Source: Inter-American Development Bank (Project ID TT-T-1037), 2015.

barriers of BA adoption in four categories – "Not a Problem", "To Some Extent", "To a Great Extent", and "No Idea". The largest single group (about 60 per cent) faced barriers to some extent. About 15 per cent said that they did not see any problem in the analytics adoption process. Nearly as many said that they faced the barriers to a great extent. About 10 per cent had no idea about these BA barriers. Firm conditions therefore appear to be more favourable to BA adoption.

The mean values of perceived BA observability are higher than the neutral value of 3.0, indicating that the results of BA is visible to top level management and other stakeholders (see table 11.5). This is a factor favourable for BA adoption in the sample.

Table 11.5. Descriptive Statistics for Perceived BA Value Observability

Perceived BA Value Observability	*N*	Mean	Standard Deviation
Senior management understands the contribution of our BA team	173	3.92	.899
The work of analytics professionals is more visible compared to a year ago	170	3.41	.958
Most of our analytics work is consumed by people outside of the analytics team	161	3.29	.990

Source: Inter-American Development Bank (Project ID TT-T1037), 2015.

The sample revealed an overall positive disposition towards BA. The question arises as to the extent to which firm factors are aligned with elements that support general BA advancement as well as improvement in the level of BA sophistication in firms.

Firm-Level BA Capabilities

Culture

The research sought to assess the extent to which company culture supported BA advancement (table 11.6). Culture was assessed by the mode of decision-making and the extent to which analytics professionals were integral to the company's strategy, growth and success. Respondents were required to assess their company's culture by responding to items on a scale of 1 to 5. Means of more than 3.5 were obtained on all dimensions of culture necessary to support BA implementation and advancement. This indicates that the cultures of organizations are aligned with the requirements for the advancement of BA. In particular, data-driven decision-making is valued by management (4.05) and there is strong appreciation for the importance of analytics to the immediate future of the company (4.51).

Table 11.6. Descriptive Statistics on Organizational Culture Elements Supportive of BA

Organizational Culture Elements	*N*	Mean	Standard Deviation
The dominant culture is gut- or intuition-driven decision-making	184	3.14	1.284
Management shows a high regard for data-driven decision-making	184	4.05	.937
I believe that analytics would be critical for our success in the near future	184	4.51	.701
Companies in my industry are benefitting from analytics in a significant way	184	3.79	1.082
Analytics professionals are respected and trusted partners in top-level management	184	3.89	1.212
Our analytical capabilities are a key element of our business model and/or strategy	184	3.61	1.232
Many of our company's business processes have analytics built into them	184	3.58	1.143
The most important decisions are based on data and analysis	184	3.66	1.022
Analytics are central to our company's products and services	184	3.68	1.046
Our analysts are used to making key decisions within the company	184	3.93	1.033
Members of the analytics group have regular conversations with other employees in the organization about the benefits of analytics	184	3.48	1.383
We use data about past, present and future events in decision-making	184	3.90	.783

Source: Inter-American Development Bank (Project ID TT-T1037), 2015.

Data Management and Skills

The data management practices and skill level of BA practitioners appear to be slightly above average and there is recognition that BA yields competitive advantage for companies (table 11.7). Though all means were above the neutral value of 3, lower values with respect to data management indicate room for improvement in this area. The achievement of actual competitive advantage attributed to analytics is a very positive signal for further BA advancement within companies.

Table 11.7. Descriptive Statistics on Organizational Data Management and Skills

Organizational Data Management and Skills	*N*	Mean	Standard Deviation
Our internal customers effectively leverage the data and results	184	3.64	1.260
Our company makes trade-offs on data quality	184	3.09	1.180
We are able to find and use the right information instantly using analytics	184	3.19	1.211
Analytics work gives our company a significant competitive advantage	184	3.98	1.169
The work of analytics professionals is more visible compared to a year ago	184	3.60	1.150
Our analyses are being used increasing by functional areas and/or business units	184	3.72	.890

Source: Inter-American Development Bank (Project ID TT-T1037), 2015.

Firm-Level BA Adoption

Overall Adoption

Table 11.8 presents the adoption rate of analytics by decision-makers in organizations included in the study. Of the total 184 respondents, only 8.2 per cent indicated that more than 75 per cent of decision-makers in their firm use analytics. This suggests a low level of adoption of BA by decision-makers. The other respondents were nearly equally split into the three lower levels of adoption, at between 25 per cent and 75 per cent, less than 25 per cent and less than 10 per cent. The data also offer an approximation of 30 per cent overall adoption rate of BA on average. The question arises as to the areas in which BA is adopted and the importance of those areas to firm competitiveness. Extending this concern to the country level, it is crucial to understand the level of BA adoption in industries of great significance to the economy.

Table 11.8. Decision-makers' Use of Analytics

Decision-Makers' Use of BA	Frequency	Per Cent	Valid Per Cent	Cumulative Per Cent
Less than 10 per cent	58	31.5	31.5	31.5
Less than 25 per cent	48	26.1	26.1	57.6
Between 25 and 75 per cent	63	34.2	34.2	91.8
More than 75 per cent	15	8.2	8.2	100.0
Total	184	100.0	100.0	

Source: Inter-American Development Bank (Project ID TT-T1037), 2015.

Figure 11.3 presents functional areas in which firms adopt BA. The figure shows that BA is used in Trinidad and Tobago mostly for pricing strategies, as almost every two out of three respondents indicated that they use BA for pricing. About 60 per cent of respondents used BA for financial performance analysis, and almost a similar percentage (55.4 per cent) indicated their use of BA for other non-financial performance management. Almost half the respondents adopted BA for sales or revenue optimization. Other areas in which BA adoption was important included customer relationship management to obtain customers' insights and satisfaction levels, supply chain management and demand forecasting. The percentage of adoption in the three aforementioned areas was 46.7, 45.7 and 40.8 per cent, respectively. Firms appear to be using BA for both internal performance management and strategic decision-making. Areas with low adoption of BA, such as warranty analytics, fraud detection and prevention and product design are likely linked to low-level firm competence in these areas.

Adoption by Industry

The data revealed significant differences in BA adoption level by industry. All industries were not considered in this comparison, and the data presented are

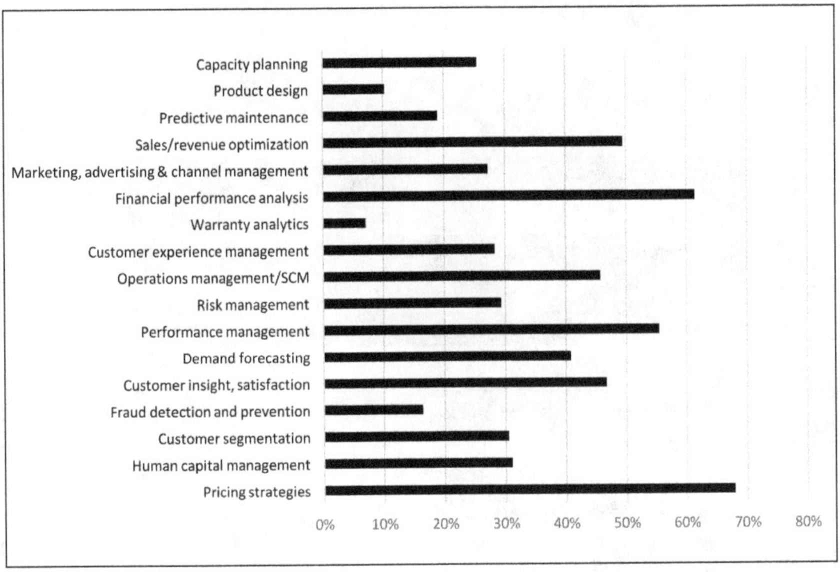

Figure 11.3. Analytics adoption in functional areas

limited to those industries with a relatively higher representation of respondents in the study. The automotive industry had the highest adoption level, as 41.7 per cent of the respondents in this industry indicated an adoption rate of more than 75 per cent (figure 11.4). The data also show that, relative to the other industries represented in the study, a small percentage of decision-makers in the automotive industry (16.7 per cent) use less BA and a large percentage of them use more of it. The BA adoption rate for the automotive industry is about 50 per cent, which is substantially higher than the sample average of 30 per cent. The food and beverage industry also showed a higher adoption level (approximately 40 per cent) compared to the overall sample average. BA adoption in banking and insurance, energy and wholesale and retail industries match the sample average benchmark. This is an area of concern given the heavy reliance of Caribbean economies on the energy and the distribution industries.

Sophistication of Adoption

The research revealed low levels of sophistication of BA adoption in general. Both predictive modelling and advanced analytics are marginally used by the

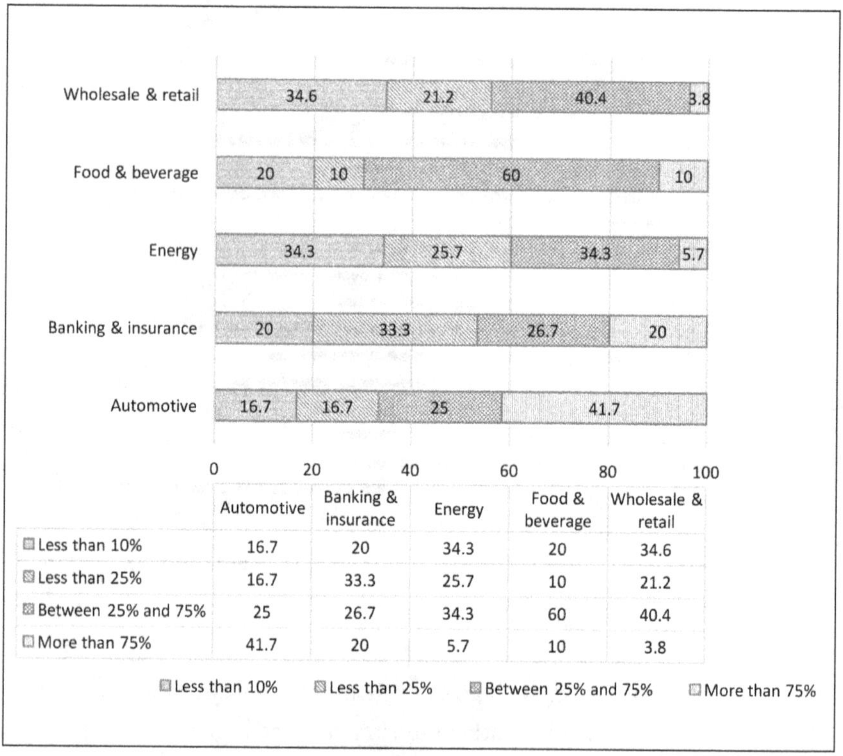

	Automotive	Banking & insurance	Energy	Food & beverage	Wholesale & retail
Less than 10%	16.7	20	34.3	20	34.6
Less than 25%	16.7	33.3	25.7	10	21.2
Between 25% and 75%	25	26.7	34.3	60	40.4
More than 75%	41.7	20	5.7	10	3.8

Figure 11.4. BA adoption level by industry

firms. Only 47 respondents of 184 indicated that they already used sophisticated software solution for storing massive data and conducting analysis. The impact level is also seen as low, indicating a higher potential for more sophisticated use of BA in firms (table 11.9).

The approach of firms for obtaining and developing BA capabilities is an indicator of the sustainability and advancement of BA within those firms. Table 11.10 presents summary statistics of respondents' preference for building or buying BA capabilities. There is a clear preference for advancing the adoption of BA based on building in-house capabilities, not on the use of contracted resources, however, the two attributes they currently use most strongly are their own experience and intuition and internal data about the past, present, and future of the business. These are critical shortcomings for firms seeking to advance their level of BA sophistication.

Table 11.9. Level of Impact of Analytics

Level of Impact	Frequency	Per Cent	Valid Per Cent	Cumulative Per Cent
Minor impact. Different solutions produce inconsistent results.	20	10.9	10.9	10.9
Some impact. We have had some success, but the impact is typically within teams or departments.	109	59.2	59.2	70.1
Strong impact. We use analytics across our core processes to inform and guide our actions.	45	24.5	24.5	94.6
Very strong impact. All our business decisions are based on information provided by analytics.	10	5.4	5.4	100.0
Total	184	100.0	100.0	

Source: Inter-American Development Bank (Project ID TT-T1037), 2015.

Advancing Business Analytics in the Caribbean

Summary of Findings

Respondents were sufficiently acquainted with BA known by various generic names and terms. The percentage of awareness of specific BA items, however, indicates that firms in Trinidad and Tobago lie somewhat at the lower level of the SAS classification of sophistication of adoption. Knowledge of spreadsheets, which is at the lowest level of sophistication, is seen among the highest in the data for all the characteristics of respondents, while advanced BA solutions, which is at the highest level of sophistication, lies at the lowest level of awareness. Further examination of the knowledge of BA items reveals that, except for a few characteristics, knowledge of most of the BA items does not differ significantly between characteristics; the characteristics referenced here were type of organization, job position, to whom reporting, length of service and academic qualifications.

In terms of awareness, therefore, the sample suggests that generally firms in Trinidad and Tobago have an appreciation of the concept of BA but do not understand what it truly is. Perceived BA usefulness that is subjectively

Table 11.10. Descriptive Statistics: Adopters' Preferences for BA Sourcing

Adopters' Preferences	*N*	Mean	Standard Deviation
We use contracted resources for analytics because they are cheaper	139	2.31	.788
Our analytical talent is centralized in a single organization	160	2.92	1.000
We use contracted resources for analytics because they provide a fresh perspective	145	2.64	.918
We have analytics teams deployed throughout the company	157	2.90	1.148
We rely exclusively on in-house analytics expertise	173	3.45	1.031
We often leverage academics for our analytics	161	2.79	.964
We use contracted resources for analytics because they provide specialized skills	149	2.83	.989
We often use our experience and intuition to look forward	180	3.94	.844
We spend substantial time and energy on data modelling before actually analysing data	181	3.29	.947
We are able to find and use the right information instantly using analytics	172	2.99	.988
Our analytics processes are embedded into our products, services or IT applications	174	3.10	.974
We spend a lot of time and energy creating graphical views (data visualization) of data to provide business insights	178	3.13	.988
We do a lot of work preparing analysis results for managers and executives	180	3.56	.987
We use data about past, present and future events in decision-making	183	3.89	.770
Our analyses are being used increasingly by functional areas and/or business units	180	3.67	.831
We already use sophisticated software solutions for storing massive data and conducting analysis	176	2.80	1.158
The volume and variety of data we deal with are causing us to consider using Hadoop-based solutions within the next twelve months for storing our data (and distributed computing solutions to analyse these data)	173	3.23	1.133

Source: Inter-American Development Bank (Project ID TT-T1037), 2015.

assessed by the adopters clearly indicates that BA adoption would increase organizational performance. The mean of all seven attribute scores in a range higher than the neutral point on the scale of "Strongly Disagree" to "Strongly Agree". The largest single group of respondents (approximately 60 per cent) faced barriers "To Some Extent". Approximately 15 per cent said they did not see any problems in the analytics adoption process. Nearly as many said that they faced the barriers "To a Great Extent". About 10 per cent had "No Idea about These BA Barriers". Mean perceived BA value observability scores are significantly higher than 3.0, indicating that the results of BA are visible to top-level management and other stakeholders. Lack of internal skill, though classified as a barrier "To Some Extent", was marginally ahead of other barriers, although there was a preference for getting BA projects done in-house. No one barrier stood out. It should be noted, though, that the options included only organizational barriers.

In terms of attitude, therefore, the sample revealed an overall positive disposition towards BA and some preference for affecting projects with in-house resources. While this approach is supported in the literature, firms must attend to their inherent dispositions that could challenge their efforts to advance BA adoption. The BA capabilities in the sampled firms were above average. These included culture as well as data management practices and skills. Management held a very positive disposition towards data-driven decision-making.

With respect to adoption, respondents' data reveal an overall firm-level adoption rate of 30 per cent, with industry rates of 50 per cent (automotive), 40 per cent (food and beverages), approximately 30 per cent (wholesale and retail) and 20 per cent (government). Other adoption-level insights include that the marginal usage of predictive modelling and advanced analytics and the impact level of sophisticated tools of BA are seen as low.

Implications for Caribbean Firms

The data suggest that Caribbean firms possess a high level of general awareness but a low level of awareness of sophisticated BA, a generally positive disposition towards BA and an average adoption level of 30 per cent. These findings have significant policy implications for Caribbean firms, showing that they could enhance their competitiveness by improving the sophistication of their business processes.

Firms can be supported by increasing their levels of awareness of the use of information and communications technologies and more sophisticated BA tools for communicating and engaging in business transactions. In the Caribbean business environment, with its small market size, the overall approach to customer acquisition and retention is critical, and BA tools and competencies can aid them in accessing customers, receiving feedback and generally improving their levels of service to customers. Caribbean firms are generally small, and cross-functional operations across the value chain are prevalent. These firms seek to become more competitive globally by expanding their presence in the value chain, and BA can serve to integrate operations across the value chain efficiently and effectively. More sophisticated tools applied in the cross-functional areas of the value chain would enhance the competitiveness of the organizations. This would require enhancement of their BA skills and competencies, both hard and soft, within their firms and across clusters and networks. Demonstration of the power of BA and support for the enhancement of BA competencies would contribute positively to the maturity of BA and to overall firm competitiveness.

Note

1. "C-level" refers to chief positions in corporate management, such as chief executive officer, chief financial officer, chief operating officer, chief technology officer and the like.

References

Best, Lloyd, and Kari Polanyi Levitt. 2010. *Essays on the Theory of Plantation Economy: A Historical and Institutional Approach to Caribbean Economic Development*. Kingston: University of the West Indies Press.

Beñat, Soumitra Dutta, and Bruno Lanvin. 2014. *The Global Information Technology Report, 2014: Rewards and Risks of Big Data*. Geneva: World Economic Forum.

Cao, Guangming. 2010. A Four-Dimensional View of IT Business Value, System Research and Behavioural Science. *Systems Research and Behavioural Science* 27 (3): 267–84.

Davenport, Thomas H., and D.J. Patil. 2012. Data Scientist: The Sexiest Job of the 21st Century. *Harvard Business Review*, October.

Kalakota, Ravi. 2012. Bloomberg on Business Analytics. *Business Analytics 3.0*. https://practicalanalytics.co/2012/04/09/bloomberg-on-state-of-business-analytics/.

Karagiannis, Nikolaos, and C.J. Polychroniou. 2015. The Scourge of Dependency and Globalization in the Caribbean. *Truth-Out,* 4 April. www.truth-out.org/opinion/item/29951-the-scourge-of-dependency-and-globalization-in-the-caribbean.

Kiron, David, Pamela Kirk Prentice and Renee Boucher Ferguson. 2014. *The Analytics Mandate.* Research Report. Cambridge, MA: MIT Sloan Management Review.

Marius, Michele. 2015. Snapshot: 2015 Update of ICT Network Readiness in the Caribbean. *ICT Pulse,* 22 April 22. www.ict-pulse.com/2015/04/snapshot-2015-update-ict-network-readiness-caribbean/.

McAfee, Andrew, and Erik Brynjolfsson. 2012. Big Data: The Management Revolution. *Harvard Business Review,* October.

Ramkissoon, Ronald. 2002. Explaining Differences in Economic Performance in Caribbean Economies. Paper presented at the international conference Iceland and the World Economy: Small Island Economies in the Era of Globalization, Center for International Development (CID), Harvard University, Cambridge, MA, 20 May.

Schwab, Klaus, and Xavier Sala-i-Martín. 2014. *The Global Competitiveness Report, 2013–2014.* Geneva: World Economic Forum.

Wang, Yu-Min, Yi-Shun Wang and Yong-Fu Yang. 2010. Understanding the Determinants of RFID Adoption in the Manufacturing Industry. *Technological Forecasting and Social Change* 77 (5): 803–15.

CHAPTER 12

Global Forces and the Role of Caribbean Trade Unions as Political Actors

Kristina Hinds-Harrison and Annita Montoute

Several debates and conceptualizations regarding globalization abounded during the 1990s. Hyper- or pro-globalists view globalization as opening extensive potential to humanity, using free markets to increase avenues for human interaction at an ever swifter pace. Meanwhile, sceptics assert that globalization has been a long historical process of the expansion and extension of capitalism that is unevenly skewed and based on the agendas of the powerful in the global political economy (see Held et al. 1999; Scholte 2005). Then there are "activist" or "transformationalist" visions of globalization that wish to refashion and utilize the beneficial tools of increasing interconnectivity while substantially reforming or rooting out the pernicious exploitative elements, assuming that such is possible (Held et al. 1999; Scholte 2005).

Rehashing these multiple discussions at length is not necessary here, but what is necessary is to highlight that globalization is generally viewed as heightened interconnectivity, facilitated and intensified by technological advances. We view these processes at present as inherently neoliberal and capitalist in orientation and as uneven, even if "global". Whether one sees these processes as new or views them positively or negatively, they certainly impact social, political and economic activities the world over.

There are also several commentaries in fields of international relations and international political economy that link globalization, the declining or changing role of the state and the growing significance of non-state actors, including corporations, non-governmental organizations (NGOs) and criminal and other networks (for example, Lipschutz 1992; Keck and Sikkink 1998; Kaldor 2003; Scholte 2005; Moghadam 2013). Trade union activities form part of the landscape of non-state actors of significance for analysis in contemporary international relations or international political economy. For instance, *Globalizations* compiled a special issue of the journal in February 2014 on Free Trade and Transnational Labour that contained articles by Bieler, Hilary, Lindberg, Park, Latimer and Hurt which addressed cross-border trade union solidarity in the face of global economic forces. Similarly, Muller, Platzer and Rub (2010) and Kowalsky (2010) discussed the difficulties faced by the union movement in addressing the intersection between labour interests and the current global economic paradigm in *International Politics and Society.* Similar discussions are presented by authors such as O'Brien (2000), Adaba (2002) and Wills (2002). Other related discussions on union politics and internationalism exist in disciplines outside of international relations or international political economy, specifically those that focus on industrial relations (see Moody 1997; Martínez 2010).

This chapter follows this trend of examining trade unions in global politics by asking questions about the ways in which the Caribbean region's entanglement in a global web has affected the conduct of the region's trade unions.[1] The chapter uses Barbados and Trinidad and Tobago as case studies and offers the view that the manner in which these types of organizations now operate as well as the ways in which they are now conceived and portrayed have been significantly altered by forces of globalization.

Caribbean Unionism in Context

Trade unionism developed along similar lines across the anglophone Caribbean in its early history. However, differences emerged post-independence as a reflection of the peculiarities of individual states (Alexander and Parker 2004). One can consider the movement to abolish slavery as the start of the regional labour movement. Then, by the start of the twentieth century, although illegal, unions began to be formed, such as the Trinidad Workingmen's Association (1897), the Bricklayers and Painters Union in Jamaica (1898) and in Guyana the British Guiana Labour Union (1919) (Lewis 1977; Bolland 2001; Randall 2003).

Yet the 1930s financial crisis and the trickle-down effects on the Caribbean created the watershed moment for Caribbean unionism. In this atmosphere, a series of uprisings spread across the region accompanied by industrial and political demands expressed at the British Guiana and West Indies Labour Congress in 1938. These demands were addressed by the Moyne Commission and laid the framework for the legal recognition of trade unions, for the creation of industrial relations frameworks and for the establishment of much employment-related legislation. The granting of the franchise, internal self-government and later independence across the region enhanced the gains of labour, and it is no secret that the region's political leadership emerged from the Caribbean workers' movement.

From the 1940s into the early post-independence period, trade unions were visibly and overtly political in their activities to mobilize for the rights of workers by negotiating with employers, striking and mobilizing for the creation of legislation which would ensure that workers were treated with dignity and fairness. Unions have stood up to private-sector operatives and, in spite of their connections to political parties or leadership, unions have also confronted Caribbean governments that have often functioned as the main employers across the region. In this regard, unions can be viewed as the champions of the "masses" of the Caribbean.

Although Caribbean trade unions have concentrated on domestic and regional industrial relations and political matters, the region's trade union movement can also be viewed as having been nestled into larger international trade union movement, even preglobalization. To begin with, delegates from the British Labour Party and the International Trades Union Congress were present at the initial meeting of the British Guiana and the West Indies Labour Congress in 1926 (Bolland 2001; Alexander and Parker 2004). This may be unsurprising since the territories involved were British colonies at the time and subject to much "tutelage". All the same, the location of Caribbean territories within the British colonial system placed them squarely within globalizing processes. Trade unionism has not been immune to this global character. The involvement of Caribbean people in the World Federation of Trade Unions from as early as 1945 illustrates this entanglement of local, regional and international trade union development (Padmore 1945; Alexander and Parker 2004).

The space in which trade unions in the Caribbean have functioned has also been significantly affected by trends in the international political economy.

For instance, many of the achievements of Caribbean trade unions, as well as the space available for union practices of agitation, were facilitated by the context of the Cold War. Socialist options and formulations of the way societies should look were open to states – as long, that is, as they were not avowedly aligned with "communism". Nevertheless, the politics of the Cold War also divided the international labour movement and, as a consequence, negatively affected the nascent attempts to build solidarity through the cooperation of trade unions across the anglophone Caribbean and also the wider Caribbean (Bolland 1997; Alexander and Parker 2004). Bolland captures this view in his discussion of the demise of the Caribbean Labour Congress as labour leaders across the region became enmeshed in the split between the "pro-Western" and "pro-communist" division that split the World Federation of Trade Unions in 1949 (Bolland 1997). The influence of the British Colonial Office was evident in support of trade union development in its West Indian colonies, but only within the fold of the anticommunist International Confederation of Free Trade Unions that emerged in 1949. These divisions across the region's unions led to some members of the Caribbean Labour Congress being affiliated with the World Federation of Trade Unions and others with the International Confederation of Free Trade Unions (Bolland 1997). This rift between the region's more moderate and more radical union leaders shows how the global insertion of the Caribbean's nascent labour unions influenced the development of regional labour solidarity.

Caribbean Unionism after the Cold War

Despite the negative impact of Cold War divisions on solidarity across the region's unions, the Cold War era was one in which moderate democratic socialism flourished in the region. Prior to decolonization the British Trade Union Congress attempted to fashion "respectable" unionism and social democracy. This sort of unionism existed in the region along with more radical union politics in some places (notably Guyana). In contrast, the entry of globalization into this Caribbean setting by the mid-1980s began to alter unions' abilities to maneuver, as a paradigm shift in the neoliberal direction began to privilege the market, economic efficiencies and capital rather than mass-based social justice. Thus unions began to be painted as economically destabilizing forces instead of as the progressive political forces on which Caribbean (social) democracies were built: "Hence, strikes and other actions against employers, which in the past were seen as actions against colonial oppressors, could now be portrayed as being against the national interest, as being a selfish use of power on behalf of particular parts of the population at the expense of the development of the economy as a whole" (Alexander and Parker 2004, 19).

The introduction of structural adjustment programmes and the normalization of neoliberal economic rationales during the 1980s and 1990s brought much downsizing, right sizing and rationalizing and thereby dramatically affected unions in the Caribbean, as well as around the world. What is more, the economic climate of financial crisis that took the global stage around 2008 led to the further prioritization of business in efforts to rescue the region. In these precarious times, where do unions stand? We posit that the globalized context has affected and, to some extent, delegitimized unions in the Caribbean in ways that are both unique to the region and in keeping with global trends.

From the mid-1990s, challenges to the preferential access to European markets awarded to ACP agricultural sectors under the Lomé conventions resulted in the erosion of preferential access for Caribbean sugar and bananas. The subsequent increased external competition that these Caribbean agricultural industries faced led to severe restructuring and even the termination of such industries in some states (ECLAC 2005; Payne and Sutton 2008). For instance, sugar production ceased in St Kitts in 2005, and Trinidad and Tobago began to close its sugar export sector in 2003. Further, Payne and Sutton note that only Belize and Guyana retain the promise of continuing worthwhile sugar export industries (Payne and Sutton 2008). Meanwhile, the Windward Islands farmers moved towards producing "fair trade" bananas in order to keep the industry alive. The declines in these sectors led to difficulties within some trade unions,[2] including the closure of some unions that were primarily comprised of agricultural workers. The All Trinidad Sugar Estates and Factory Workers' Trade Union is an example of a trade union that ceased to exist following the demise of sugar in Trinidad and Tobago.

Declines in agriculture for export in the region can also be linked to the movement in the Caribbean towards service-oriented pursuits ranging from tourism to the provision of "offshore" financial services. These trends have complicated the landscape of the Caribbean labour force and may incline some workers to be less willing to join unions or to avoid seeing themselves as having interests aligned with "labour". Morris notes of Caribbean unions that "trade unions have developed great expertise and experience in organizing and relating to white collar workers in the public sector. However, there has been a slower response in organizing workers into trade unions in areas such as finance and banking" (Morris 2002, 5).

What is more, the development of human resources professionals often employed in corporate settings tends to function to shift the focus away from industrial relations and towards "managing" human resources, thus posing a challenge to workers' organizations (Morris 2002). Labour has been transformed linguistically into the more neutral category "human resources", a term that is not associated with the history of tensions often inherent in relations between labour and capital.

To these occurrences we can add the trend towards what was once viewed as "atypical work" in the form of contract-based work, short-term and temporary jobs often facilitated by technological advances that have been used as cost-cutting strategies. These strategies have deprived workers of several benefits and may make them less inclined or less able to unionize (Morris 2002; Nurse 2004; de Peiza 2013). O'Brien (2000), Gallin (2001) and Palley (2009) are among the authors who indicate the ways in which such forms of work that increase business profitability but reduce the abilities of workers to organize are not unique to the Caribbean (O'Brien 2000; Gallin 2001; Palley 2009).

Notable also is the International Labour Organization's promotion of tripartite arrangements both within the workplace and at the national level. Such tripartite arrangements encourage discussion and conciliation between labour and capital and the state towards the goal of supporting the best outcomes for all (see ILO 2011). Yet one may ask questions about the ways in which the interests of labour in such arrangements may be shaped, or even tamed, particularly in light of the preponderance of "the market" in the current global political economy and even more so following the 2008 global financial crisis, which necessitated recovery on the back of corporate profitability.

It is against the backdrop of these implications that we now look at the ways in which occurrences in the global political economy have influenced trade union activities in two case studies from the English-speaking Caribbean. These cases, though not representative of the entire Caribbean or even the entire English-speaking Caribbean, offer glimpses into the ways in which global forces have altered the climate in which trade unions function and, by extension, the ways in which trade unions operate.

The Trinidad and Tobago Case

Trinidad and Tobago has a total of twenty-eight registered trade unions, the four largest ones being the National Union of Government and Federated Workers, having a membership of 21,515; the Public Service Association of Trinidad and Tobago, 17,954 members strong; the Oil Field Workers Trade Union, with a membership of 13,654; and the Trinidad and Tobago Unified Teachers Association, with 13,588 members. With the exception of the Trinidad and Tobago Unified Teachers Association, which was registered in 1980, they were all registered in the context of the 1937 labour riots: the Public Service Association of Trinidad and Tobago in 1938 and the Oilfields Workers' Trade Union (OWTU) and the National Union of Government and Federated Workers in 1937 (Ministry of Labour 2015).[3]

Although historically there had been divisions within the Trinidad and Tobago trade union movement, the formation of the National Trade Union Centre of Trinidad and Tobago in 1990 bridged these differences by uniting the Trinidad and Tobago Labour Congress and the Council of Progressive Trade Unions. Up to 2000, the National Trade Union Centre was the only umbrella trade union. However, differences among union leadership caused the OWTU to break away and, along with some smaller unions, join with some civil society organizations to form the Federation of Independent Trade Unions and NGOs. Additionally, the newly formed Joint Trade Union Movement represents an informal alliance of members and non-members of both the National Trade Union Centre of Trinidad and Tobago and the Federation of Independent Trade Unions and NGOs. Despite these developments, the National Trade Union Centre remains the only officially recognized trade union federation by the International Labour Organization. Membership in the National Trade Union Centre of Trinidad and Tobago stands at fifty thousand from fourteen trade unions.

Modern Trade Unionism: The Beginnings of Political Activism

Trade unions in Trinidad, like the rest of the Caribbean, by virtue of their role in the labour riots of 1937, were not only instrumental in advancing legislative changes in industrial relations but also broad social and political change. Trade union political activism was bolstered by poor social and economic conditions which were an outcome of external consideration, such as dominance of the economy by colonial capitalist interests, colonial rule and exploitation (Jacobs 1977).

However, unlike in other anglophone Caribbean countries, trade unions were not included in designing the plan for independence. This was because the political leadership emerged from outside of the trade union movement and the approach to independence was "cautious". Trinidad's strategy towards independence was one of non-violence, utilizing "political compromises"; therefore, "drastic inputs such as militant collaboration with organized labor" were not necessary (Johnson 1980, 244). Further, in the post-independence era Dr Eric Williams excluded trade unions from the political process, convinced that it would be in the best interest of the country if the former prioritized addressing the needs of their members above broader social and political issues (Johnson 1980). "The. . . program of development . . . failed to integrate the industrial relations system into the formal processes of industrial organization and economic growth" (Johnson 1980, 245). This is the environment from which trade unions emerged in the post-independence era – formally isolated from wider social and political processes. Kiely argues, however, that this formal separation did not always mean that trade unions were "apolitical", because in many instances their action impacted political processes, albeit indirectly (Kiely 1996). Kiely's thesis is supported by developments in trade union activity throughout the 1960s and 1970s, which in some cases were directly political or had significant political implications (Institute of Commonwealth Studies 2004). Additional proof of the interest of trade unions beyond matters of industrial relations was the formation of the first political party – the Leftist Council of Progressive Trade Unions – along trade union lines and the continuation of progressive elements within the trade union movement (see, for example, Meighoo 2008).

Trade Unions' Political Activism in an Era of Neoliberal Globalization

Structural adjustment policies from the 1980s and continuing forces of globalization from the 1990s served to weaken trade unions. The closing down of businesses and cuts in the public and private sectors led to a decline in the number of trade unions. It is noteworthy that thirty unions in Trinidad and Tobago were either "cancelled or dissolved" in a one-year period, 1996–97.

There was also a decline in trade union membership, partly arising from the developments mentioned earlier, the emergence of new sectors which were not traditionally inclined to union membership and changing attitudes towards unions. With the practice of privatization which accompanied structural adjustment, efficiency and profitability became central, with negative implications for the strength of trade unions within these settings (Moonilal 1998).

In the 1990s the deepening of neoliberal policies – reciprocal trade preferences, the dismantling of unilateral trade preferences through the World Trade Organization and the onslaught of external competition – led to the closure of some sectors of the economy, leading to further decline in trade union membership and the demise of some unions. Arguably, the most striking case is in the agricultural sector with the closure of the sugar industry and dissolution of Caroni 1975 Limited in 2003. Consequently, approximately ten thousand sugar workers lost their jobs, gravely reducing the membership of the All Trinidad Sugar and Factory Trade Union. Its rebranding to the All Trinidad General Workers' Trade Union reflects the loss of its membership from the sugar sector.

Another example of the impact of globalization on trade unions is the effect of global deregulation and privatization on the Caribbean airline industry. Although 9/11 worsened the crisis of the airline industry, deregulation of the global industry since the end of the 1970s had been forcing the Caribbean aviation industry to take steps to lower fares and improve quality in the midst of external competition – all of which raised costs (Guy 1991). These developments led to the closure of British West Indian Airways (BWIA), and many employees lost their jobs. Some BWIA employees were offered separation packages and the opportunity to work with Caribbean Airlines; however, employment would now be on a contract basis (Frederick 2013). This affected close to two thousand workers and led to the demise of unions which had represented BWIA workers.[4]

This reduction in membership has resulted in declining revenue for unions. For example, in 1990, the OWTU reported that the reduction of membership from retrenchment and early retirement severely affected the union's income. Also, the introduction of a value-added tax resulting from International Monetary Fund conditionality increased the union's expenses and consequently reduced its income (OWTU 1990).

The prevalence of precarious employment has intensified in recent times and has adversely impacted trade unions all over the world.[5] In the face of competitive forces and restructuring, short-term and temporary contracts have been utilized as a strategy by companies worldwide to cut costs (O'Brien 2000; Gallin 2001; Palley 2009). Contract employment has risen phenomenally in Trinidad and Tobago. In the public service, for example, in 2010 more than ten thousand persons were employed on a contract basis compared to fewer than a hundred in 1990 (Government of Trinidad and Tobago News 2013). This trend has also emerged in the private sector, especially in cases in which smaller firms have linked with larger ones (Moonilal 1998).

Precarious employment denies workers the right to join or form unions for fear of being fired (International Labor Rights Forum 2010). In Trinidad and Tobago, although contract workers have the right to join trade unions and to be represented on rights-related issues in the industrial court, they are not part of the bargaining units of trade unions as permanent employees under the Industrial Relations Act. Unions in this sense are not as "useful" to contract workers as they are to permanent employees, which reduces the degree to which unions are sought out by contract workers (Frederick 2013).

The shift towards services which comes with the increasing use of telecommunications technologies has changed the nature of work and has led to declines in membership and a further weakening of unions. For example, in Trinidad and Tobago the use of technology in the banking sector, in particular, has reduced the need for workers (Frederick 2013).

What has been the result of these developments in this new climate? One result has been a "softening" of trade unions and a shift towards conciliation. One union reflected on their approach at the Fifty-first Annual Conference of Delegates in 1990as follows:

> We questioned whether we had become "soft" or had become too engrossed in the legality of Industrial Relations. We said that perhaps our approach differs vastly to that of our predecessors in that they used struggle as a means to resolve their disputes and then formalised their victory with meetings of agreements, whereas we use meetings to settle and only occasionally, use struggle as a means when we have gone through a ritual of meetings and the situation has deteriorated to crisis proportions. (OWTU 1990, 23)[6]

This approach has been accompanied by greater collaboration with employers and the state around labour issues. The International Labour Organization has been promoting social dialogue through tripartite arrangements (involving employers, employees and the state) in the context of its decent work agenda. In this vein, Trinidad and Tobago created the International Labour Organization's 144 tripartite Consultations Committee in 1996. The committee comprises individuals with expertise in economic, social and labour issues who examine national law and practice in light of conventions being considered for ratification (ILO 2011). This approach towards more and institutionalized dialogue obviously has advantages but also poses the danger of compromising independent union action.

This emerging culture of trade unions' moving towards greater consultation is seen in the approach of a wide section of the labour movement that works within existing structures to try to achieve as much as is possible or feasible within them. We see this globally, and it is reflected in Trinidad and Tobago in trade union advocacy for the insertion of the core labour standards in the development agenda, for example, in trade agreements.

Fewer trade unions are confronting globalization and rejecting the ideological basis and underlying philosophy of economic globalization. In Trinidad and Tobago, the OWTU has historically been engaged in ideological struggles from its birthing to its attack on neoliberal globalization starting in the structural adjustment era (see, for example, Meighoo 2008). The OWTU has been addressing national challenges through antiglobalization processes such as the World Social Forum, in which participants advocate for an alternative global economic order.

An additional response to neoliberal globalization has been to broaden and deepen linkages with like-minded organizations in civil society at the national and regional levels. The OWTU has increasingly formalized alliances with civil society to overcome the existing challenges of this new global dispensation. The pioneering of the Assembly of Caribbean Peoples in 1994 was one such example (OWTU 1995). The OWTU also collaborates with the Caribbean Policy Development Centre, the umbrella civil society organization in the region (OWTU 2006). Arguably, the most striking case of trade union–NGO collaboration was the formation of the Federation of Independent Trade Unions and NGOs, which participated in the anti-EPA campaign.

Trade unions and the workers they represent have always been confronted by challenges that emanate from external developments. Trade unions have traditionally responded with various strategies that are for the most part political, albeit indirectly, even when efforts have been made to neutralize their progressive posture. Neoliberal globalization has been posing a unique set of challenges that are threatening the ability of trade unions to remain political and progressive. These challenges and responses to them in the Trinidad and Tobago case are seen in both similar and contrasting ways in the case of Barbados, the details of which we now turn to.

The Barbados Case: Between Conciliation and Confrontation

In Barbados there are two major unions and several other small ones. These are the Barbados Worker's Union (BWU) and the National Union of Public Workers. The BWU boasts a membership of approximately twenty-five thousand workers across the private sector and in some areas of the public sector and is the country's oldest legally registered union, dating from 4 October 1941. The National Union of Public Workers, with at least ten thousand government employees comprising its membership, was established in 1944 and legally registered in 1964. There is also a national umbrella organization of unions called the Congress of Trade Unions and Staff Associations of Barbados (CTUSAB), comprising twelve workers' representative organizations in Barbados (Fashoyin 2001; BWU 2015; NUPW 2015).

If one considers the history of the two major unions, the BWU and the National Union of Public Workers, the linkages to the crystallization of political parties in Barbados becomes clear. For instance, Sir Grantely Adams was the BWU president between 1941 and 1954. During this time the BWU and the Barbados Labour Party, which Adams helped to create, were fused (BWU 1983). Union active mobilization on behalf of workers via negotiation and strike actions and their roles in labour education using their labour colleges are also undeniable. For example, the BWU notes its role in creating the Holidays with Pay Act (1952) and the Severance Pay Act (1973) and also in amending the Trade Union Act to allow for peaceful picketing and modifying the Workmen's Compensation Act to incorporate domestics, both in the 1970s. The BWU also lists several other pieces of legislation created since the 1970s among its achievements (BWU 1983, 2015; Fashoyin 2001).

In the early 1990s, the BWU and the National Union of Public Workers were also of critical importance in mobilizing against negotiations between the Government of Barbados and the International Monetary Fund. This joint activism led to the formation of CTUSAB. CTUSAB then played an important role in the establishment of the social partnership in Barbados through its engagement with the Barbados Private Sector Agency on the national economic situation. This collaboration between CTUSAB and the Barbados Private Sector Agency was an important step in negotiating the social partnership in Barbados (Fashoyin 2001; Charles-Soverall and Khan 2004).

The social partnership was established in 1993 as the Protocol on Prices and Incomes Policy, a tripartite arrangement for addressing the economic problems of the time. The consultative type of arrangement that this protocol began was in part a response to neoliberal demands of the emerging globalized post–Cold War era. This tripartite framework, now over twenty years old and in its sixth protocol, altered the way that unions fit into the Barbadian social and political landscape. The social partnership brought unions, employers and the private sector, and the government of Barbados together as partners in a conciliatory framework for socioeconomic development and discussion. As previously stated, such partnerships and collaborative practices are viewed in a positive light by the International Labour Organization. The social partnership can be seen as one of the means by which Barbadian unions can advocate for workers in the context of a global economy in which Barbados is a marginal and heavily dependent player. Unions have been formally integrated into processes of political consultation that are important in the Barbadian political decision-making context.

Despite the creation of this formal structure in response to the encroachments of neoliberal globalization, though, one can also assert that the creation of the social partnership was not a radical shift in governance but more of a continuation of an industrial relations bargain characterized by voluntarism. Although labour legislation exists and enshrines workers' rights in Barbados, voluntary approaches are generally used to address a variety of industrial relations issues (Fashoyin 2001). This bargain allowed for a precarious post-1960s peace as follows: "The state, capital and organised labour orchestrated a social peace under the norms of a Keynesian strategy that valorised redistribution as just reward for worker co-operation in accumulation schemes" (Marshall 2002, 735). Therefore, the social partnership, while it opens space for labour in decision-making, may also function to subdue the demands of workers in the spirit of cooperation and compromise if their representatives are not careful.

In Barbados much emphasis has also been placed on fostering a strong services-based economy. Tourism-dependent from the 1980s, Barbados has at least a forty-year history of concentrating on service provision focused on (though not exclusively) attracting foreign investment. From the 1990s in particular, the emphasis on attracting "offshore" financial institutions or "international business" entities also intensified, along with the decline in sugar production for export. Although there are debates surrounding the contribution of service investment to economic well-being and to the employment landscape of the island (Marshall 2002), maintaining a stable industrial relations climate has been high on the agenda in Barbados in order to maintain an attractive setting for potential investors. Barbados has fashioned itself as operating as a provider of services, including "international business" and "offshore finance", within a globalized economy. Therefore, Barbados's placement within the global economy requires a level of "harmony" that aligns well with the sustenance of the social partnership. Unions have worked to foster this accommodating climate, in particular from the 1990s, when globalizing shifts were viewed as potentially making Barbados a less attractive site for international investment in both manufacturing and services. Griffith makes the point, noting that "trade union leaders in Barbados realized the disadvantage in which Barbados found itself and they therefore adopted a new approach to industrial relations to help prevent the closure of foreign manufacturing plants in Barbados. They began to work with firms to increase worker productivity in order to restore and maintain the competitiveness of Barbadian products and services" (Griffith 2002, 99). He continues to note that Sir Roy Morris, former general secretary of the BWU, indicated the need for labour in Barbados in order to adapt to meet the needs of foreign capital, which was increasingly footloose and able to easily relocate to more competitive geographical locations (Griffith 2002, 99). Similarly, the general secretary of CTUSAB, Dennis de Peiza, noted that "militancy has its place in time", and thus an adversarial approach had been "lowered almost to its final resting place" (de Peiza 2013).

Nevertheless, to argue that unions in Barbados have been converted from champions of workers to partners with the employers from the private sector and the state is not altogether accurate. On the one hand, one can assert that within trade unions there is a view that confrontation and militancy should be avoided, particularly in the turbulent context of a "globalized" economy. In important ways, then, unions may recognize that they must help to facilitate capital movement to make Barbados attractive to investors, help their membership to facilitate the improvement of the business climate and make public-sector entities operate effectively and efficiently. On the other hand, unions continue to employ their tools of militancy as needed.

Indeed, if one assesses the data available from the Barbados Labour Department it becomes clear that in the globalization era strikes may have been on the increase even though the number of work stoppages have fluctuated (figure 12.1).

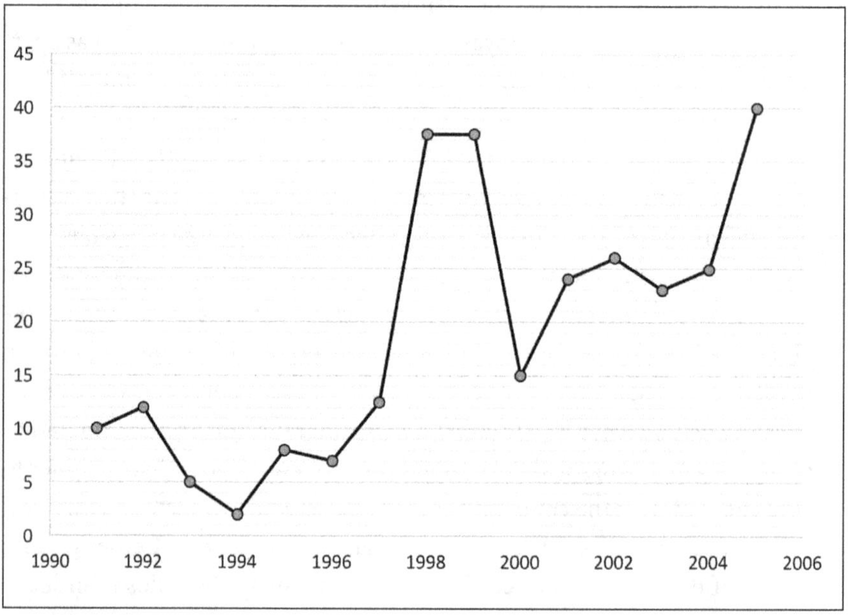

Figure 12.1. Total number of work stoppages, 1991–2005
Source: Government of Barbados, Ministry of Labour, https://labour.gov.bb/statistics/dynamic/.
Note: These statistics are unfortunately incomplete, with no published information available prior to 1991 or after 2005.

The social partnership may have created an ethos of cooperation across competing interests and even among competitor private-sector entities and unions in order to adapt to a changing global environment, but this bargain has not negated the strike option. Additionally, the bargain has been a fragile one. So, despite the many ways in which the social partnership has been applauded as a model for developing countries to follow, in April of 2013, the year marking the twentieth anniversary of the social partnership, the BWU left CTUSAB and, by extension, the social partnership. This exit occurred in spite of the pivotal role of the BWU in both establishing CTUSAB and pioneering the social partnership. The BWU's exit from CTUSAB shows the fragility of this cooperative arrangement, especially in the post-2008 climate of financial crisis. The fragility of the social bargain became ever more clear following the government's 2013 budget, which initiated swift and painful austerity measures, which combined with private-sector job cuts and preexisting issues surrounding poor working conditions and terms of employment to create an atmosphere ripe for confrontation and indeed militancy.

As a result, unions have, in very visible ways, supported the rights of workers to withdraw their labour in protest just as the private sector and employers have been able to withdraw employment or ignore problematic employment matters because of "hard times". Several recent examples of the willingness of unions to support their members in withdrawing their labour or in threatening to withdraw their labour in protest can be found in the Barbadian news media since 2012. Job losses in the public and private sectors have been particularly important in forcing unions to exercise or threaten the option of the strike. However, the industrial relations climate became even more chilly following the implementation of a December 2013 plan announced by the minister of finance, the Honourable Christopher Sinckler, to cut three thousand public-sector jobs during 2014. These employment cuts were part of the government's efforts to strengthen the country's fiscal position by drastically decreasing state expenditure. Some of the more contentious union-led actions in response have included

- a threatened BWU national strike in January 2013 over the alleged unfair dismissal of ninety-seven employees of Lime (a branch of the telecommunications multinational Cable and Wireless);
- an eight-day strike by sugar workers employed by the state-run Barbados Agricultural Management Company in April 2014 that delayed the start of the sugar harvest;
- a day-long strike by state-employed air traffic controllers on 17 November 2014 that raised public fears about the negative economic impact of this action at the start of the winter tourist season;

- a strike lasting six hours on 6 May 2015 by bus drivers employed at the state-run Barbados Transport Board over retrenchment concerns; and
- BWU-mooted strikes and possibly even a general strike over varied outstanding workers' matters in May 2015.[7]

Despite the views of the general secretary of CTUSAB on militancy as a historical relic, the member organizations of CTUSAB (as well as the BWU) continued to find it fitting to utilize such as needed.

What is noticeable in this climate of palpable labour discontent is the way in which movements in the direction of militancy, in the form of strike action, have at times been portrayed in Barbados. An editorial in *Nation News* on 10 May 2015 titled "Tension Not Good for Economy" encourages conciliation between workers and employers in the face of a newly rebounding economy. The editorial cites the crippling strike by bus drivers on 6 May 2015 and depicts threatened work stoppages at Barbados Light and Power as potentially damaging to the local economy. The author urges "all players in the industrial relations sphere to recognise the impact which their every action can have on the economic situation of our island".

Similarly, on 22 May 2015, Tony Walcott, the executive director of the Barbados Employers' Confederation, is reported to have stated: "Any disruption to the economic activity in an economy, which is struggling to recover, is not welcomed" (Joseph 2015). Walcott's comments came in response to the BWU's proposing a general strike to protest a series of outstanding labour concerns, as previously mentioned. The actions of the Barbados Employers' Confederation in January 2013, when the BWU threatened a general strike, are also worthy of consideration here. This organization issued a press release advising against strike action on 11 January 2013, stating: "While the employees' accredited bargaining agent reserves the right to threaten to take strike action, we believe that in this case, the call for a general strike is not warranted! Such strike action can/will inflict irreparable damage to the economy of Barbados and the long-term sustainability of several business ventures, exacerbating an already weak employment environment" (BEC 2013, para. 6).

News reports also indicated that the Barbados Employers' Confederation distributed a circular to members advising that they should dissuade employees from participating in a general strike but warning that employees choosing to participate in a strike should not be penalized for this apart from being denied wages for the days that they were not at work. The Barbados Employers' Confederation is reported to have advised employers: "Be sure that you impress on staff the damage which such action can have on the sustainability of not only the company, but the economy of Barbados" (Cumberbatch 2013, para. 1). What is significant here is that the Barbados Employers' Confederation is one of the participants in the social partnership as a member of the Barbados Private Sector Agency. These comments and recommendations provided by the Barbados Employers' Confederation are further indicators of the fragility of this social partnership, in which contentious interests exist.

While unions were once viewed as champions of Barbadian advancement and vital for social progress, calls for action by Barbadian workers are portrayed as actions that are damaging to the economy and even irresponsible. Consequently, the need to defend workers' rights has been juxtaposed with arguments about productivity losses, global competitiveness and the national interest. What such commentaries ignore is that it is the ability of labour to jeopardize business profitability, the sugar crop, the tourist sector, the supply of electricity and such that provides workers with their bargaining power.

The neoliberal world in which unions operate seems to have weakened the legitimacy of the strike option and may be changing perceptions about the purpose and relevance of unions, while the priorities of competitiveness and efficiency have been elevated. Stated differently, the dictates of capital are given priority over those of labour. This coincides with assertions about labour in the Caribbean presented by Alexander and Parker (2004) and in the European Union presented by Kowalsky (2010). The primacy awarded to capital stems from the contention that emerged during the 1980s, that capital is single-handedly responsible for economic advancement in a highly competitive world (Gill and Law 1989).

Ironically, it is in this climate of neoliberal globalization, particularly with financial crisis, that the exercise of more militant unionism may be needed. Since facilitating capital along with trimming public expenditure are framed as ever more critical, workers are asked to be all the more compliant in order to facilitate such processes. However, such compliance may mean that workers' rights can be ignored. It is this contradiction that may demand forceful union action.

Conclusion

The two case studies suggest to us that Caribbean unions have been facing challenges while navigating a swiftly changing globalized world. The global financial crisis that commenced in 2008, along with continued technological advances, continues to complicate this world. Caribbean trade unions understand and acknowledge that the context of the world is different and that they must adapt to global forces. In significant ways many support neoliberal constructions of globalization. They seek to educate workers about their rights, they focus on ensuring that labour standards are created and upheld, and they participate in partnership agreements with the state and capital.

However, the insertion of core labour standards and adaptation to a business-dominated global economic structure based on the suggestion that these activities can make neoliberal globalization better are insufficient for Caribbean societies. Similarly, "win-win" tripartite partnership arrangements for collaboration and conciliation allow for compromise as well as a measure of interest fulfilment. However, like core labour standards, tripartite arrangements do not confront the philosophical foundations of the market-driven vision of the global economy, which is more focused on capital accumulation than on people.

Therefore, we question the ways in which the region's unions challenge structures of inequality at this point in time. While it is clear that they do continue to advocate for workers, they walk a tightrope by simultaneously submitting to the dictates of global capital. Undoubtedly, unions continue to be politically important in advocating for workers' rights within the workplace and contributing to the construction of social legislation. All the same, one might ask whether unions, in navigating the now-dominant political-economic paradigm, can be of sufficient use in challenging the roots of global inequalities which market-oriented globalization perpetuates.

Notes

1. We focus specifically here on the anglophone Caribbean in light of the shared history of British colonization, which has allowed for similarities in the development of trade unions and "labour parties" in these countries.
2. Data on trade union membership and density over time in the Caribbean are limited.

3. This information is current up to 31 March 2015.
4. The Airline Superintendents Association; the Aviation, Communication and Allied Workers Union; and the Communication, Transport and General Workers Union. The Trinidad and Tobago Pilots Association continues to exist, and the others either have been subsumed or continue to exist to look into remaining issues with former BWIA workers
5. "Involuntary part-time work and temporary employment are on the increase in the majority of countries where employment growth has resumed" (ILO 2011, 1).
6. At this meeting, the union identified plans to change this approach and revert to more militant action.
7. In the absence of data, the foregoing commentary presented the cases of industrial action that were given news coverage between 2012 and May 2015. See the following sources for information on these and other union actions: Gilkes 2014; Henry 2014; *Nation News* 2014; Thompson 2014; Wedderburn 2014; Bradshaw 2015a, 2015b; Yearwood, 2015.

References

Adaba, G. 2002. Trade Unions and the Promotion of Socially Sustainable Global Finance. In *Civil Society and Global Finance*, edited by Jan Aart Scholte and Albrecht Schnabe, 181–98. London: Routledge.

Alexander, R.J., and E.M. Parker. 2004. *A History of Organized Labor in the English-Speaking West Indies*. Westport, CT: Greenwood.

BEC (Barbados Employers' Confederation). 2013. Lime/BWU Impasse, Barbados Employers' Confederation. Press Statement. http://barbadosemployers.com/wp-content/uploads/2013/01/Press-Statement-on-LIME-BWU-Impasse.pdf.

BWU (Barbados Workers Union). 1983. Brief Outline of Trade Union Development in Barbados. www.bwubb.org/index.php?option=com_docman&task=doc_download&gid=2&Itemid=25.

———. 2015. About Us. www.bwubb.org/index.php?option=com_content&view=article&id=15&Itemid=5.

Bolland, O.N. 1997. Democracy and Authoritarianism in the Struggle for National Liberation: The Caribbean Labour Congress and the Cold War, 1945–52. *Comparative Studies of South Asia, Africa and the Middle East* 17 (1): 99–117.

———. 2001. *The Politics of Labour in the British Caribbean*. Kingston: Ian Randle.

Bradshaw, M. 2015a. Bosses Warned. *Nation News* (Bridgetown, Barbados), 7 May. www.nationnews.com/nationnews/news/67092/bosses-warned.

———. 2015b. Workers Air Their Grouses. *Nation News* (Bridgetown, Barbados), 21 May. www.nationnews.com/nationnews/news/67676/workers-air-grouses.

Charles-Soverall, W., and J. Khan. 2004. Social Partnership: New Public Management Practice in Barbados. *African Journal of Public Administration and Management* 15 (1): 22–36.

Cumberbatch, S. 2013. Strike Back. *Barbados Today*, 23 January. http://www.barbadostoday.bb/2013/01/23/strike-back/.

de Peiza, D. 2013. Author interview, CTUSAB offices, St Michael, Barbados, 4 June.

ECLAC (Economic Commission for Latin America and the Caribbean). 2005. Restructuring Caribbean Industries to Meet the Challenges of Trade Liberalisation. Santiago de Chile. www.cepal.org/publicaciones/xml/7/23747/L.77.pdf.

Fashoyin, T. 2001. Barbados: Fostering Economic Development through Social Partnership. Working Paper No. 351408. International Labour Organization, Geneva. www.ilo.org/public/libdoc/ilo/2001/101B09_340_engl.pdf.

Frederick, L. 2013. Author interview, Cipriani Labour College, Valsyn, St Joseph, Trinidad and Tobago. 16 May.

Gallin, D. 2001. Propositions on Trade Unions and Informal Employment in Times of Globalisation. *Antipode* 33 (3): 531–49.

Gilkes, R. 2014. BCC Strike. *Barbados Today* (Bridgetown), 26 June. www.barbados today.bb/2014/06/26/bcc-strike/.

Gill, S.R., and D. Law. 1989. Global Hegemony and the Structural Power of Capital. *International Studies Quarterly* 33 (4): 475–99.

Government of Trinidad and Tobago News. 2013. Relief Comes for Contract Employees in the Public Service. News.gov.tt, 15 April. http://www.news.gov.tt/archive /index.php?news=12682.

Griffith, W.H. 2002. A Tale of Four CARICOM Countries. *Journal of Economic Issues* (Association For Evolutionary Economics) 36 (1): 79–106.

Guy, H. 1991. The Caribbean Airline Industry in a Restructured International Airline Industry: Strategic Human Resource Management as an Option for Achieving Competitive Advantage. MA Research Paper, Institute of Social Studies, the Hague.

Held, D., A. McGrew, D. Goldblatt and J. Perraton. 1999. *Global Transformations: Politics, Economics and Culture*. Stanford, CA: Stanford University Press.

Henry, A. 2014. UCAL Workers Honour Strike Threat. *Barbados Today* (Bridgetown), 26 March. www.barbadostoday.bb/2014/03/26/ucal-workers-honour-strike-threat/.

Institute of Commonwealth Studies. 2004. Trinidad and Tobago: Trade Unions Material. www.aim25.ac.uk/cgi-bin/vcdf/detail?coll_id=7535&inst_id=16.

ILO (International Labour Organization). 2011. Promote Tripartite Consultation: Ratify and Apply Convention No. 144. Industrial and Employment Relations Department, Geneva. www.ilo.org/wcmsp5/groups/public/@ed_dialogue/@dialogue /documents/publication/wcms_159700.pdf.

International Labour Rights Forum. 2010. Freedom at Work: Campaign Toolkit. http://digitalcommons.ilr.cornell.edu/cgi/viewcontent.cgi?article=1808&context =globaldocs.

Jacobs, W.R. 1977. The Politics of Protest in Trinidad: The Strikes and Disturbances of 1937. *Caribbean Studies* 17 (April–July): 5–54.

Johnson, C.L. 1980. Political Unionism and Autonomy in Economies of British Colonial Origin: The Cases of Jamaica and Trinidad. *American Journal of Economics and Sociology* 39 (3): 237–48.

Joseph, E. 2015. Now Is Not the Time to Strike, Warns Employers. *Barbados Today* (Bridgetown), May 2. www.barbadostoday.bb/2015/05/22/now-is-not-the-time-to -strike-warns-employer/.

Kaldor, M. 2003. *Global Civil Society: An Answer to War*. Cambridge: Polity Press and Blackwell Publishers.

Keck, M.E., and K. Sikkink. 1998. *Activists Beyond Borders: Advocacy Networks in International Politics*. Ithaca, NY: Cornell University Press.

Kiely, R. 1996. *The Politics of Labour and Development in Trinidad*. Kingston: University of the West Indies Press.

Kowalsky, Wolfgang. 2010. Trade Unions and European Integration: Between Naïve Endorsement and Undifferentiated Rejection. *International Politics and Society* 3: 128–44.

Lewis, W.A. 1977. *Labour in the West Indies: The Birth of a Workers' Movement*. London: New Beacon.

Lipschutz, R.D. 1992. Reconstructing World Politics: The Emergence of Global Civil Society. *Millennium: Journal of International Studies* 21 (3): 389–91.

Marshall, Don D. 2002. At Whose Service? Caribbean State Posture, Merchant Capital and the Export Services Option. *Third World Quarterly* 23 (4): 725–51.

Martínez, L.M. 2010. Dimensions of Internationalism and the Politics of the Labour Movement: Understanding the Political and Organisational Aspects of Labour Networking and Co-ordination. *Employee Relations* 32 (6): 538–56.

Meighoo, K. 2008. Putting Up a New Resistance: The OWTU and the Emergence of an Open, Plural and Democratic Left in Trinidad and Tobago. In *Selected Issues and Problems in Social Policy*, edited by Deryck R. Brown, 222–70. Kingston: Canoe Press.

Ministry of Labour. 2015. *Micro Enterprise and Development*. Port of Spain: Government of Trinidad and Tobago.

Moghadam, V.M. 2013. *Globalization and Social Movements: Islamism, Feminism, and the Global Justice Movement*. Lanham, MD: Rowman and Littlefield.

Moody, K. 1997. *Workers in a Lean World: Unions in the International Economy*. London: Verso.

Moonilal, R. 1998. Changing Labour Relations and the Future of Trade Unions: A Case Study of Trinidad and Tobago. PhD thesis, Institute for Social Studies, the Hague.

Morris, R.L. 2002. Trade Union Administration: A Caribbean Workers' Education Guide. International Labour Office, Port of Spain. http://www.ilo.org/wcmsp5/groups/public/@americas/@ro-lima/@sro-port_of_spain/documents/publication/wcms_224177.pdf.

Muller, T., H.W. Platzer and S. Rub. 2010. Global Trade Union Federations Facing the Challenges of Globalization. *International Politics and Society* 3: 111–27.

Nation News (Bridgetown, Barbados). 2014. Workers Off Job. 19 November, Nation Publishing. www.nationnews.com/nationnews/news/59522/workers-job.

NUPW (National Union of Public Workers). 2015. Join Our Union. http://www.nupwbarbados.com/member-services/newmember/?doing_wp_cron=1433112873.0482699871063232421875.

Nurse, L. 2004. Different Faces of Participation in Trade Union Activity in Barbados: A Research Note. *Social and Economic Studies* 53 (3): 111–25.

O'Brien, R. 2000. Workers and World Order: The Tentative Transformation of the International Union Movement. *Review of International Studies* 26 (4): 533–55.

OWTU (Oilfields Workers' Trade Union). 1990. Report of the 51st Annual Conference of Delegates, San Fernando, Trinidad and Tobago, 13–14 July.
———. 1995. General Council's Report. OWTU Headquarters, San Fernando, Trinidad and Tobago.
———. 2006. General Secretaries Report. OWTU Headquarters, San Fernando, Trinidad and Tobago.
Padmore, G. 1945. *The Voice of Coloured Labour: Speeches and Reports of Colonial Delegates to the World Trade Union Conference – 1945.* Manchester, UK: PANAF Services. www.marxists.org/archive/padmore/1945/labour-congress/index.htm.
Palley, T.I. 2009. A Labor Perspective on Globalization. *International Politics and Society* 2: 22–39.
Payne, A., and P. Sutton. 2008. Repositioning the Caribbean within Globalization. In *The Caribbean Community in Transition: Functional Cooperation as a Catalyst for Change,* edited by K. Hall and M. Chuck-A-Sang, 76–113. Kingston: Ian Randle.
Randall, S.J. 2003. The Historical Context. In *Understanding the Contemporary Caribbean,* edited by R.S. Hillman and T.J. Agostino, 51–84. Boulder: Lynne Rienner.
Scholte, J.A. 2005. *Globalization: A Critical Introduction.* New York: Palgrave MacMillan.
Thompson, R. 2014. $1/2 Million Pay Pack. *Nation News* (Bridgetown, Barbados), 16 April. www.nationnews.com/nationnews/news/30338/usd1-million-pay-pack.
Wedderburn, F. 2014. Surprise Strike at BHL. *Barbados Today* (Bridgetown), 25 October. www.barbadostoday.bb/2014/10/25/surprise-strike-at-bhl/.
Wills, J. 2002. Bargaining for the Space to Organize in the Global Economy: A Review of the Accor-IUF Trade Union Rights Agreement. *Review of International Political Economy* 9 (4): 675–700.
Yearwood, T. 2015. General Strike a BWU Option. *Nation News* (Bridgetown, Barbados), 22 May. www.nationnews.com/nationnews/news/67715/-strike-bwu-option.

Contributors

Debbie A. Mohammed is Senior Lecturer in International Trade, Institute of International Relations and the Arthur Lok Jack Graduate School of Business, the University of the West Indies, St Augustine, Trinidad and Tobago. Her publications include (co-edited with Nikolaos Karagiannis) *The Modern Caribbean Economy* (2 volumes).

Nikolaos Karagiannis is Professor of Economics, Winston-Salem State University, North Carolina, and co-editor of the journal *American Review of Political Economy*. His publications include *The US Economy and Neoliberalism: Alternative Strategies and Policies*; *Europe in Crisis: Problems, Challenges, and Alternative Perspectives*; and (co-edited with Debbie A. Mohammed) *The Modern Caribbean Economy* (2 volumes).

Jacqueline A. Braveboy-Wagner is Professor of Political Science, the Graduate School and University Center, and the City College of the City University of New York. Her publications include *Diplomatic Strategies of Leading Nations in the Global South* and *Institutions of the Global South*.

Georgina Chami is Research Fellow, Institute of International Relations, the University of the West Indies, St Augustine, Trinidad and Tobago.

Russell Foote is a professionally trained educator, social researcher, and social scientist. His published work has been on topics such as ethical issues, Carnival, teenage aggression, qualitative research, Caribbean studies and sociology.

Anthony Peter Gonzales is honorary Senior Fellow, Institute of International Relations, the University of the West Indies, St Augustine, Trinidad and Tobago, and former World Trade Organization director and representative of the Caribbean Regional Negotiating Machinery. He has published several articles on international trade and investment policy.

Wendy C. Grenade is Lecturer in Political Science and Deputy Dean (Outreach), Faculty of Social Sciences, the University of the West Indies, Cave Hill, Barbados. Her publications include *Grenada Revolution: Reflections and Lessons.*

Kristina Hinds-Harrison is Lecturer in Political Science and International Relations, the University of the West Indies, Cave Hill, Barbados. Her published work has been on the role of civil society in Caribbean regional integration, political protest in the Caribbean Community, and women and gender in Caribbean politics/political economy.

Ronald Marshall is Senior Lecturer attached to the Sociology Unit, the University of the West Indies, St Augustine, Trinidad and Tobago. His publications include *Alcoholism: Genetic Culpability or Social Irresponsibility* and *Return to Innocence: A Study of Street Children in the Caribbean.*

Indianna D. Minto-Coy is Senior Research Fellow, Mona School of Business and Management, the University of the West Indies, Mona, Jamaica. Her publications include (co-edited with Evan Berman) *Public Administration and Policy in the Caribbean.*

Annita Montoute is Lecturer, Institute of International Relations, the University of the West Indies, St Augustine, Trinidad and Tobago. Her published work has been on issues relating to civil society, emerging powers, ACP–EU relations, and crime and security in the Caribbean.

Kamla Mungal is Director for Academic Development and Accreditation and Director of the Leadership Institute, Arthur Lok Jack Graduate School of Business, the University of the West Indies, St Augustine, Trinidad and Tobago.

Emilio Pantojas-García is Senior Researcher, Center for Social Research, and Professor of Sociology, University of Puerto Rico. His publications include *Development Strategies as Ideology: Puerto Rico's Export-Led Industrialization Experience* and *Crónicas del Colapso: Economía Política y Sociedad de Puerto Rico en el Siglo Veintiuno.*

Gour C. Saha is Professor and Director of the Centre for Business Analytics and Intelligence, Arthur Lok Jack Graduate School of Business, the University of the West Indies, St Augustine, Trinidad and Tobago.

Dave Seerattan is Lecturer in International Money and Finance, Institute of International Relations and Officer in Charge, Caribbean Centre for Money and Finance, the University of the West Indies, St Augustine, Trinidad and Tobago. He is an assistant editor of the *Journal of Business, Finance and Economics in Emerging Economies.*

Ron R. Sookram is Deputy Academic Director and Senior Faculty, Arthur Lok Jack Graduate School of Business, the University of the West Indies, St Augustine, Trinidad and Tobago. His publications include articles in peer-reviewed and professional journals on corporate responsibility, sustainability and cultural history.

CPSIA information can be obtained
at www.ICGtesting.com
Printed in the USA
LVHW030036261120
672689LV00002B/63